AGE of EMPIRES

UNAUTHORIZED GAME SECRETS

LAWRENCE T. RUSSELL

PRIMA PUBLISHING
Rocklin, California
(916) 632-4400
www.primagames.com

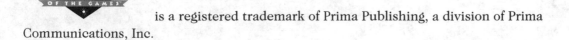
Project Editor: Brooke Raymond

ISBN: 0-7615-1053-2
Library of Congress Catalog Card Number: 97-066003
Printed in the United States of America

97 98 99 00 BB 10 9 8 7 6 5 4 3 2

Acknowledgments

This project came to me out of the blue. I had heard rumors of a great new game and I had read teasers in trade magazines but the name *Age of Empires* didn't mean much to me at the time. Well—that was then . . . this is now.

I consider myself very fortunate to have been asked to write a strategy guide on such a fine product. Truthfully, there were times when I couldn't stop playing long enough to put words down on paper. I can't remember the number of meals I ate seated in front of the computer trying to hustle my way into the Tool Age.

This strategy guide represents the collaborative efforts of a great many people. I just happen to be the point man. It's only fair, then, that I should take a moment and thank them publicly for their help.

First on the list of people I need to thank are Roxanne Roberts and Tony Winston. This intrepid pair came to southern California on vacation expecting to tour Hollywood and surf the break off Malibu. Imagine their surprise when they found themselves playtesting *Age of Empires* scenarios around the clock for two straight weeks. What a vacation! I don't think they ever did get to the beach but you know—they loved every minute of it.

Next I'd like to thank Sue Roberts, Creative Director/ The Russell Group. Sue spent many hours laboring over the graphics, creating scenarios, and playing the campaigns. Equally important is the contribution made by Mary Christensen, Senior Editor/ The Russell Group. Mary put her keen editorial eye to the manuscript and ultimately made numerous suggestions and important corrections.

Last, but certainly not least, my heartfelt thanks goes out to Amy Raynor and Brooke Raymond at Prima Publishing. Amy and I both had occasion to remark how surprised we were that everything worked out as well as it did. It's largely because of the efforts of Amy and Brooke that you have the opportunity to enjoy this strategy guide today.

Lawrence T. Russell
(The Russell Group)
September 1997

Contents

Introduction 1

CHAPTER 1   THE CIVILIZATIONS (THE 12 TRIBES) 3

The Asian Group 5
The Babylonian Group 14
The Hellenic (Greek) Group 23
The Egyptian Group 31

CHAPTER 2   THE AGES 41

Nomad 42
Stone Age 43
Tool Age 45
Bronze Age 48
Iron Age 52

CHAPTER 3   THE TECHNOLOGIES 57

Stone Age Technology 58
Tool Age Technology 58
Bronze Age Technologies 67
Iron Age Technologies 80

CHAPTER 4   THE BUILDINGS 95

Stone Age Buildings 97
Tool Age Buildings 107
Bronze Age Buildings 117
Iron Age Buildings 129

CHAPTER 5   THE PEOPLE 133

Character Summary Format. 134
Civilians 135
Infantry Units 140
Archer Units 156
Calvary Units 168
Siege Weapons 177
Naval Vessels. 185
Heroes. 201

CHAPTER 6   GENERAL PLAY
TIPS AND HINTS. 207

Gathering Resources. 208
Movement and Exploration 217
Combat 219
Using Terrain Features 224
Victory Conditions (Ways to Win) 227
End of Game Achievement Summary 230
Multiplayer Strategies. 232
Dirty Tricks. 237

CHAPTER 7   SCENARIO HINTS AND TIPS 239

The Campaign Games. 240
Multiplayer Scenarios 302

Introduction

Welcome to *Age of Empires*. It's not every day that a game of this magnitude, with this much depth, comes along. Centuries of human history and development are all rolled into one presentation that is not only informative, but also . . . fun to play.

Consider for a moment, what your life would be like in 12,000 BCE. The Ice Age has just ended, the continents are drifting apart, and there's no cable TV. From this humble beginning you must build an empire—not just any empire but an empire to last through the Ages.

Age of Empires is principally a game about exploration. You must create and manage a primitive society then use it to forge a technologically advanced and militarily strong civilization. You're not alone in the world, however, there can be up to seven other players each trying to do the same thing—win the game through economic, military, or diplomatic means.

CHAPTER 1

The Civilizations
(The 12 Tribes)

Choosing what civilization to play is only the first of many decisions you need to make when starting a new game. What's in a name? Plenty. There are 12 different civilizations (also known as tribes) in *Age of Empires*. Each one has a special set of advantages and disadvantages—characteristics that make each one different from all the others.

It is important to understand the fundamental impact that these characteristics have on gameplay. Certain strategies work well for some civilizations but are disastrous if tried by others. For example, if you like to build powerful fleets of ships, you should choose the Minoan, Persian, or Phoenician civilization. On the other hand, if you prefer to build city walls and fortifications, the Sumerian and Babylonian empires are more in line with your style.

More important, each civilization has its own method of advancement, unless you play with the *Full Tech Tree* option enabled. Some are limited in the kinds of research they can conduct; as a result, they may be prevented from building certain military Units. With the *Full Tech Tree*, all of the civilizations have their unique attributes switched off, and each has access to all the technologies in the game.

As you can readily see, choosing a civilization requires more thought than just picking a cool name. This chapter is designed to help you select a civilization that best matches your particular style of play. It is divided into four sections, corresponding to the groups of civilizations—Asian, Babylonian, Hellenic (Greek), and Egyptian. Each section contains a summary on the three civilizations that belong in each group.

THE ASIAN GROUP

Asian civilizations are probably the least familiar. Chalk it up to being educated in the West, but most of us breeze through school with just a cursory look at anything east of Hawaii. But it's safe to say that, after playing *Age of Empires* for a while, you will be the only one on your block who can discuss these ancient cultures intelligently. As a matter of fact, you will get to know these civilizations quite well. They are interesting to play and have such ornate and beautiful structures that it is almost a shame to destroy them.

CHOSON

The Choson civilization grew out of the Korean mainland and came to be known for its fierce warriors. The fact that it was able to maintain itself as a separate entity—especially with its proximity to China—says something about the strength of this civilization.

When playing the Choson, be prepared to build large numbers of sword-wielding infantry Units. Although you are prevented from equipping them with chain mail or iron shields, your Long Swordsman and Legion Units possess 80 extra Hit Points. This sustainability compensates for their lack of armor and keeps them in the fight a bit longer. These Units should constitute the bulk of your army.

The Choson can and should build all of their allowable cavalry Units. You want to use cavalry to protect your infantrymen from enemy cavalry and siege weapons. Do note, however, that the Choson are precluded from researching *Nobility*, and, therefore, their cavalry Units are somewhat weaker than other civilizations' cavalries.

Choson Priests cost 30 percent less to build than other Priests and have access to all of the religious technologies of the Iron Age.

You should build between four and six Priests to act as medics for your infantry. Choson Priests will not win battles against Egyptian or Babylonian Priests, but they can aid in healing damaged Units.

The Choson should stay with dry land wherever possible. This civilization lacks the ability to construct heavy transports and powerful warships like the Catapult Trireme and Juggernaught. Aside from building a few fishing boats, the Choson should situate their structures well inland.

One advantage enjoyed by the Choson is the additional range of their towers (two extra tiles). Surround your buildings with walls, and let the superior range of your towers keep the enemy at bay. Because the Choson also lack the ability to research *Engineering*, this initial advantage will be nullified once other civilizations reach the Iron Age.

Winning the game with the Choson undoubtedly will be difficult—just be sure to have plenty of Barracks and Stables prepared to produce Units the instant you reach the Iron Age. The longer you wait to strike once your Long Swordsman and Heavy Cavalry Units begin to appear, the more difficult your task will be.

Choson Advantages

- The amount of damage Choson Long Swordsman and Legion can sustain is 80 more Hit Points (Long Swordsman: 160 Hit Points; Legion: 320 Hit Points).

- The missile range from Choson towers is two tiles greater than other civilizations' towers. The Watch Tower has a range of seven tiles. The Sentry Tower has a range of eight tiles. The Guard Tower and Ballista Tower have a range of nine tiles.

- The cost of Choson Priest Units is 30 percent less (85 RPs of gold) than the cost in other civilizations.

Choson Disadvantages

- The Choson army is limited by its lack of some high-end Units, namely, the Phalanx, Centurion, and Heavy Catapult.
- Choson Stables and Archery Ranges cannot build any chariot or elephant Units. These include the Chariot, Chariot Archer, War Elephant, and Elephant Archer.
- The Choson navy cannot build the Heavy Transport, Catapult Trireme, or Juggernaught.
- The Choson cannot research the following Bronze and Iron Age technologies: *Nobility, Aristocracy, Alchemy, Engineering, Chain Mail* or *Iron Shield.*

SHANG

The Shang is one of the weaker civilizations in the game. Never volunteer to play the Shang unless you can get everyone to agree to use the *Full Tech Tree* option. The Shang has no real advantages whatsoever—save for the strength of its walls. Its Villagers cost less to produce in terms of food (35 RPs), but this benefit amounts to little. If you build 20 Villagers over the course of a game, you save only 300 RPs of food.

The Shang army consists mainly of mounted Units and siege weapons. With the exception of the War Elephant and Elephant Archer, the Shang can produce all archer and cavalry Units in the game. There is nothing particularly noteworthy about the Shang infantry as a class, except that the Shang cannot build the Long Swordsman, Legion, Phalanx, or Centurion.

While the Shang army is relatively nondescript, the Shang navy is pathetically weak. Aside from a little fishing, its vessels should avoid the water. Its strongest warship is the War Galley. The Shang can build fishing and merchant ships, but cannot build the Heavy Transport.

Shang Priests are neither good nor bad. All Iron Age religious technologies are open to them, so you may consider building them for this reason alone. But trying to mix the slow-walking Priest with a mounted army causes coordination problems that are difficult to resolve. Depending on which other civilizations are in the game, you may have some measure of success with Priests.

All other Iron Age technologies are open as well, except those which originate at the Government Center. The prohibited technologies include *Aristocracy, Alchemy, Engineering,* and *Ballistics.* You can probably live without these technologies anyway. By the time these normally become available, it is likely that the Shang are already toast.

If you draw the short straw and have no other choice but to play as the Shang, be aware that your chances of victory are slim. Your best strategy is to build as many Heavy Cavalry and Heavy Catapult Units as quickly as you can. Keep your army hidden from view until you are ready to attack. When the time is right, flood the enemy with a massive cavalry charge. Have your cavalry concentrate on attacking enemy Units, then move your siege engines in to finish off the buildings. Good luck. You'll need it.

Shang Advantages

- The cost of Shang Villagers is reduced by 30 percent to 35 RPs of food.
- Shang wall sections can sustain double the normal amount of damage (Small Wall: 400 Hit Points; Medium Wall: 600 Hit Points; Fortification: 800 Hit Points).

Shang Disadvantages

- The biggest Shang disadvantage is the fact that, as a civilization, it has no real advantages. The Shang builds terrific walls, but not every game involves extensive field fortifications.
- The Shang navy has trouble facing a school of tuna. Stay away from water!

YAMATO

In stark contrast to the Shang, the Yamato civilization is one of the most powerful—if not *the* most powerful—civilization in the game. Not only can it field a huge mounted army, but its ships are quite strong as well. Yamato Villagers must be on skates because they move about the map at great speeds. This speed allows the Yamato civilization to develop very quickly into a formidable economic and military force.

Like the Shang, the Yamato army is made up almost entirely of mounted Units with the exception of some War Elephants and Elephant Archers. The cost to produce mounted Units is reduced by 25 percent (see below); therefore, the army will be large and able to sweep across the map like the Mongol horde. All naval vessels are available to the Yamato civilization, including the Juggernaught. The Yamato is as strong at sea as it is on land.

One of the greatest Yamato advantages is the 30 percent increase in the speed of its Villagers (from 1.1 tiles to 1.46 tiles per second). You can actually see the difference in speed. Use this advantage during the Stone Age to explore uncharted areas of the map. The Villagers' speed is equally useful for hunting and foraging

because it reduces the time spent in transit between resource sites and storage structures. This reduction in time lets you build your inventories of food and wood quickly and virtually propels you into the Tool Age.

The only serious weakness of the Yamato lies in the inability of its Priests to research many technologies available to other civilizations. Because they can only research *Polytheism* and *Afterlife*, Yamato Priests are unable to convert enemy Priests and buildings. Ultimately, this shortcoming may lead to the Yamato's defeat. Keep a few Priests around as medics, but don't expect them to last very long.

All things considered, the Yamato is one of the easier civilizations to play. In games without religiously strong civilizations (such as Egypt or Babylon), the Yamato should prove to be nearly unstoppable. Their first opportunity for victory comes in the Bronze Age. Be ready to make your move.

Yamato Advantages

 The cost of Yamato Horse Archer, Scout, Cavalry, Heavy Cavalry, and Cataphract Units is decreased by 25 percent. Consult the table below for the exact cost (in resources) of each Unit.

YAMATO UNIT	RESOURCE COST TO PRODUCE
Horse Archer	37 RPs of food, 52 RPs of gold
Scout	75 RPs of food
Cavalry	52 RPs of food, 60 RPs of gold
Heavy Cavalry	52 RPs of food, 60 RPs of gold
Cataphract	52 RPs of food, 60 RPs of gold

- The speed of Yamato Villagers is increased by 30 percent to 1.46 tiles per second. This speed allows them to outrun most foot soldiers.

- The amount of damage Yamato naval vessels can sustain is 30 percent greater than what other civilizations' navies can withstand. Consult the table below for the exact number of Hit Points each Yamato vessel has.

YAMATO VESSEL	HIT POINTS
Fishing Boat	59 Hit Points
Fishing Ship	99 Hit Points
Trade Boat	259 Hit Points
Merchant Ship	324 Hit Points
Light Transport	194 Hit Points
Heavy Transport	259 Hit Points
Scout Ship	155 Hit Points
War Galley	207 Hit Points
Trireme	259 Hit Points
Catapult Trireme	155 Hit Points
Juggernaught	259 Hit Points

Yamato Disadvantages

- The biggest disadvantage the Yamato tribe has is the fact that it is so strong—it frightens other civilizations and may cause them to team up to defeat it.

- The Yamato are prevented from upgrading Medium Walls to Fortifications and Sentry Towers to Guard Towers.

- The only research open to Yamato Priests is *Polytheism* and *Afterlife*.

THE BABYLONIAN GROUP

Some groups of civilizations are known for producing ships and fighting great naval battles. Other civilizations are known for building large land armies. The civilizations in the Babylonian group are commonly considered to be the "builder" tribes. The villages and town they construct are among the largest and most elaborate of any civilization's in the game.

BABYLON

The Babylonians were known as prodigious builders. This characteristic is reflected in the game by doubling the strength of their walls and towers plus increasing the stone mining ability of its Villagers. From the very beginning of each game, send Villagers out to explore the countryside. For Babylon to survive, it must settle in areas with abundant supplies of nearby stone and gold. Without these materials, Babylon will be hard-pressed to protect itself later on.

Because the Babylonian army lacks the ability to build many of the top Units, it needs to build walls and towers instead. Even sections of Small Wall (with 400 Hit Points) make you invulnerable to attack during the Tool and Bronze Ages. Once you have secured large deposits of stone and gold, consider walling in large portions of the map. Create impediments to enemy movement and deny them access to you and your resources.

Unfortunately, later in the game, walls and towers become less relevant as military Units become more powerful and more mobile. Since the Babylonians cannot build elephant Units or Heavy Cavalry, they are unable to fight this kind of war. They are able to respond, however, by building very strong Priests and artillery (minus the Ballista and Helepolis).

You will find that, when you play Babylon, you come to rely on Priests more than when you play other civilizations. Their rejuve-

nation rate is among the fastest in the game, and Babylonian Priests have access to all Priestly research of the Iron Age.

Although they can build all the top Barracks-trained infantry Units, the Babylonians lack certain research technologies (*Chain Mail, Metallurgy,* and *Iron Shield*) which limits their effectiveness in hand-to-hand combat.

Babylonian Advantages

Babylonian walls and towers can sustain twice as much damage as walls and towers of other civilizations. Consult the table below for the exact number of Hit Points each structure possesses.

STRUCTURE	HIT POINTS
Small Wall	400 Hit Points
Medium Wall	600 Hit Points
Fortification	800 Hit Points
Watch Tower	200 Hit Points
Sentry Tower	300 Hit Points
Guard Tower	400 Hit Points

- Babylonian Priests take 30 percent less time (35 seconds) to rejuvenate between conversion attempts.

- Babylonian stone miners are 30 percent more efficient than other civilizations. They can mine and carry 13 RPs of stone in the same time that others take to mine 10 RPs.

Babylonian Disadvantages

- The Babylonian navy is comparable to that of the Shang. It is weak, ineffectual, and limited to fishing vessels, merchant ships, the Light Transport, and the War Galley.

- Babylonians cannot research *Metallurgy, Chain Mail,* or *Iron Shield*. The lack of these Iron Age technologies makes their troops more vulnerable in hand-to-hand combat.

- Many of the top military Units in each class are unavailable. These Units include the Heavy Cavalry, War Elephant, Phalanx, Centurion, Elephant Archer, Ballista, and Helepolis.

ASSYRIA

The Assyrian empire grows very quickly at first and then tapers off. If it is to win the game, it must do so quickly. Fortunately, Assyria's greatest advantages come early in the game when its chance for victory is greatest. They must achieve a quick, military conquest. Don't look for the Assyrians to build Wonders late in the Iron Age.

Assyrian Villagers move across land with the speed of a swift fishing boat (almost). While this advantage remains with you throughout the game, it becomes less meaningful in later Ages. Since your Villagers are faster (almost 1.5 tiles per second), you can place your storage pits and granaries further away from resource sites. This strategic placement lets you keep the position of your buildings a secret while you build up an army.

Alternatively, you can quickly build your stockpile of resources by putting storage pits and granaries directly adjacent to the resource sites. Your Villagers zip along chopping, picking, and mining, so that your inventories grow at amazing speed.

Sometime during the Stone Age, send one or two of your

Villagers abroad to explore the map. Their increased speed allows them to quickly reveal vast areas of uncharted territory quickly. This early exploration pays off during the Tool and Bronze Ages when the real scramble for resources begins. You already will know where all the choice spots are located.

The rest of your Villagers should collect food and wood. The Assyrians have only a brief window of opportunity to expand, so make the most of it. Quickly establish your housing, then begin building Archery Ranges—lots of them. The biggest advantage Assyrians have is a 40 percent increase in the rate of fire of their Archery Range Units (Bowman, Chariot Archer, and Horse Archer). Assyrian archers let loose volleys of missiles with the rapidity of an automatic weapon—one round every second (actually 1.07 seconds).

Now, whether this is enough to overcome some very serious military restrictions is a different story. In most cases, it will not be enough. The Assyrian civilization is prohibited from researching a few very important Bronze and Iron Age technologies. These limitations keep Assyria from fully developing as an empire and lets other civilizations begin to overtake it late in the game.

Assyrian Advantages

- Assyrian Villagers have their speed increased by 30 percent (from 1.1 tiles per second to 1.46 tiles per second.)
- Assyrian archery range Units have their rate of fire increased by 40 percent. They are able to fire one volley approximately every second.

Assyrian Disadvantages

- Assyria is definitely a land power. Its navy lacks the Heavy Transport and the two most advanced warships—the Catapult Trireme and Juggernaught.

- Assyrian Archery Range Units are limited to the Bowman, Chariot Archer, and Horse Archer.

- The Hoplite is the only academy-trained infantry Unit available to Assyria. Assyria cannot build the Legion or Centurion.

- Assyria lacks the ability to research many Bronze and Iron Age technologies. These technologies include *Nobility, Architecture, Aristocracy, Alchemy,* and *Engineering*.

- Assyrian military Units are limited to wearing Scale Mail and may not carry either the Bronze or Iron Shield.

SUMER

Sumer was the first of the 12 civilizations and, for the game, is one of the easier ones to play. Like the Assyrians and Yamato, the Sumerians possess Villagers with special attributes. These abilities allow Sumer to use these advantages to get a jump on the competition. The Sumerians are usually among the first to enter the Tool Age.

As a Sumerian, your Villagers are a hardy lot, able to withstand an extra 15 Hit Points worth of damage. Because your Villagers can sustain more damage than neighboring Villagers, you can send a few of them off to explore the countryside without fear of losing them. It also means that there is no reason to build Sumerian clubmen. Since clubmen cannot be used to perform other tasks, save the food resources for building more Villagers.

Sumerian Villagers cause the same amount of attack damage and have the same number of Hit Points as clubmen from other civilizations. Designated as hunters, Sumerian Villagers actually cause more attack damage than clubmen (4 vs. 3). Look at the following two comparative charts:

TABLE 1-1 Basis of Comparison for the Most Common Stone and Early Tool Age Military Units

Unit	HP*	Attack Damage	Time required to kill a Sumerian villager
Standard Villager**	25	3 (4)	19.9 seconds (15 sec)
Standard Clubman	40	3	19.9 seconds
Standard Axeman	50	5	12 seconds
Standard Scout	60	3	19.9 seconds
Standard Bowman	35	3	19.9 seconds

*HP: Hit Points

**Damage inflicted and time required when the Villager is designated as a Hunter.

TABLE 1-2 Requirements to Kill a Sumerian Villager

UNIT	HP*	TIME REQUIRED FOR A SUMERIAN VILLAGER TO KILL ANOTHER UNIT
Standard Villager**	25	12.4 seconds (9.3 sec)
Standard Clubman	40	19.9 seconds (15 sec)
Standard Axeman	50	24.9 seconds (18.7 sec)
Standard Scout	60	30 seconds (22.5 sec)
Standard Bowman	35	17.4 seconds (13.1 sec)

*HP: Hit Points

**Time required to kill another Unit when a Sumerian Villager is designated as a Hunter is shown in parenthesis.

The first table sets the basis for comparing the most common Stone and early Tool Age military Units. It provides the number of Hit Points they possess, the amount of damage they inflict, and the length of time it takes them to inflict 40 Hit Points of damage on a Sumerian Unit. The second table shows the length of time required for a Sumerian Villager to kill a particular Unit.

These tables illustrate the advantage Sumerian Villagers have over other Stone and Tool Age Units by virtue of their additional Hit Points. As you can see, it takes the standard Clubman almost 20 seconds to eliminate a Sumerian Villager. The Sumerian Villager, on the other hand, needs only 15 seconds to kill the Clubman. In combat against other Villagers, clubmen, or bowmen, Sumerian Villagers (when designated as hunters) always come out on top. If two Sumerian Villagers decide to team up, they can beat any of the military Units listed without any problems.

The best use of Sumerian Villagers, however, is not to have them traipse across the countryside. Sumerians are farmers, not Hunters or foragers. Their farms are tremendously productive, generating a base of 500 food RPs. Find a way to keep your Sumerian boys "down on the farm." Once you are able to build farms, there no longer is a need to search the map for food. Even fishing becomes unnecessary when you consider that each Sumerian farm produces twice the amount of food as a prime salmon run or school of tuna.

You must lay the ground work during the Stone and Tool Ages when your Villagers and farms are at their point of greatest advantage. These early economic benefits become less significant during the Bronze and Iron Ages and are replaced by military considerations.

For the most part, there is nothing special about the Sumerian army. It is a bland mix of the standard Units, neither good nor particularly bad with one exception—siege weaponry. Sumerian artillery pieces (Stone Thrower, Catapult, and Heavy Catapult) have their rate of fire increased by 50 percent. Instead of hurling a projectile every five seconds, these Units can fire one round approximately every 3.3 seconds.

Though its military has its moments, in most cases the Sumerians need to field an army and navy only in self-defense. They are not equipped to win and should not fight wars of conquest. Look for the Sumerians to win the game by building a Wonder before other civilizations.

Sumerian Advantages

- The damage that Sumerian Villagers can sustain is increased from 25 Hit Points to 40 Hit Points.
- Sumerian farms have their food generation doubled from 250 RPs of food to 500 RPs of food.
- Sumerian Stone Throwers, Catapults, and Heavy Catapults have their rates of fire increased by 50 percent; that is, one round every 3.3 seconds.

Sumerian Disadvantages

- Sumerian Priests cannot benefit from many Bronze and Iron Age technologies. These include *Afterlife, Astrology, Fanaticism,* and *Monotheism*.

- Two other important technologies are closed to the Sumerians as well—*Craftsmanship* and *Coinage*. This precludes the Sumerians from being able to pay tribute without being subjected to the 25% tax.

- Sumerian troops cannot benefit from Metallurgy and *Iron Shield*. They should avoid hand-to-hand combat during the Iron Age whenever possible.

THE HELLENIC (GREEK) GROUP

The Hellenic Group consists of three civilizations (Greek, Minoan, and Phoenician) that were situated in the eastern Mediterranean. Two of these three, the Minoan and Phoenicians, were known for their prowess as sailors. These "sea peoples" confidently moved about in fishing and trade vessels. The Greek civilization is perhaps the most familiar to most of us. While names like Suppiluliuma and Sargon leave us scratching our head, almost everyone has heard the name Alexander the Great. (This is a minor point, but Alexander was actually Macedonian, not Greek.)

GREEK

The Greek civilization is strong economically, militarily, and intellectually. Although they have no early advantages, the Greeks come into their own during the late Bronze and Iron Ages. For this reason, when playing this civilization you should lay low at the start of the game and avoid doing things that attract too much attention.

As a Greek, the Market is one of the most important buildings you can construct because of the four Tool Age technologies that it makes available. These technologies (*Domestication, Gold Mining, Stone Mining, Woodworking*) help your civilization acquire resources faster and, thus, keep pace with other civilizations.

The Archery Range, on the other hand, is a building that can and should be ignored—at least initially. Since the only archer Unit you can build is the Bowman and since the Bowman is too weak to contribute much beyond the Tool Age, the Archery Range is an unnecessary expense. Don't waste your resources building one until you reach the Bronze Age. At this point, the Archery Range becomes important because it lies on the construction path to the Siege Workshop, which you very definitely want to build.

The inability to build Archers (other than the Bowman) is a serious liability. It forces the Greeks to close with, and destroy, opposing armies in hand-to-hand combat, rather than shoot at the

enemy from a distance. To make matters worse, Greeks are prevented from researching *Metallurgy*—a technology that would allow them to inflict three extra Hit Points of damage per round of hand-to-hand combat.

The Greek navy is a superb fighting force. Their warships (Scout, War Galley, Trireme, Catapult Trireme and Juggernaught) move 30 percent faster than their counterparts in other navies. At 2.6 tiles per second, this speed advantage lets them escape trouble as fast as they enter it. This speed also allows them to choose the time and place of Greek naval battles.

Use Greek warships to conduct Viking-like raids on neighbors who are foolish enough to build their civilizations near the coast. These nuisance raids will harass and annoy your enemies and, at the very least, cause them to spend resources building towers for protection. If you see this happen, simply move on to a new location.

Greek Advantages

- Greek Hoplite, Phalanx, and Centurions have their speed increased by 30 percent (from 0.9 tiles to 1.2 tiles per second.)
- All Greek warships speed along at 2.6 tiles per second, 30 percent faster than their counterparts in other civilizations.

Greek Disadvantages

- Greek Priests cannot benefit from several Iron Age technologies. These include *Jihad* and *Monotheism*.
- The Greeks are prohibited from building several top infantry Units. These include the Board Swordsman, Long Swordsman, and Legion.
- The Bowman is the only Archery Range Unit available to the Greeks.

MINOAN

For all the many strengths of the Minoan civilization, it has some very serious shortcomings. And while these glaring deficiencies may not be enough to cause it to lose many games, Minoan advantages may not be great enough to cause it to win many either. Nothing about the Minoan civilization is middle-of-the-road. Almost every aspect of this civilization is extreme—either excellent or horribly atrocious.

Playing the Minoan in a multi-player game requires that you emphasize the positive features while seeking to minimize the negatives. This advice sounds obvious enough—and perhaps even a bit trite—but it is nonetheless true. To be successful as a Minoan requires that you approach the game with some forethought and that you not plan to get by on brute force.

If your idea of problem solving is to reach for a sledgehammer, the Minoan civilization is not for you. Manage this superb civilization correctly, and the Minoan is a match even for the Yamato. But watch out—make a mistake and the other players will bury you.

The only available Cavalry Units for the Minoan player are Scout and Cavalry Units. Likewise, you cannot build mounted Archers such as the Chariot, Horse, and Elephant Archer Units. This lack of Cavalry and Archer Units is a serious shortcoming. It condemns the Minoan to fielding armies comprised primarily of slow-moving infantry Units.

Fortunately, the Minoan can build a full array of siege weaponry, so positional warfare will be to their liking. The added firepower of a few catapults gives the infantry some teeth. Whether a couple of siege weapons are enough to prevent the Minoan infantry from being overrun early in a battle is a legitimate question to ask.

Although the Minoan civilization is prevented from building Legion Units, they can (and should) produce all of the academy-

trained professional Unit types (Hoplite, Phalanx, and Centurion). These Units will not make up for the lack of cavalry, but they are capable of inflicting heavy damage at a reasonable cost. In short, these Units give the Minoan the biggest bang for the buck.

The ideal strategy for a Minoan player is to settle on an island somewhere—or at the very least, a peninsula. Once this is accomplished, the Minoan should begin building walls, towers, and—most importantly—warships. (Minoan ships are 30 percent cheaper than they would otherwise be.) The Minoan civilization also should begin making good use of their farm advantage. The Minoan objective should be total control over large bodies of water while stockpiling resources toward construction of a Wonder.

Minoan Advantages

- The cost of Minoan ships is decreased by 30 percent. Consult the table below for the exact cost of each ship.

TABLE 1-3 Minoan ships

MINOAN VESSEL	COST TO CONSTRUCT
Fishing Boat	34 RPs of wood
Fishing Ship	34 RPs of wood
Trade Boat	60 RPs of wood
Merchant Ship	69 RPs of wood
Light Transport	104 RPs of wood
Heavy Transport	104 RPs of wood
Scout Ship	94 RPs of wood
War Galley	94 RPs of wood
Trireme	94 RPs of wood
Catapult Trireme	94 RPs of wood, 52 RPs of gold
Juggernaught	94 RPs of wood, 52 RPs of gold

- Minoan Composite Bowman have their range increased by two tiles to nine tiles.

- Minoan farms have their food production increased by 25 percent to a base output of 310 RPs of food.

Minoan Disadvantages

- Minoan Priests are among the worst in the game. They are prevented from researching any technology (except *Polytheism*) that would make them effective and practical Units.

- The Minoan army is incapable of producing advanced Cavalry Units or mounted Archers.

- Minoans are prohibited from building Fortifications, Guard Towers, or Ballista Towers.
- The Minoan civilization doesn't stand a chance, unless you play on one of the following land features: Small Island, Large Island, or Coastal Maps.

PHOENICIA

The Phoenician civilization had the historical misfortune to settle in one of the most heavily traveled and hotly contested corridors in the ancient world. Eventually they got tired of being pushed around, so they took to their boats and moved on. In the process of moving, the Phoenicians gained a reputation as excellent sailors.

Playing the Phoenicians can be frustrating, until you realize that, in *Age of Empires,* most of the advantages that belong to this renowned sea-faring civilization are land-based. You will win or lose as a result of events that happen on land, even though, as a Phoenician, you can build a powerful navy.

Phoenician Priests, like their Egyptian counterparts, have access to all of the beneficial Bronze and Iron Age technologies. This means that they can begin to convert enemy Units and buildings at some point in the game. While this tactic is not nearly as important to Phoenicia as it is to Egypt (and other civilizations), it nonetheless is a significant aspect of this culture.

The Phoenician army is well-balanced and features a nice mixture of high-end Units. Their only shortcoming in this otherwise excellent force is the almost total absence of Siege Weaponry. You can build the Catapult, but all other types of siege weapons are prohibited. Phoenicia also is prevented from training Heavy Cavalry and Cataphract Units. This situation, however, is not nearly as severe as the lack of artillery.

In compensation for having no elite Cavalry, the Phoenician army can build War Elephants and Elephant Archers for 25 percent less than other civilizations. Make good use of the advantage. If you are lucky, your Priests can convert a few mounted Units over to your side to round out your force.

The Phoenician navy is given its first opportunity to rule the waves in the Iron Age with the introduction of the Catapult Trireme. These vessels have their rate of fire increased from once every five seconds to once every three seconds. You need only a few of these warships to begin an awesome barrage that ravages a coastal community. Never overlook this capacity to lay waste to enemy structures that have been foolishly situated in places where you can attack them.

Phoenician Advantages

- The cost to produce Phoenician War Elephants and Elephant Archers is 25 percent less than it is in other civilizations. War Elephant Units cost 127 RPs of food and 30 RPs of gold. Elephant Archer Units cost 135 RPs of food and 45 RPs of gold.

- Phoenician Catapult Triremes and Juggernaughts have their rates of fire increased by 65 percent. Both vessels fire one volley approximately every three seconds.

Phoenician Disadvantages

- Phoenician Siege Workshops are only capable of producing the Catapult Unit. The inability to manufacture advance siege engines—including the Ballista and Helepolis—is a major liability.

- Phoenician Stables are prohibited from producing advanced Cavalry Units such as the Heavy Cavalry and Cataphract.

- Phoenicia cannot research *Metallurgy* or *Chain Mail*. This limits the effectiveness of their Units in hand-to-hand combat.

THE EGYPTIAN GROUP

The three civilizations that make up the Egyptian category (Egypt, Hittite, and Persia) are interesting to play. They present numerous challenges because they are quite different from the others. The

Hittites are a mysterious tribe, even today. If you like building massive fortifications, then you might want to give the Hittites a try. Count on the Persians to build a huge army of elephants and mounted archers. If you like to play aggressively, then Persia is for you. (You must run it better than Darius ever could, though.) Finally, there is Egypt—the jewel of the Nile. You owe it to yourself—at least once—to play Egypt in a multi-player game with eight other people.

EGYPT

To play the Egyptian civilization is to recall its past glories. One thinks of massive chariot armies, mountains of gold, and pyramids rising from the desert. (*Just for the record, Egypt is my personal favorite*.) Egypt is among the strongest civilizations in the game. It has its share of weaknesses, to be sure, but it is forgiving of mistakes like no other civilization.

Egypt is very good at accumulating supplies of gold. Egyptian Villagers have a gold mining ability which is 20 percent better than that of other civilizations. Unfortunately, Egypt is not allowed to research *Coinage* which would further increase this ability. No matter. As it turns out, there is little that Egypt can build that requires lots of gold. You wind up sitting on a pile of money with nothing to buy save for Priests and Priestly research (and the Wonder notwithstanding).

Basically, the Egyptian military is unique. It is characterized more by the Units it cannot produce, rather than the ones that it can. The strongest Units it can deploy are Chariots and Elephants. Chariots provide Egypt with some semblance of mobility, while the Elephants provide the muscle. Even though the Hit Points of Egyptian Chariots and Chariot Archers are increased by 30 percent, they are still only chariots after all. They may move fast, but they lack attack strength. The hey-day of the chariot passes once most civilizations enter the Bronze.

One positive aspect of playing Egypt is the strength of its Priests. All Bronze and Iron Age technologies are open to Egyptian research. One tactic that seems to work well is to use Priests to convert enemy Units and buildings. (I call it the *Cleopatra syndrome*. Enemy Units just can't wait to join up with Egypt for some reason.) This tactic, incidentally, is a convenient way around the limitations of Egypt's home-grown army. Think of it as using Priests to attract mercenaries to your cause.

As poor as Egypt is on land, the Egyptian navy is quite good. Egyptian Docks can build all of the high-end warships, including the Juggernaught. Since enemy ships are more resistant to conversion than land Units, keep a powerful Egyptian navy on hand to deal with them. Convert what you can—sink the rest.

Egyptian Advantages

- The gold mining ability of Egyptian gold miners is increased by 20 percent. They can mine and carry twelve (12) RPs of gold in the same amount of time as other Villagers can mine ten (10) RPs.

- The Egyptian Chariot and Chariot Archer have the amount of damage they can absorb increased by 33 percent. Egyptian Chariot Units can withstand 133 Hit Points, and Chariot Archer Units can withstand 93 Hit Points.

- The conversion range of Egyptian Priests is increased by three tiles to thirteen tiles. All Bronze and Iron technologies are available.

Egyptian Disadvantages

- The Egyptian military lacks diversity. It cannot produce a great number of Unit types. These Unit types include the Phalanx, Centurion, Cavalry, Heavy Cavalry, Cataphract, Broad Swordsman, Long Swordsman, Legion, Horse Archer, Heavy Catapults, Ballista and Helepolis.

- Egypt cannot research *Iron Shield*.

HITTITE

The Hittite empire was a powerful entity in its day leaving historians to wonder what happened to it—one minute it was here, the next minute (forgive the pun) it was history. Fortunately, the Hittites left some documents lying around that modern-day scholars have used to lend credence to Homer's version of the Trojan War.

Hittite archers use a special recurved bow that lets them inflict one additional Hit Point per attack. Whether this advantage is all that significant is open to debate. During the Tool Age, the only Archer available is the Bowman. Is the fact that a Hittite Bowman

inflicts four Hit Points of damage instead of three Hit Points a big deal? Not really.

One undeniably important advantage is the doubling of their Stone Thrower, Catapult, and Heavy Catapult Hit Points. Siege weapons are the most lethal weapons available to you as a Hittite player. Anything that keeps these weapons on the battlefield longer is a significant advantage. Typically, siege weapons are fragile Units that break after just a few hits. Hittite artillery pieces, however, can withstand twice as much damage and continue operating.

Despite the War Galley's increased range, the Hittite navy is weak overall. The inability to produce warships stronger than the War Galley is a fatal liability. Aside from building fishing vessels, the Hittites should remain on dry land. Don't let the War Galley's increased range tempt you into building a bunch of them. The advantage is a minor one compared to the increased speeds or increased rates of fire enjoyed by other civilizations' navies.

In addition to having a poor navy, the Hittites are further hampered by having poor religious figures. Except for *Astrology*, Hittite Priests are prevented from researching Bronze and Iron Age technologies that would make them effective. Keep a few Priests around to act as medics.

Like the Babylonians, Hittites are mean builders. They have access to all of the Iron Age technologies that help a civilization create monumental settlements. One thing the Hittites should build is defensive structures such as walls and towers. None of their important advantages come into play until later in the game. Building fortifications during the Tool Age is one way to ensure survival.

In fact, when you play the Hittite civilization, never embark on wars of conquest—they are un-winnable. Plan on stockpiling resources and protecting yourself (and your resources) behind thick walls while saving to build a Wonder. Let the enemy come to you. While your enemies expend their energies trying to breach your fortifications, pound them into dust with your siege weapons.

Hittite Advantages

- Hittite Stone Thrower, Catapult, and Heavy Catapult Units can absorb twice as much damage as their counterparts in other civilizations (Stone Thrower: 150 Hit Points; Catapult: 150 Hit Points; Heavy Catapult: 300 Hit Points).

- The Hittite archery Units' attack damage is increased by one Hit Point due to their use of a recurved bow (Bowman: four Hit Points; Chariot Archer: five Hit Points; Horse Archer: eight Hit Points; Elephant Archer: six Hit Points; Heavy Horse Archer: nine Hit Points).

- The range of Hittite War Galleys is increased by four tiles to ten tiles.

Hittite Disadvantages

- Hittite Priests rival those in the Minoan civilization for being among the worst in the game. They are prevented from researching any technology (except *Astrology*) that would make them worthwhile.

- The Hittite Siege Workshop cannot produce Ballista or Helepolis Units.

- The Hittites cannot train some advanced infantry and Cavalry Unit types. These include the Long Swordsman, Legion, Heavy Cavalry, and Cataphract.

- The Hittite navy is limited to building fishing vessels, merchant vessels, Light Transports and the War Galley.

PERSIA

As civilizations go, Persia was a monster—one of the largest empires in the ancient world. It is best remembered, however, for getting the stuffing kicked out of it by Alexander the Great and his Macedonians. If you get a thrill seeing a herd of War Elephants go racing through an enemy camp, then playing as Persia is for you.

This civilization comes with some meaningful advantages starting with a 30 percent increase in the hunting ability of its Villagers. This early benefit speeds Persian development. The 500 Resource Points of food needed to enter the Tool Age does not seem so far away when your Villagers are able to hunt and haul 30 percent more food. Eventually, all the wild game in your vicinity turns into T-bones, and your stockpile of food dwindles. The poor productivity of Persian farms only makes matters worse.

Usually, the Persian army will be large and diverse. In Persia's wars with Alexander the Great, it became known for using Elephants in battle. In *Age of Empires*, Persia is likely to build a massive army of Elephant Units once again. The movement speed of

Persian War Elephants and Elephant Archers is increased to 1.2 tiles per second. This means that these normally sluggish Units can now catch and kill all Priests, siege weapons, and infantry Units.

Although the Persian army will be large, it unfortunately will be stupid, too. The Persian Academy is useless and unable to build military Units, including the Hoplite, Phalanx, and Centurion. As a result, Persian players are tempted to substitute quantity for quality, foregoing these elite Units for massive mediocrity.

Besides building a force of War Elephants, the Persian player should concentrate on training Cavalry and Archer Units as well. The Elephant Archer is the perfect partner for these plodding pachyderms. The Persian Horse Archer is another "must-build" Unit.

The Persian navy also will be a force to reckon with. It can build all ship types, including the Juggernaught. Persian Triremes have their rate of fire increased by 50 percent, so that they can fire a missile volley every 1.5 seconds.

Persia is one civilization that needs to win by conquest. The lack of some critical Iron Age technologies makes it difficult to win by building a Wonder. Count on building a huge army and then using it. Don't play Persia unless you have a militaristic personality and hate wasting time on diplomacy.

Persian Advantages

- Persian Villagers have their hunting ability increased by 30 percent. They can hunt and carry 13 RPs of food per trip in the same amount of time as Villagers from other civilizations take to hunt 10 RPs.

- Persian War Elephants and Elephant Archers have their speeds increased by 30 percent. Both Units move at 1.2 tiles per second.

- Persian Trireme Units have their rate of fire increased by 50 percent, firing one missile volley every 1.5 seconds.

Persian Disadvantages

- Persian farm production is decreased by 30 percent, giving Persian farms a basic output of only 175 RPs of food.

- Persians may not research any Bronze or Iron Age technologies at the Market. The prohibited technologies include *Artisanship, Plow, Wheel, Irrigation, Craftsmanship, Coinage* and *Siegecraft*.

- Persians may not research *Aristocracy* or *Ballistics*.

- The Siege Workshop can produce only Catapult and Heavy Catapult Units.

CHAPTER 2
The Ages

Age of Empires spans 12,000 years of human history—from the end of the last great Ice Age to the end of the Iron Age around 100 A.D. This time period is divided into four distinct Ages (Stone, Tool, Bronze, and Iron). Your job is to guide the development of one of twelve different civilizations through the four Ages and, eventually, to gain dominance over the ancient world.

Each Age represents a different stage in the development of your civilization. As your people advance to the next Age, new Units, buildings, and research become available. This chapter summarizes the four Ages and presents this information in convenient, easy-to-use tables.

NOMAD

Nomad is not technically an Age—it's just a different way of beginning the game. If you choose to begin the game as a Nomad, you start all alone in the world with only one single Villager. Fortunately, you begin the game with resources already in your stockpile (200 wood resource points, 200 food resource points, 0 gold resource points, and 150 stone resource points).

Even though you are faced with building an empire from such an inauspicious beginning, do not be daunted by the magnitude of the task. By beginning the game as a Nomad, you have an opportunity to put down roots, as it were, anywhere on the map. Since you have no immediate need to build a Town Center, you should spend some time exploring the nearby terrain.

Your primary concern at this stage of the game should be security and access to food. Whenever possible, you want to build your early structures on high ground or in remote areas of the map. Always try to incorporate impassable terrain features into your settlement plans, so that—in case of conflict—enemy movement into your area will be restricted.

After you settle down, the first order of business is to obtain a steady supply of food. Since you have only the one Villager, you will want to begin expanding your population as soon as possible. This expansion means that you will need to use wood resources to build a Town Center and then use the Town Center to produce new Villagers.

STONE AGE

The Stone Age is characterized by a low population density of humans across the vast untouched riches of an unexplored world. Each civilization begins with three Villagers and a Town Center already placed on the map. If you are fortunate, the Town Center will be situated near food resources. If you are not so fortunate, your Villagers must start scouting the countryside right away. Once again, you start with resources already in your inventory (200 wood RPs, 200 food RPs, 0 gold RPs, 150 stone RPs).

The rudimentary structures available in the Stone Age will not be of much immediate help, but they will get your civilization started down the path of development.

TABLE 2-1 Stone Age Structures

STONE AGE STRUCTURES	CONSTRUCTION COST (RPS)	HIT POINTS
Barracks	125 wood	350
Dock	100 wood	350
Granary	120 wood	350
House	30 wood	75
Storage Pit	120 wood	350
Town Center	200 wood	600

With your Town Center in place, you should look to expand your population. This growth requires that you begin to build housing for your people and Storage Pits or Granaries for stockpiling their food. You will want to build a Dock and begin fishing right away. Once the Barracks is completed, you can begin to build your army.

TABLE 2-2 Stone Age Units

Unit	Construction Cost (RPs)
Clubman	50 food
Villager	50 food

The single Stone Age military Unit (the Clubman) is not much better than the average Villager. The level of protection may not be great, but there is a certain comfort that comes from having these club-wielding cavemen roaming around.

Since your primary concern during the Stone Age is to acquire resources and to construct primitive buildings, you will have few resource points left over for research. Research is unavailable during this Age anyway, so you shouldn't be too distracted by it.

TABLE 2-3 Stone Age Technology

Type	Research Cost (RPs)
None	N/A

As soon as your people locate a suitable body of water, you should spend the wood resources to build a Dock. Once again, your primary concern is getting food; at this point, military considerations take second place. Build the Dock close to good fishing sites, and don't worry about defending it—at least initially. Besides fishing boats, trading skiffs are also available during this Age.

TABLE 2-4 Stone Age Naval Units

Unit	Construction Cost (RPs)
Fishing Boat	50 wood
Trade Boat	100 wood

Throughout the Stone Age, you want to increase your population and add to your stockpile of resources. As you build Villagers (at 50 Rps of food each), keep in mind that you will need to spend 500 resource points to enter the next Age. Arriving at the next Age is important, but not at the expense of your population base. Try to develop a work force of at least six Villagers before entering the Tool Age. There is no sense in having the tools to succeed if there is no one around to use them.

TOOL AGE

Now that you have reached the Tool Age, a number of new buildings and military Units appear. The most important new aspect of the game, however, is the introduction of technologies. The Tool Age is an exciting time in the life of your civilization—one of the more enjoyable periods to play. Your civilization should start to branch out into new areas of the map. You may even bump into a neighbor or two.

For the most part, Tool Age buildings serve two purposes: (1) they broaden the kinds of military Units you can build, and (2) they introduce new and better ways to acquire resources, particularly food.

TABLE 2-5 Tool Age Structures

Tool Age Structures	Construction Cost (RPs)	Hit Points
Archery Range	150 wood	350
Farm	75 wood	50
Market	150 wood	350
Small Wall	5 stone	200
Stable	150 wood	350
Watch Tower	150 stone	100

In addition to spending resources on buildings, your civilization should begin to spend resources on research. Tool Age technologies accelerate your civic development by improving your Villagers and military Units.

TABLE 2-6 Tool Age Technology

Type	Research Cost (RPs)
Domestication	200 food, 50 wood
Gold Mining	120 food, 100 wood
Leather Armor for Archers	100 food
Leather Armor for Cavalry	125 food
Leather Armor for Infantry	75 food
Small Wall	50 food
Stone Mining	100 food, 50 stone
Toolworking	100 food
Watch Tower	50 food
Woodworking	120 food, 75 wood

Even with new Units, Tool Age armies are nothing more than mobs of unskilled men carrying weapons. By upgrading your Clubmen to Axeman status, however, you give your people a slight advantage in hand-to-hand combat. The introduction of the first archer Unit allows you to begin engaging targets from a distance.

TABLE 2-7 Tool Age Land Units

UNIT	CONSTRUCTION COST (RPs)
Axeman	100 food
Bowman	40 food, 20 wood
Scout	100 food

TABLE 2-8 Tool Age Upgrades

UNIT	UPGRADE COST (RPs)
Upgrade to Axeman	100 food

With improvements on land come developments at sea. You may now build a transport vessel to carry Units across water. For protection, you may build a crude warship, a forerunner to the Trireme.

TABLE 2-9 Tool Age Naval Units

VESSEL	CONSTRUCTION COST (RPs)
Light Transport	150 wood
Scout Ship	135 wood

As your population and work force increase, so does your need for food. Even with the appearance of farms, your food consumption likely exceeds your supply. By the time you are ready to advance from the Tool Age to the Bronze Age, you already should know where all the good hunting, foraging, and fishing spots are located.

BRONZE AGE

Once you reach the Bronze Age, most of the map will have been explored by one or more civilizations. Ruins will have been discovered (and guarded); artifacts will have been found (and carted away). The population density of the map will have increased significantly. Resources become scarce, but one thing does not diminish in the Bronze Age—the competition! The first truly professional armies are about to emerge on the plains of the battlefield.

By this time, your civilization should have created an extensive infrastructure. The Bronze Age gives you an opportunity to expand the power and reach of your government. New buildings improve your ability to threaten your neighbors and, at the same time, to defend your empire.

TABLE 2-10 Bronze Age Structures

BRONZE AGE STRUCTURES	CONSTRUCTION COST (RPS)	HIT POINTS
Academy	200 wood	350
Government Center	175 wood	350
Medium Wall	5 stone	300
Sentry Tower	150 stone	150
Siege Workshop	200 wood	350
Temple	200 wood	350

In addition to new buildings, the Bronze Age offers an array of new research. The introduction of religious technologies adds a spiritual dimension to your civilization that has not existed before.

TABLE 2-11 Bronze Age Technology

TYPE	RESEARCH COST (RPs)
Architecture	150 food, 175 wood
Artisanship	170 food, 150 wood
Astrology	150 gold
Bronze Shield	150 food, 180 gold
Improved Bowman	140 food, 80 wood
Metalworking	200 food, 120 gold
Mysticism	120 gold
Nobility	175 food, 120 gold
Plow	250 food, 75 wood
Polytheism	120 gold
Scale Armor for Archers	125 food, 50 gold
Scale Armor for Cavalry	150 food, 50 gold
Scale Armor for Infantry	100 food, 50 gold
Short Swordsman	120 food, 50 gold
Wheel	175 food, 75 wood
Writing	200 food, 75 gold

The role of the military dramatically increases during the Bronze Age as the encroachment of neighboring civilizations becomes more and more prominent. You probably will have to use force to get what you want from now on.

TABLE 2-12 Bronze Age Land Units

Unit	Construction Cost (RPs)
Broad Swordsman	35 food, 15 gold
Cavalry	70 food, 80 gold
Chariot	40 food, 60 wood
Chariot Archer	40 food, 70 wood
Composite Bowman	40 food, 20 gold
Hoplite	60 food, 40 gold
Improved Bowman	40 food, 20 gold
Priest	125 gold
Short Swordsman	35 food, 15 gold
Stone Thrower	180 wood, 80 gold

TABLE 2-13 Bronze Age Upgrades

Unit	Upgrade Cost (RPs)
Upgrade to Broad Swordsman	140 food, 50 gold
Upgrade to Composite Bowman	180 food, 100 gold
Upgrade to Medium Wall	180 food, 100 stone
Upgrade to Sentry Tower	120 food, 50 stone
Upgrade to Short Swordsman	120 food, 50 gold

Bronze Age navies, like their land counterparts, take on new responsibilities. Vessel upgrades ensure that more activity will take place at sea in the near future.

TABLE 2-14 Bronze Age Naval Units

Vessel	Construction Cost (RPs)
Fishing Ship	50 wood
Merchant Ship	100 wood
War Galley	135 wood

TABLE 2-15 Bronze Age Naval Upgrades

Unit	Upgrade Cost (RPs)
Upgrade to Fishing Ship	50 food, 100 wood
Upgrade to Merchant Ship	200 food, 75 wood
Upgrade to War Galley	150 food, 75 wood

By the end of the Bronze Age, it should be apparent which civilizations have prospered and which civilizations seem destined for destruction. Although the tools to eliminate a civilization are certainly present, the proverbial ax normally does not fall until the Iron Age. The Bronze Age is also known as the Age of Diplomacy. You had better talk with your neighbors now because, once everyone reaches the Iron Age, armies march and navies go to sea.

IRON AGE

Welcome to the Iron Age, the fourth and last epoch in the game. Hopefully, by this point, you have learned a thing or two about running a civilization. Unfortunately, you are now competing directly against other civilizations (gameplayers) with similar knowledge. In earlier Ages, food and wood were important; during the Iron Age, the search for gold will control your actions as the game nears its conclusion.

No new buildings come into existence during this final stage of the game. There are two new types of towers, however. You should pay to upgrade your existing towers.

TABLE 2-16 Iron Age Structures

IRON AGE STRUCTURES	CONSTRUCTION COST (RPS)	HIT POINTS
Guard Tower	150 stone	200
Ballista Tower	150 stone	200

Technology now takes the forefront. This Age is characterized by a continued strengthening of spiritual faith and an increased emphasis on religious conversion. Priests assume awesome powers as a result of the technologies available to them. Other research expands the role of government and further improves the military.

TABLE 2-17 Iron Age Technology

Type	Research Cost (RPs)
Afterlife	275 gold
Alchemy	250 food, 200 gold
Aristocracy	175 food, 150 gold
Ballistics	200 food, 50 gold
Catapult Trireme	300 food, 100 wood
Chain Mail for Archers	150 food, 100 gold
Chain Mail for Cavalry	175 food, 100 gold
Chain Mail for Infantry	125 food, 100 gold
Coinage	200 food, 100 gold
Craftsmanship	240 food, 200 wood
Engineering	200 food, 100 wood
Fanaticism	150 gold
Iron Shield	200 food, 320 gold
Irrigation	300 food, 100 wood
Jihad	120 gold
Metallurgy	300 food, 180 gold
Monotheism	350 gold
Siegecraft	190 food, 100 stone

Most visible military Units during this Age are upgrades from previous Units. They are extremely expensive but fantastically strong. Increased armor protection is offset by an increased ability to inflict damage. Defensive benefits enjoyed by some Units (due to increased speed, for example) are offset by larger missile ranges of other Units.

TABLE 2-18 Iron Age Land Units

Unit	Construction Cost (RPs)
Ballista	100 wood, 80 gold
Cataphract	70 food, 80 gold
Catapult	180 wood, 80 gold
Centurion	60 food, 40 gold
Elephant Archer	180 food, 60 gold
Heavy Catapult	180 wood, 80 gold
Heavy Cavalry	70 food, 80 gold
Heavy Horse Archer	50 food, 70 gold
Helepolis	100 wood, 80 gold
Horse Archer	50 food, 70 gold
Legion	35 food, 15 gold
Long Swordsman	35 food, 15 gold
Phalanx	60 food, 40 gold
War Elephant	170 food, 40 gold

The number of Unit upgrades available in the Iron Age is significant. The cost of some upgrades makes them affordable to only the most economically successful civilizations.

TABLE 2-19 Iron Age Upgrades

Unit	Upgrade Cost (RPs)
Upgrade to Ballista Tower	1,800 food, 750 stone
Upgrade to Long Swordsman	160 food, 50 gold
Upgrade to Legion	1,400 food, 600 gold
Upgrade to Phalanx	300 food, 100 gold

Upgrade to Centurion	1,800 food, 700 gold
Upgrade to Heavy Catapult	1,800 food, 900 wood
Upgrade to Heavy Cavalry	350 food, 125 gold
Upgrade to Helepolis	1,500 food, 1,000 wood
Upgrade to Guard Tower	300 food, 100 stone
Upgrade to Cataphract	2,000 food, 850 gold
Upgrade to Catapult	300 food, 250 wood
Upgrade to Heavy Horse Archer	1,750 food, 800 gold

Any civilization situated near the coast is in for a rough time. The abilities and prowess of naval vessels finally match—and exceed—those of their land counterparts. With the advent of these new vessels, control of the seas is mandatory.

TABLE 2-20 Iron Age Naval Units

VESSELS	CONSTRUCTION COST (RPs)
Catapult Trireme	135 wood, 75 gold
Heavy Transport	150 wood
Juggernaught	135 wood, 75 gold
Trireme	135 wood

TABLE 2-21 Iron Age Naval Upgrades

VESSELS	UPGRADE COST (RPs)
Upgrade to Heavy Transport	150 food, 125 wood
Upgrade to Juggernaught	2,000 food, 900 wood
Upgrade to Trireme	250 food, 100 wood

CHAPTER 3
The Technologies

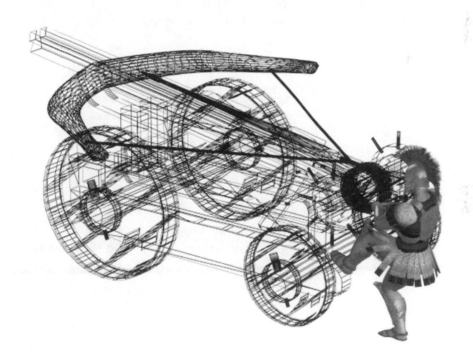

Your success in *Age of Empires* will be determined by your ability to guide the development of your people. Part of this development occurs as a result of acquiring resources (peaceably or forcefully) and constructing buildings. But the largest share of this development, by far, comes from using resources to research advancement technologies.

This chapter is an in-depth look at these technologies. It answers questions concerning cost, location of these researches, and benefits your people derive from them. The technologies are presented in alphabetical order according to the Age in which they first become available.

STONE AGE TECHNOLOGY

During the Stone Age, people are barely surviving. Their main concerns are focused on gathering food and other resources, so they can make it through another day. In most cases, the surplus of resources—if there are any at all—will be small. Hardly anything will be left over for idle research into new technologies.

Fortunately, most civilizations do not remain in the Stone Age for long. If you have settled your tribe in even a remotely habitable region of the map, your Villagers can hunt for, and forage, enough food to make the jump into the Tool Age in a reasonable amount of time.

TOOL AGE TECHNOLOGY

It only takes 500 resource points (RPs) of food and the construction of two Stone Age buildings to enter the Tool Age. Once you reach this Age, be prepared to spend additional food right away.

Wondrous new technologies are available to your people, but they all require research—and research requires food. This presents somewhat of a problem.

These new technologies appear at a time when you are trying to build your population base. So, do you spend the food resources on building new Villagers or on improving the Villagers you already have? This question obviously must be answered on a case-by-case basis, but keep it in mind as you examine the Tool Age technologies below.

DOMESTICATION

COMPOSITE	DESCRIPTION
Age	Tool
Prerequisite Buildings	Town Center, Granary, Market
Prerequisite Technologies	None
Cost	200 RPs of food, 50 RPs of wood
Research Location	Market

Benefit of Technology

Domestication adds 75 RPs of food to the total amount of food generated by your farms. The base amount of food produced on your farms is 250 RPs. Sometimes this base is modified by your civilization's special attributes and research in other technologies. Unless you are surrounded by abundant wild life or foraging sites, you will want to research this technology as soon as it becomes available. Build the Market, do the research, and start creating Farms. The 75 extra points of food that *Domestication* makes available represents a 30 percent increase in your farms' overall productivity. **Note:** This only affects new farms created after the research is done.

GOLD MINING

COMPOSITE	DESCRIPTION
Age	Tool
Prerequisite Buildings	Town Center, Granary, Market
Prerequisite Technologies	None
Cost	120 RPs of food, 100 RPs of wood
Research Location	Market

Benefit of Technology

Gold Mining adds three resource points to your Villagers' ability to mine and transport gold. A Villager normally can mine and carry ten RPs of gold per trip. This technology allows your Villager to mine and carry 13 RPs.

Whether this ability is necessary during the Tool Age is debatable. Acquiring food, wood, and stone resources is usually more important at this stage of the game. Try to hold off for a while before researching this technology. Build a couple Villagers and a fishing boat (or two) instead.

LEATHER ARMOR FOR ARCHERS

COMPOSITE	DESCRIPTION
Age	Tool
Prerequisite Buildings	Town Center, Storage Pit
Prerequisite Technologies	None
Cost	100 RPs of food
Research Location	Storage Pit

Benefit of Technology

Leather Armor for Archers reduces the amount of damage your archer (Archery Range) Units suffer by two Hit Points per attack. Leather Armor is the first of three armor technologies that become available to your archers. You must complete research on this technology before you can move to the more advanced types of armor.

Typically, archers can withstand less damage than other kinds of units. If you are considering building a number of archer units, you definitely should spend the 100 RPs of food to research this technology. Unless you are threatened with imminent attack, you can afford to delay researching this technology.

LEATHER ARMOR FOR CAVALRY

COMPOSITE	DESCRIPTION
Age	Tool
Prerequisite Buildings	Town Center, Storage Pit
Prerequisite Technologies	None
Cost	125 RPs of food
Research Location	Storage Pit

Benefit of Technology

Leather Armor for Cavalry reduces the damage your Cavalry (Stable) Units sustain by two Hit Points per attack. Leather Armor is the first of three armor technologies available to your Cavalry. You must complete research on this technology before you can move to the more advanced types of armor.

Cavalry Units are most effective when they charge the enemy and engage in hand-to-hand combat—they obviously require protection. Remember that infantry Units can dish out a great deal of damage in return. Making Leather Armor available to your Cavalry Units for only 125 RPs of food is a bargain. Still, unless you are threatened with imminent attack, you can afford to delay researching this technology.

LEATHER ARMOR FOR INFANTRY

COMPOSITE	DESCRIPTION
Age	Tool
Prerequisite Buildings	Town Center, Storage Pit
Prerequisite Technologies	None
Cost	75 RPs of food
Research Location	Storage Pit

Benefit of Technology

Leather Armor for Infantry reduces the amount of damage your infantry (Barracks and Academy) Units suffer by two Hit Points per round of attack. Leather Armor is the first of three armor technologies available to your infantry units. You must complete research on this technology before you can move to the more advanced types of armor.

Since infantry Units spend most of their time in close proximity to the enemy, any protection you can give them extends their usefulness. Researching *Leather Armor for Infantry* is a no-brainer. For little more than the cost of a Clubman, you can prolong the life of your infantry Units by, at least, several rounds of combat. Once again, unless you are threatened with imminent attack, you can afford to delay researching this technology.

SMALL WALL

COMPOSITE	DESCRIPTION
Age	Tool
Prerequisite Buildings	Town Center, Granary
Prerequisite Technologies	None
Cost	50 RPs of food
Research Location	Granary

Benefit of Technology

Small Wall allows your civilization to begin building sections of Small Wall. These structures are stone obstructions that prevent Units (both friendly and enemy) from moving through a particular tile. Multiple sections of Small Wall can be arranged, so that they form a solid row extending as far as you want.

During the Tool Age, when your military strength is low, you may want to make good use of these defensive structures. Small Walls can channel or block enemy movement, keeping them away from areas you wish to inhabit. The modest research cost of 50 RPs of food will not impede your development nearly as much as failing to build walls and letting enemy troops ransack your civilization.

STONE MINING

COMPOSITE	DESCRIPTION
Age	Tool
Prerequisite Buildings	Town Center, Granary, Market
Prerequisite Technologies	None
Cost	100 RPs of food, 50 RPs of stone
Research Location	Market

Benefit of Technology

Stone Mining adds three resource points to your Villagers' ability to mine and transport stone. Normally, a Villager can mine and carry ten RPs of stone per trip. This technology allows your Villagers to mine and carry up to 13 RPs of stone, thus increasing your Villagers' mining speed by 30 percent over their counterparts' rate without this technology.

Stone Mining is a critical technology.

TOOLWORKING

COMPOSITE	DESCRIPTION
Age	Tool
Prerequisite Buildings	Town Center, Storage Pit
Prerequisite Technologies	None
Cost	100 RPs of food
Research Location	Storage Pit

Benefit of Technology

Toolworking adds two additional Hit Points of damage per round of attack to all of your Barracks, Academy, and Stable Units (with the exception of the War Elephant). For some units, like the Clubman and Axeman, this increase almost doubles the amount of damage they inflict per round.

Toolworking is quite important because it benefits all your Units. If you have *Toolworking* researched, you can buy yourself some insurance; you will be able to compete if someone attacks. It is a must-buy by the mid-Tool Age.

WATCH TOWER

COMPOSITE	DESCRIPTION
Age	Tool
Prerequisite Buildings	Town Center, Granary
Prerequisite Technologies	None
Cost	50 RPs of food
Research Location	Granary

Benefit of Technology

Watch Tower allows your civilization to begin building Watch Towers. These structures become available as soon as you build a Granary and reach the Tool Age. Considering the tactical and strategic advantages that come from owning towers, spending 50 RPs of food on researching *Watch Tower* is a bargain.

Towers are stationary structures that can fire missiles (projectiles) at enemy troops that wander within its range. The Watch Tower is just the first (and weakest) of four different towers in the game. It has an attack strength of 3 Hit Points, a range of 5 tiles, and can withstand 100 Hit Points of damage. Each of the subsequent tower upgrades cause more damage, have a greater range of fire, and possess more Hit Points than its predecessor.

WOODWORKING

Composite	Description
Age	Tool
Prerequisite Buildings	Town Center, Granary, Market
Prerequisite Technologies	None
Cost	100 RPs of food, 75 RPs of wood
Research Location	Market

Benefit of Technology

Woodworking adds two resource points to your Villagers' ability to cut and transport wood. A Villager can typically cut and carry ten RPs of wood per trip. This technology allows your Villagers to cut and carry up to 12 RPs of wood, increasing your Villagers' woodcutting speed by 20 percent.

Woodworking also adds one tile to the range of all Archery Range units, towers, Scout Ships, War Galleys, and Triremes (for Archer Strategies, all range upgrades are crucial). Although the increased range will not be that significant to you, the cost of this research is cheap in relation to its added benefits. *Woodworking* is a prerequisite technology for researching Artisanship.

BRONZE AGE TECHNOLOGIES

Tool Age technologies were designed mainly to help your people survive and to stock some resources for a rainy decade or two. Having survived the Tool Age, it is time for your civilization to begin diversifying and expanding into new areas. Bronze Age technologies build on the research you have conducted thus far by improving your ability to collect resources. They also strengthen your military units. From a developmental standpoint, however, the most important benefit of entering the Bronze Age is the introduction of religion and its technologies.

ARCHITECTURE

COMPOSITE	DESCRIPTION
Age	Bronze
Prerequisite Buildings	Town Center, Granary, Market, Government Center
Prerequisite Technologies	None
Cost	150 RPs of food, 175 RPs of wood
Research Location	Government Center

Benefit of Technology

Architecture increases the damage your buildings can sustain by 20 percent. For example, your Town Center can withstand 600 Hit Points of damage before being destroyed. After researching *Architecture*, your Town Center will absorb 720 Hit Points.

Architecture also decreases construction time of your buildings by 33 percent. A building that normally takes 90 seconds of game time to construct only take 60 seconds after researching *Architecture*. The real beauty of this technology is that its effects are retroactively applied to existing structures. It is relatively expensive in terms of resources, and it's a fairly low priority technology. Use it when resources are available. It's a must before building a Wonder.

(Not every civilization has access to this technology, however. Those without it are at a slight disadvantage.)

ARTISANSHIP

COMPOSITE	DESCRIPTION
Age	Bronze
Prerequisite Buildings	Town Center, Granary, Market
Prerequisite Technologies	*Woodworking*
Cost	170 RPs of food, 150 RPs of wood
Research Location	Market

Benefit of Technology

Artisanship adds two RPs to your Villagers' ability to cut and carry wood. Coupled with the increase your Villagers already enjoy from *Woodworking*, this technology turns them into little "Agent Oranges"—no matter what their color in the game happens to be. (Just remember the saying, *"Only YOU can prevent forests."*)

Not only does this technology raise your basic "cut-and-carry" capacity to 14 RPs of wood, it also gives you a military advantage. *Artisanship* increases the missile range of your Archery Range Units, towers, Scout Ships, War Galleys, and Triremes by one tile. Against moving targets, the practical effect of being able to shoot one extra tile may not seem like much. When dealing with stationary targets like buildings, however, the extra range allows you to set and maintain a safe distance from your enemies. It also gives the relatively fragile Archers more time to shoot advancing infantry before it can attack.

ASTROLOGY

COMPOSITE	DESCRIPTION
Age	Bronze
Prerequisite Buildings	Town Center, Granary, Market, Temple
Prerequisite Technologies	None
Cost	90 RPs of gold
Research Location	Temple

Benefit of Technology

Astrology, one of the cheaper religious technologies in the game, increases the effectiveness at which your Priests convert enemy Units by 30 percent. You should research it as soon as it becomes available. If you plan to spend 125 RPs of gold to train a single Priest, why not spend the additional 150 RPs to make all of your Priest Units even better?

Usually, an enemy player will hear the "Yo-Yo-Yo" chant and immediately move in to kill the Priest. If your Priest fails to convert the Unit—or cannot convert it in time—the Priest is usually a dead man. Though powerful, these old guys do not last very long in hand-to-hand combat. *Astrology* raises the chance that the Priest will succeed at conversions and possibly even survive. This is a must research if you plan to build Priests, but as a number of tribes don't even get most of the Priest technologies, your planned strategy is key in this decision.

BRONZE SHIELD

COMPOSITE	DESCRIPTION
Age	Bronze
Prerequisite Buildings	Town Center, Storage Pit
Prerequisite Technologies	None
Cost	120 RPs of food, 140 RPs of gold
Research Location	Storage Pit

Benefit of Technology

Bronze Shield is a defensive accessory which reduces the damage your infantry Units suffer by one Hit Point per round of attack—but only when you are attacked by missile Units (Ballista, Helepolis, Archery Range units, towers, Scout Ships, War Galleys and Triremes). Because the *Bronze Shield* is only good against missile attacks, the protection it offers its bearer is referred to as a Piercing Armor bonus.

This technology is expensive, and its protection is not that significant compared to the damage that most Bronze Age missile Units can inflict. You can usually pass it up without suffering any noticeable effect. Bear in mind that the *Bronze Shield* is a prerequisite technology for researching the *Iron Shield*, but it's only really useful if you are playing an infantry-based strategy such as Greek Phalanx or chosen Long Swords.

IMPROVED BOW

COMPOSITE	DESCRIPTION
Age	Bronze
Prerequisite Buildings	Town Center, Barracks, Archery Range
Prerequisite Technologies	None
Cost	140 RPs of food, 80 RPs of wood
Research Location	Archery Range

Benefit of Technology

Improved Bow is a prerequisite technology for training the Improved Bowman Unit. This Unit does four Hit Points of damage per attack and has a range of seven tiles. It can absorb 40 Hit Points of damage and moves at a speed of 1.2 tiles per second.

Although Improved Bowman Units are only marginally better than the basic Bowman, you still want to research the *Improved Bow*. This research is costly—even for a Bronze Age technology—so pick the proper time. This research gives a certain military advantage to its recipient. This is most important because it opens the door to the Composite Bow. It is a must buy if you are planning on making archers. If you're not, it's a waste.

METALWORKING

COMPOSITE	DESCRIPTION
Age	Bronze
Prerequisite Buildings	Town Center, Storage Pit
Prerequisite Technologies	*Toolworking*
Cost	200 RPs of food, 120 RPs of gold
Research Location	Storage Pit

Benefit of Technology

Metalworking adds two Hit Points of damage per attack round to all Units that engage in hand-to-hand combat. This benefit is applied to all Barracks, Academy, and Stable Units (except the War Elephant).

An Axeman that normally inflicts five Hit Points of damage per attack round, for example, would inflict nine Hit Points after research in *Metalworking* is completed. (This damage total reflects the Axeman's base damage [5], plus *Toolworking* [+2], plus *Metalworking* [+2]). Notice that the Axeman inflicts almost twice as much damage as a result of *Metalworking*. Consider this technology as a "must have." It is the second of three such hand-to-hand combat technologies and a prerequisite technology for researching Metallurgy.

MYSTICISM

COMPOSITE	DESCRIPTION
Age	Bronze
Prerequisite Buildings	Town Center, Granary, Market, Temple
Prerequisite Technologies	None
Cost	120 RPs of gold
Research Location	Temple

Benefit of Technology

Mysticism doubles the amount of damage your Priests can absorb before elimination. A Priest Unit normally can withstand 25 Hit Points of damage. With *Mysticism*, the total is increased to 50. Don't forget: A Priest, despite his power, is just some geezer in a robe when it comes to hand-to-hand combat—they don't have a prayer. (*Okay, you got me—pun intended*).

Priest Units attract a lot of attention, especially when they attempt to convert an enemy unit. Their distinctive chanting stands out against the normal background noises, and the enemy usually has no trouble homing in on them. In general, killing Priests is a priority because their conversion ability can be quite devastating. Anything you can do to help your Priests survive—at least a bit longer—is worth the expense.

NOBILITY

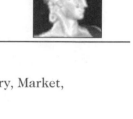

COMPOSITE	DESCRIPTION
Age	Bronze
Prerequisite Buildings	Town Center, Granary, Market, Government Center
Prerequisite Technologies	None
Cost	175 RPs of food, 120 RPs of gold
Research Location	Government Center

Benefit of Technology

Nobility increases the Hit Points of certain Cavalry Units by 15 percent. (Cavalry Units affected by this research include the Chariot, Chariot Archer, Horse Archer, and Heavy Horse Archer.) Considering the cost of replacing even a single Cavalry Unit (not to mention the entire Calvary), *Nobility* is a necessity (depending on your Calvary, Heavy Cavalry, and Catapult strategy. Alway pick technology based on your goal.

Unfortunately, this technology is not universally available. Only certain tribes can make good use of its benefits. The Greek, Persian, and Yamato civilizations are the three main beneficiaries. *Nobility* is particularly important for the Yamato. This one technology alone can make the Yamato's mounted armies close to invincible.

PLOW

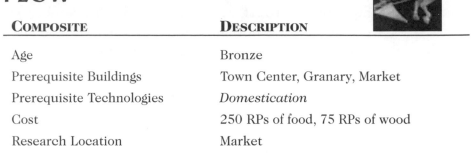

COMPOSITE	DESCRIPTION
Age	Bronze
Prerequisite Buildings	Town Center, Granary, Market
Prerequisite Technologies	*Domestication*
Cost	250 RPs of food, 75 RPs of wood
Research Location	Market

Benefit of Technology

Plow is one of several technologies that agrarian civilizations should research. The base amount of food produced on your farms is increased from 250 RPs to 325 RPs (+75) as a result of researching *Domestication*. By researching *Plow* now, you can increase the food output of your farms by an additional 75 resource points to 400.

Consider for a moment what 400 points of food equals in terms of berry bushes or gazelle. Soon, the government will step in and begin paying your Villagers not to grow anything. When you play the Persian civilization, you should always research these technologies. Persians cannot research beyond domestication. They only have Tool Age market research available. Persians have no plow options.

POLYTHEISM

COMPOSITE	DESCRIPTION
Age	Bronze
Prerequisite Buildings	Town Center, Granary, Market, Temple
Prerequisite Technologies	None
Cost	120 RPs of gold
Research Location	Temple

Benefit of Technology

Polytheism increases the movement speed of your Priests by 40 percent from 0.8 tiles per second to 1.12 tiles per second. Priests never move fast enough to suit your needs, but at least after researching this technology, they will be able to outrun enemy siege weapons.

In some scenarios, you will have control of a Blind Lame Priest. No matter how many Gods you believe in, this Unit never moves. The Hittites are the only civilization unable to research *Polytheism*. The Babylonians and Egyptians, with their strong reliance on religious conversion, should make this research a priority.

SCALE ARMOR FOR ARCHERS

COMPOSITE	DESCRIPTION
Age	Bronze
Prerequisite Buildings	Town Center, Storage Pit
Prerequisite Technologies	*Leather Armor for Archers*
Cost	125 RPs of food, 50 RPs of gold
Research Location	Storage Pit

Benefit of Technology

Scale Armor for Archers reduces the damage your Archery Range Units suffer by two Hit Points per attack. Scale Armor is the second of three armor technologies available for archers. Before you can research *Scale Armor for Archers*, you must research *Leather Armor for Archers*.

By the time you have outfitted your archers with Scale Armor, the damage they suffer per round of attack is reduced by four Hit Points. Lacking substantial Hit Points to begin with, archers have the most to gain by wearing armor. If your civilization intends on producing archers in numbers, consider this technology a "must."

SCALE ARMOR FOR CAVALRY

COMPOSITE	DESCRIPTION
Age	Bronze
Prerequisite Buildings	Town Center, Storage Pit
Prerequisite Technologies	*Leather Armor for Cavalry*
Cost	150 RPs of food, 50 RPs of gold
Research Location	Storage Pit

Benefit of Technology

Scale Armor for Cavalry reduces the amount of damage your Stable Units suffer by two Hit Points per round of attack. Scale Armor is the second of three armor technologies available to Cavalry. Before you can research *Scale Armor for Cavalry*, you must first research *Leather Armor for Cavalry*.

By the time you have outfitted your Cavalry Units with Scale Armor, the damage they suffer per attack is reduced by four Hit Points.

SCALE ARMOR FOR INFANTRY

COMPOSITE	DESCRIPTION
Age	Bronze
Prerequisite Buildings	Town Center, Storage Pit
Prerequisite Technologies	*Leather Armor for Infantry*
Cost	100 RPs of food, 50 RPs of gold
Research Location	Storage Pit

Benefit of Technology

Scale Armor for Infantry reduces the damage your Barracks Units suffer by two Hit Points per round of attack. Scale Armor is the second of three armor technologies to become available to your Infantry. Before you can research *Scale Armor for Infantry*, you must first research *Leather Armor for Infantry*.

By the time you have outfitted your infantry Units with Scale Armor, the amount of damage they suffer per round of attack is reduced by four Hit Points. Your foot soldiers will get killed off fairly quickly without adequate protection, especially during the Bronze and Iron Ages.

SHORT SWORD

COMPOSITE	DESCRIPTION
Age	Bronze
Prerequisite Buildings	Town Center, Barracks
Prerequisite Technologies	None
Cost	120 RPs of food, 50 RPs of gold
Research Location	Barracks

Benefit of Technology

Short Sword is a prerequisite for training the Short Swordsman. This technology opens the way to producing the first half-way decent infantry Unit in the game. Both the Clubman and Axeman are inferior Units to the sword-wielding, semi-professional infantry types that begin to appear in the Bronze Age.

Unless you intend to build a strictly mounted army, consider researching *Short Sword*. Although they require gold to produce, Short Swordsman Units inflict twice as much damage as the Clubman and can endure 60 hits points of damage before succumbing to the inevitable. These warriors represent a significant advancement in power.

WHEEL

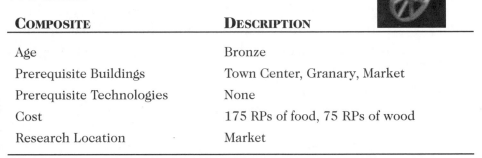

COMPOSITE	DESCRIPTION
Age	Bronze
Prerequisite Buildings	Town Center, Granary, Market
Prerequisite Technologies	None
Cost	175 RPs of food, 75 RPs of wood
Research Location	Market

Benefit of Technology

Wheel increases your Villagers' speed by 30 percent. It is arguably the most important technology in the game because of the far-reaching implications associated with any increase in the speed of your Villagers.

If your Villagers can move 30 percent faster, you can acquire resources 30 percent faster than you could otherwise, which means you can afford to erect buildings at a rate 30 percent faster, which means you advance to the next Age 30 percent faster, which means new technologies become available to you 30 percent faster . . . and so forth. It is difficult to overestimate the significance of the *Wheel*. This technology comes available at the Market as soon as you enter the Bronze Age. No other research is so singularly important at this stage of the game. Spend the resources to research the *Wheel*. This one technology truly will get your civilization rolling along. It is also a prerequisite for Chariot and Archer Chariot Units.

WRITING

COMPOSITE	DESCRIPTION
Age	Bronze
Prerequisite Buildings	Town Center, Granary, Market
Prerequisite Technologies	None
Cost	200 RPs of food, 75 RPs of gold
Research Location	Government Center

Benefit of Technology

Writing allows you and your allied civilizations to exchange maps, revealing all areas that have been explored by one or more of the parties involved. As you acquire more allies, more of the map is revealed.

Whether this technology is worth its cost obviously depends on the civilizations with which you are allied. If your civilization has not explored much of the map by this point in the game, this technology comes in handy. Knowing the lay of the land will save you time and effort in locating resources. Consider researching this technology as an alternative to provoking your neighbors with Villagers or military Units on scouting missions. However, it's useless if you aren't allied.

IRON AGE TECHNOLOGIES

The seventeen Iron Age technologies in this section represent the culmination of human development in *Age of Empires*. Though expensive, these technologies are all worthwhile in that they unleash the full might of the ancient world and bestow potential game-winning advantages upon the civilizations that research them.

AFTERLIFE

COMPOSITE	DESCRIPTION
Age	Iron
Prerequisite Buildings	Town Center, Granary, Market, Temple
Prerequisite Technologies	None
Cost	175 RPs of gold
Research Location	Temple

Benefit of Technology

Afterlife is a religious technology that increases the conversion range of your Priests by three tiles to a total of 13. It allows Priests to conduct their conversion attempts beyond the reach of enemy archers and siege weapons.

One of the biggest problems with converting Units is the fact that Priests usually are killed before the conversion is complete. Because of the distance, this technology increases the Priest's time to complete the conversion. At a distance of 3 tiles, the Priest remains out of visibility of most units. Concealment may be the Priest's best protection, allowing him to maintain his distance and to strike like a "bolt from the blue."

ALCHEMY

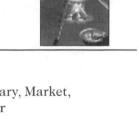

Composite	Description
Age	Iron
Prerequisite Buildings	Town Center, Granary, Market, Government Center
Prerequisite Technologies	None
Cost	250 RPs of food, 200 RPs of gold
Research Location	Government Center

Benefit of Technology

Alchemy adds one Hit Point to the damage caused by all missile units, including warships and Units produced at the Archery Range and Siege Workshop. For an Iron Age technology, the additional Hit Point of damage is relatively minor. A Stone Thrower, for example, already inflicts 50 Hit Points of damage per attack. Is researching *Alchemy* so that you inflict 51 Hit Points, instead of 50, worth the cost? Consider what 200 RPs of gold could otherwise buy you and then decide for yourself.

ARISTOCRACY

Composite	Description
Age	Iron
Prerequisite Buildings	Town Center, Granary, Market, Government Center
Prerequisite Technologies	None
Cost	175 RPs of food, 150 RPs of gold
Research Location	Government Center

Benefit of Technology

Aristocracy increases the speed of your Academy Units by 25 percent. (Academy Units include the Hoplite, Phalanx, and Centurion.) These Units are elite school-trained professionals. They are skilled in hand-to-hand combat, heavily armored, and able to withstand a great deal of punishment.

In the ancient world, only the very wealthy upper crust of society—the aristocracy—could afford the training, arms, and armor. By researching *Aristocracy*, you raise the movement rate of these Units from 0.9 tiles per second to 1.12 tiles per second. Instead of ambling about the map turtle-like in their armored shells, *Aristocracy* gives Academy Units a practical movement rate. They still are not fast enough to escape danger entirely, but at least this lets them catch a Priest on occasion. If this isn't reason enough, remember that *Aristocracy* is a prerequisite technology for upgrading your existing Phalanx Units to Centurion status.

BALLISTICS

COMPOSITE	DESCRIPTION
Age	Iron
Prerequisite Buildings	Town Center, Granary, Market, Government Center
Prerequisite Technologies	None
Cost	200 RPs of food, 50 RPs of gold
Research Location	Government Center

Benefit of Technology

Ballistics improves the accuracy of your missile units, including all Archery Range units, towers, warships, and siege weapons. Normally, a Unit can sometimes avoid a hit by a projectile simply by moving after it has been fired. The projectile lands at the spot where the Unit was, not where the Unit has since moved. *Ballistics* changes all that. It improves the accuracy of missile fire by "taking into account" the fact that the target moves. *Ballistics* allows the missile Unit to "predict" where the target is moving, so that it "leads" the target. *Ballistics* is only critical when a large portion of your army is made up of siege weapons and when the enemy is primarily a mounted force. In most cases, the blast radius of your weapons still will inflict damage on moving units. *Ballistics* is a prerequisite technology for upgrading your Guard Towers to Ballista Tower status.

CHAIN MAIL FOR ARCHERS

COMPOSITE	DESCRIPTION
Age	Iron
Prerequisite Buildings	Town Center, Storage Pit
Prerequisite Technologies	*Leather Armor for Archers,* *Scale Armor for Archers*
Cost	150 RPs of food, 100 RPs of gold
Research Location	Storage Pit

Benefit of Technology

Chain Mail for Archers reduces the damage your Archery Range Units suffer by two Hit Points per attack. Chain Armor is the most advanced—and, therefore, offers the most protection—of the three armor technologies. Before you can research *Chain Mail for Archers* you first must research both *Scale Armor for Archers* and *Leather Armor for Archers*.

By the time you have outfitted your Archers with Chain Mail, the amount of damage they suffer per round of attack is reduced by six Hit Points, or two Hit Points for each of the three Armor types. *Chain Mail for Archers* is a prerequisite technology for upgrading your Horse Archers to Heavy Horse Archer status.

CHAIN MAIL FOR CAVALRY

COMPOSITE	DESCRIPTION
Age	Iron
Prerequisite Buildings	Town Center, Storage Pit
Prerequisite Technologies	*Leather Armor for Cavalry, Scale Armor for Cavalry*
Cost	175 RPs of food, 100 RPs of gold
Research Location	Storage Pit

Benefit of Technology

Chain Mail for Cavalry reduces the amount of damage your Stable Units sustain by two Hit Points per attack. Chain Armor is the most advanced—and, therefore, offers the most protection—of the three Armor technologies. Before you can research *Chain Mail for Cavalry*, you first must research both *Scale Armor for Cavalry* and *Leather Armor for Cavalry*.

By the time you have outfitted your cavalry Units with Chain Mail, the damage they sustain per attack is reduced by six Hit Points, or two Hit Points for each of the three Armor types.

CHAIN MAIL FOR INFANTRY

COMPOSITE	DESCRIPTION
Age	Iron
Prerequisite Buildings	Town Center, Storage Pit
Prerequisite Technologies	*Leather Armor for Infantry, Scale Armor for Infantry*
Cost	125 RPs of food, 100 RPs of gold
Research Location	Storage Pit

Benefit of Technology

Chain Mail for Infantry reduces the amount of damage your Barracks and Academy Units sustain by two Hit Points per attack. Chain Armor is the most advanced—and, therefore, offers the most protection—of the three armor technologies available to Infantry. Before you can research *Chain Mail for Infantry*, you first must research both *Scale Armor for Infantry* and *Leather Armor for Infantry*.

By the time you have outfitted your Barracks and Academy Units with Chain Mail, the amount of damage they suffer per attack is reduced by six Hit Points, or two Hit Points for each of the three armor types.

COINAGE

COMPOSITE	DESCRIPTION
Age	Iron
Prerequisite Buildings	Town Center, Granary, Market
Prerequisite Technologies	*Gold Mining*
Cost	200 RPs of food, 100 RPs of gold
Research Location	Market

Benefit of Technology

Coinage increases the productivity of your gold mines by 25 percent. Initially, gold mines produce 400 RPs of gold before depletion. *Coinage* increases this total to 500 RPs of gold. As you can see, this technology pays for itself very quickly.

   An additional benefit of *Coinage* is that it allows you to pay tribute to other players in the game without incurring the standard 25 percent tax (fee) on resources. This is one of technologies you should research at your leisure. The extra gold it makes available is nice to have, but this technology should not take precedence over more pressing matters, especially those of a military nature.

CRAFTSMANSHIP

COMPOSITE	DESCRIPTION
Age	Iron
Prerequisite Buildings	Town Center, Granary, Market
Prerequisite Technologies	*Woodworking, Artisanship*
Cost	240 RPs of food, 200 RPs of wood
Research Location	Market

Benefit of Technology

Craftsmanship adds two RPs to your Villagers' ability to cut and carry wood. This is the third of three technologies dealing with woodcutting. Together with the increases from *Woodworking* and *Artisanship, Craftsmanship* raises your Villagers' "cut-and-carry" capacity to 16 RPs per trip. Like the other two technologies, it also increases the missile range of your Archery Range units, towers,

Scout Ships, War Galleys, and Triremes by one tile. *Craftsmanship* is a prerequisite technology for upgrading your existing Ballista Units to Helepolis status.

ENGINEERING

COMPOSITE	DESCRIPTION
Age	Iron
Prerequisite Buildings	Town Center, Granary, Market, Government Center
Prerequisite Technologies	None
Cost	200 RPs of food, 100 RPs of wood
Research Location	Government Center

Benefit of Technology

Engineering increases the range of your Catapult Triremes, Juggernaughts, and siege weaponry (Stone Throwers, Catapults, Heavy Catapults, Ballistas, Helepoli) by two tiles. Naturally, any technology that extends the range of your most potent weapons is worth looking at.

All civilizations can take full advantage of *Engineering*.

Engineering is a prerequisite technology for upgrading your Catapult Triremes to Juggernaught status.

FANATICISM

COMPOSITE	DESCRIPTION
Age	Iron
Prerequisite Buildings	Town Center, Granary, Market, Temple
Prerequisite Technologies	None
Cost	150 RPs of gold
Research Location	Temple

Benefit of Technology

Fanaticism decreases the time a Priest needs to rejuvenate between conversion attempts by 50 percent. The normal rejuvenation rate of 50 seconds is cut in half with *Fanaticism*. This powerful technology effectively doubles the power of your Priests. For those civilizations that use the Priest as the centerpiece of their late game strategy, *Fanaticism* is a must. Used in conjunction with *Monotheism*, this technology tends to create a ripple effect. As you convert enemy Priests, they in turn begin conversions of their own.

Enemy Priests can eventually halt the spread because of the limitations imposed by lengthy rejuvenation periods. After researching *Fanaticism*, however, the rate at which you are able to effect conversions is magnified, leaving enemy Priests helpless and vulnerable. *Fanaticism* is a prerequisite technology for upgrading your Long Swordsman to Legion status.

IRON SHIELD

COMPOSITE	DESCRIPTION
Age	Iron
Prerequisite Buildings	Town Center, Storage Pit
Prerequisite Technologies	*Bronze Shield*
Cost	160 RPs of food, 180 RPs of gold
Research Location	Storage Pit

Benefit of Technology

Iron Shield is a defensive accoutrement that reduces the damage your Units suffer by one Hit Point per attack by missile Units (including Ballista, Helepolis, Archery Range units, towers, Scout Ships, War Galleys and Triremes). Because this armor is only good against missile attacks, the protection it gives the wearer is referred to as a Piercing Armor Bonus.

Researching *Iron Shield* is expensive. Iron Age missile troops are an order of magnitude more effective than their predecessors. Instead of facing down a row of Bowmen, your troops are much more likely to face a group of Horse Archers or Ballistas. If this happens, you want all the protection you can get.

IRRIGATION

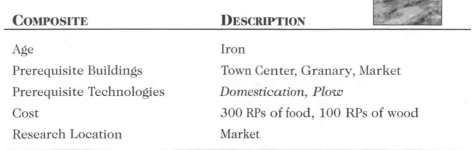

COMPOSITE	DESCRIPTION
Age	Iron
Prerequisite Buildings	Town Center, Granary, Market
Prerequisite Technologies	*Domestication, Plow*
Cost	300 RPs of food, 100 RPs of wood
Research Location	Market

Benefit of Technology

Irrigation is the third of three technologies designed to improve the productivity of your farms. This technology, like the previous two, raises the output of each farm by 75 food Resource Points. Since the cost of the research does not involve gold, you may want to consider *Irrigation*.

By this point, hunting and foraging will have long since reached a point of diminishing returns. Farming is likely to be your only source of food. Between the three technologies, your farms will produce 475 RPs of food. Multiply this considerable sum by the number of farms you have in operation, and you can see just how beneficial this technology really is. *Irrigation* is not sexy like some of the other technologies, so it is easily overlooked. The cost is minimal. By all means, if your civilization can do this research, do it!

JIHAD

COMPOSITE	DESCRIPTION
Age	Iron
Prerequisite Buildings	Town Center, Granary, Market, Temple, Research, *Jihad*
Prerequisite Technologies	None
Cost	120 RPs of gold
Research Location	Temple

Benefit of Technology

Jihad turns your Villagers into militant little warriors consumed by religious fervor. They are bent on making the world a better place by eliminating everyone who disagrees with them. They don't wanna eat, and they don't wanna sleep—all they wanna do is pray . . . and then go kill somebody!

After researching *Jihad*, your Villagers can inflict ten Hit Points of damage per attack round, instead of the normal three Hit Points. They move at a rate of 1.5 tiles per second and can withstand 65 Hit Points of damage, instead of the normal 25 Hit Points.

This technology, however, does have a drawback. It decreases the resource-gathering ability of your Villagers from ten RPs per trip to four. Certain tribes may not make use of this religious zeal. These enlightened civilizations include the Greeks, Hittites, Minoans, Sumerians, and Yamato. The gathering upgrades still apply, so the numbers may vary.

METALLURGY

COMPOSITE	DESCRIPTION
Age	Iron
Prerequisite Buildings	Town Center, Storage Pit
Prerequisite Technologies	*Toolworking, Metalworking*
Cost	300 RPs of food, 180 gold
Research Location	Storage Pit

Benefit of Technology

Metallurgy adds three Hit Points of damage per attack round to all Units that engage in hand-to-hand combat. This benefit is applied to all Barracks, Academy, and Stable Units (except the War Elephant). For example, a Phalanx Unit that normally causes 20 Hit Points of damage per attack would be able to inflict 14 Hit Points once *Metallurgy* is researched—twice its normal amount! (Phalanx base damage [7], [+2] for *Toolworking* [+2] for *Metalworking*, [+3] for *Metallurgy* = 14.)

Consider this technology a "must-have." The three extra Hit Points of damage per round of attack is significant, as you can see. This technology is a prerequisite for upgrading your Heavy Cavalry Units to Cataphract status.

MONOTHEISM

COMPOSITE	DESCRIPTION
Age	Iron
Prerequisite Buildings	Town Center, Granary, Market, Temple
Prerequisite Technologies	None
Cost	350 RPs of gold
Research Location	Temple

Benefit of Technology

Monotheism allows your Priests to make conversion attempts against enemy Priests and buildings. How delightfully insidious this technology is! It drives your opponents absolutely crazy with worry just wondering when your Priests will strike, and they always imagine the worst. Of all the religious technologies in the game, this is the one that makes your Priests an awesome force.

Consider the typical amount of effort that goes into bashing down an enemy structure. Now consider how easy it becomes to send a Priest over to "pick up the keys," so to speak. No more extended Catapult barrages or swarms of infantry. No more War Elephants or massive expenditures on armor. Not only that, you take control of the structure. Think of what this means when you encounter a row of enemy towers. Converting them turns the enemy's own defensive network against him!

In terms of gold resources, this technology is the most expensive in the game. Frankly, it would be cheap at three times the cost. Unfortunately, not all civilizations are allowed to research this wonderful technology. These civilizations include the Greeks, Hittites, Minoans, Sumerians, and Yamato. Sorry 'bout that guys!

SIEGECRAFT

COMPOSITE	DESCRIPTION
Age	Iron
Prerequisite Buildings	Town Center, Granary, Market
Prerequisite Technologies	*Stone Mining*
Cost	190 RPs of food, 100 RPs of stone
Research Location	Market

Benefit of Technology

Siegecraft adds three resource points to your Villagers' capacity to mine and transport stone. A Villager typically can mine and carry ten RPs of stone per trip. The prerequisite technology, *Stone Mining*, raises this capacity to 13 RPs of stone. *Siegecraft* further increases this ability to 16 RPs of stone per trip. Villagers now mine these 16 RPs in the same amount of time as others mine only ten RPs of stone.

Siegecraft also gives your Villagers the ability to inflict full damage on wall structures and towers. (Without this technology, the amount of damage Villagers can inflict on walls is reduced to one fifth of their normal amount of Hit Points.)

CHAPTER 4
The Buildings

There are 21 different buildings (including walls and towers) in *Age Of Empires*. Each one plays a specific part in helping your civilization to advance. Some buildings, like the Barracks or Archery Range, allow you to train specialized military forces. Other structures, like the Government Center and Temple, are important for the intrinsic benefits they bestow.

Ultimately, the strength of your civilization depends on the number and type of buildings you possess. The infrastructure you create determines your civilization's nature and tribal characteristics. For example, a landlocked civilization may concentrate on developing buildings that can assist in amassing a large land army. A tribe confined to an island may wish to forego land forces in favor of building docks and ships.

As the game progresses, each civilization places buildings on the map as it gathers the necessary resources to do so. It is important to note that many buildings come with prerequisites and are not always available. Once a building is placed, however, it becomes a permanent feature of the landscape—so consider the placement of new structures carefully. Once built, they cannot be moved.

When choosing a building site, it is a good idea to balance your short-term needs with long-term security. Although much about placing buildings comes down to using good common sense, there are two main considerations in choosing a site for a new building. First, you should seek sites that maximize the building's effectiveness; second, pick a location that is naturally defensible or one which can easily be incorporated into your overall defense plan.

This chapter contains summaries on all available buildings and structures in the game. They are listed in alphabetical order. The summaries have been divided into four separate sections based on the structures in a particular Age. Within each summary is a list of

building prerequisites (if any), the cost of construction in resource points (RPs), and other general information. When appropriate, tactical guidelines on the placement of the structure are given as well.

STONE AGE BUILDINGS

Stone Age buildings are rudimentary structures that are inexpensive to build. They represent your tribe's first attempts at progressing beyond a purely nomadic existence. For the most part, Stone Age buildings merely assist the tribe in gathering foodstuffs and other resources. They offer little in the way of advancement and provide only a modicum of protection. Their placement, however, sets the tone for the entire game and lays the foundation on which your civilization will either rise or fall.

BARRACKS

Building Attributes	Details
Age	Stone
Prerequisite Buildings	Town Center
Construction Time	30 seconds (with one Villager)/ 20 seconds (with one Villager and *Architecture*)
Construction Procedure	build a Barracks
Cost	125 RPs of wood
Hit Points	350 (420 with *Architecture*)
Size of Structure	3 × 3 (9 tiles)
Outward Range of Visibility	4 tiles

The Barracks represents your tribe's first military structure and should be considered the centerpiece of your early land strategy. This structure is used to train and build common infantry foot soldiers. These Units include the Clubman, Axeman, Short Swordsman, Broad Swordsman, Long Swordsman, and Legion.

The Barracks is comparatively inexpensive to construct, costing only 125 wood resource points. It is well within the reach of your economy soon after the game begins. Its initial importance depends largely on the location of your tribe. If you are surrounded by neighboring tribes, you want to start building a Barracks right away. The Clubmen Units it generates—and Axemen when upgraded—will be your only defense against hostile neighbors.

On the other hand, if your tribe is located in an area that is difficult to reach, such as an island or forest clearing, you can afford to delay construction on a Barracks. Eventually, you must build a Barracks so that more advanced military structures—such as the Archery Range, Siege Workshop, Stable, and Academy—can be established. In this respect, the Barracks is a lynchpin to the eventual construction of all your high-end Units.

If you plan a major offensive with foot soldiers, you want to build a Barracks close to the "front." In fact, if you anticipate heavy casualties, you may even want to build two to ensure a steady supply of troops. These structures can sustain considerable damage (350 Hit Points). An enemy force using Stone Age weapons requires a significant amount of time to destroy a Barracks. Therefore, this is time better spent going after Villagers or other buildings.

DOCK

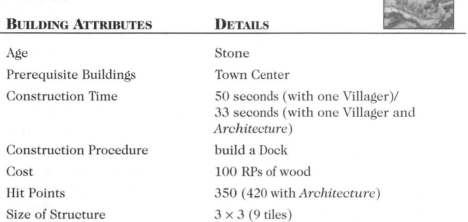

BUILDING ATTRIBUTES	DETAILS
Age	Stone
Prerequisite Buildings	Town Center
Construction Time	50 seconds (with one Villager)/ 33 seconds (with one Villager and *Architecture*)
Construction Procedure	build a Dock
Cost	100 RPs of wood
Hit Points	350 (420 with *Architecture*)
Size of Structure	3 × 3 (9 tiles)
Outward Range of Visibility	4 tiles

Like the Barracks, the Dock is key to your early military strategy. This structure is used to build naval vessels and to train their crews. It is a deceptively simple structure. During the Stone Age, a Dock is nothing more than a place to moor small fishing skiffs and trading vessels. As you progress into later Ages, however, the Dock is transformed into a mighty port able to service great fleets of warships.

Besides serving as a base for naval operations, the Dock has an economic value, which should not be overlooked. Initially, a Dock can construct only two types of ships: Fishing Boats and Trade Boats. Later, Docks can build a variety of naval vessels, such as the Fishing Ship, Merchant Ship, Light Transport, Heavy Transport, Scout Ship, War Galley, Trireme, Catapult Trireme, and Juggernaught.

You want to build a Dock as soon as possible, as the small investment of wood resources (100 RPs) is insignificant when you consider the amount of food that one fishing boat alone can haul.

As the game opens, send a Villager to scout the surrounding countryside. When the Villager discovers a stretch of coastline, explore it with an eye toward building a Dock nearby.

During the Stone and Tool Ages, when you need to stockpile food quickly, place your Docks near areas where fish appear to be plentiful. This action reduces the time it takes your boats to reach the fish and to return to the Dock. (Look for fish jumping or whales surfacing—either one is a good sign.) During the later two Ages, when stockpiling food is less significant, you should place Docks within a more military and economic (trade) context.

Docks allow you to begin trading your stockpiled resources for gold. Initially, the Dock enables you to build a Trade Boat. By sending the Trade Boat to another player's Dock, a trade route is established. The placement of your Docks is important in regard to the trade model. The amount of gold your trade vessels collect is based on the distance they must travel. The greater the distance between Docks, the more gold you acquire on a trip. The calculation is a simple linear progression which starts at 5 gold RPs (given a distance of 10 tiles). The maximum amount of gold that a single trip can generate is 75 RPs (given a distance of 141 tiles or greater).

It is best to build your Docks within small inlets or coves where they can be protected by towers and walls. Missile fire from several towers should suffice in discouraging marauding enemy ships. Docks should never be built close to the frontier. Although they can sustain the same damage as a Barracks (350 Hit Points), Docks tend to attract attention and draw enemy fire. As more powerful warships are built in later Ages, an exposed Dock will not last very long. Researching *Architecture* increases this structure's Hit Points by 20 percent and decreases its construction time by one third.

GRANARY

BUILDING ATTRIBUTES	DETAILS
Age	Stone
Prerequisite Buildings	Town Center
Construction Time	30 seconds (with one Villager)/ 20 seconds (with one Villager and *Architecture*)
Construction Procedure	build a Granary
Cost	120 RPs of wood
Hit Points	350 (420 with *Architecture*)
Size of Structure	3 × 3 (9 tiles)
Outward Range of Visibility	4 tiles

The Granary is a storage place where foraging and farming Villagers can deposit food resources rather than carry them all the way to the Town Center. More importantly, the Granary lies on the critical path that leads to the Market and such defensive structures as the Small Wall, Medium Wall, Fortification, Watch Tower, Sentry Tower, Guard Tower, and Ballista Tower.

Place your Granaries close to natural resources (berry bushes). This placement reduces the time it takes to move food resources into your tribal stockpile. During the Stone Age, this transit time can be critical. The more quickly you are able to harvest food and store it in your Granary, the sooner you will be able to use it to acquire additional Villagers.

Granaries can withstand the same damage as other Stone Age buildings, but their loss is less significant. Units are not built at these locations. The Granary is only useful in that it allows you to build the Market and to research other structures mentioned above. Should you lose a Granary due to enemy action after the Market has been built, all you really lose is a storage depot. You lose neither your marketplace (retroactively) nor your research once it has been conducted.

Because of their relative dispensability, Granaries should be placed adjacent to berry bushes even if the location comes with some measure of risk. The modest investment of wood (120 RPs) can easily be made up. (You may feel the loss of Villagers at such a location more keenly than the loss of the Granary.) You should consider building multiple Granaries—perhaps as many as one at each grove of berry bushes. This way the loss of a single Granary will not impede your development. Researching *Architecture* increases this structure's Hit Points by 20 percent and decreases its construction time by one third.

STORAGE PIT

BUILDING ATTRIBUTES	DETAILS
Age	Stone
Prerequisite Buildings	Town Center
Construction Time	30 seconds (with one Villager)/ 20 seconds (with one Villager and *Architecture*)
Construction Procedure	build a Storage Pit
Cost	120 RPs of wood
Hit Points	350 (420 with *Architecture*)
Size of Structure	3 × 3 (9 tiles)
Outward Range of Visibility	3 tiles

The Storage Pit is a storage location for certain natural resources (food, stone, and gold). It functions as the Granary does, except that *foraged* food resources cannot be stored. In other woods, only food derived from hunting animals can be stored here. Hunters and Miners can deposit the resources they harvest at the Storage Pit, instead of carrying them all the way to the Town Center.

Like the Granary, the Storage Pit is more than a place to deposit resources. Granaries allow you to research technologies that improve your military units. These technologies include Toolworking, Metalworking, Metallurgy, the Bronze Shield, the Iron Shield, Leather Armor for Infantry, Scale Armor for Infantry, Chain Mail for Infantry, Leather Armor for Cavalry, Scale Armor for Cavalry, Chain Mail for Cavalry, Leather Armor for Archers, Scale Armor for Archers, and Chain Mail for Archers.

As you can see by the list, if you ever hope to become a military power, the Storage Pit is essential. It costs the same in resource points (RPs) as the Granary and can sustain the same amount of damage. Both storage locations are necessary for your tribe's advancement. Do not think you can get by building only one and not the other storage center. Placement issues remain the same for the Storage Pit as they are for the Granary. Researching *Architecture* increases this structure's Hit Points by 20 percent and decreases its construction time by one third.

TOWN CENTER

BUILDING ATTRIBUTES	DETAILS
Age	Stone
Prerequisite Buildings	Granary, Market, Government Center
Construction Time	60 seconds (with one Villager)/ 40 seconds (with one Villager and *Architecture*)
Construction Procedure	build a Town Center
Cost	200 RPs of wood
Hit Points	600 (720 with *Architecture*)
Size of Structure	3 × 3 (9 tiles)
Outward Range of Visibility	6 tiles

Unless you're starting the game as a nomadic tribe (one Villager and no buildings), you have no control over the placement of your Town Center. If you are lucky, you will be blessed with a Town Center that lies close to abundant resources and far from jealous neighbors. If you are less fortunate, your Town Center will be situated in the middle of a dry, dusty desert. After you build a Government Center, you can contruct additional Town Centers.

During the Stone and Tool Ages, the Town Center represents the focal point—the nerve center—of your civilization's activity. Treat it as if it were your tribe's headquarters. In absence of Storage Pits and Granaries, the Town Center is the one place where you can stockpile all of your resources.

The Town Center combines the ability to store resources with the ability to create Villagers. By itself, it can support four villagers or any combination Unit without having to construct additional housing. Its most important feature is its ability to advance your civilization into the next Age. Without a Town Center, your tribe is stuck in the present.

Should your only Town Center be destroyed, you need to build another one right away. At a cost of 200 RPs worth of wood, it is one of the more expensive Stone Age buildings to construct. Still, the chance of losing a Town Center early in the game is minimal. It takes many club- and ax-wielding troops to beat a Town Center into submission. Only a full-scale enemy assault by a formidable force would inflict 600 Hit Points of damage in a relatively short period of time.

Later, as troops become more lethal, the chance of losing a Town Center to enemy action increases. Even though they are immune to priestly conversion attempts, these structures are still vulnerable to high-class troops backed by siege weaponry. A handful of heavy cavalry Units or legionnaires can ransack a Town Center with unbelievable efficiency. Researching *Architecture* increases this structure's Hit Points by 20 percent and decreases its construction time by one third.

Having expanded from your original Town Center, extra centers come in handy as a way to increase your control over new areas of the map.

HOUSE

BUILDING ATTRIBUTES	DETAILS
Age	Stone
Prerequisite Buildings	Town Center
Construction Time	20 seconds (with one Villager)/ 14 seconds (with one Villager and *Architecture*)
Construction Procedure	build a House
Cost	30 RPs of wood
Hit Points	75 (90 with *Architecture*)
Size of Structure	2 × 2 (4 tiles)
Outward Range of Visibility	3 tiles

As structures go, the House is small and drab. If you lose one—who cares? Right? True, the House is rather inconsequential (costing only 30 RPs of wood or three trips to the forest), but it represents living quarters for your population. The House is a good measure of the size of your civilization.

If your intention is to build a great army or navy, you first must build the necessary infrastructure to support it. This is where the House comes in. Each House supports four Villagers, military units, or naval vessels. For example, if you currently have eight houses and a Town Center, your civilization can have as many as 36 Units (9 × 4 = 36).

Houses can sustain seventy-five (75) Hit Points of damage. Considering that these are mere dwellings, they can withstand a fair share of warfare before they are destroyed. Researching *Architecture* increases this structure's Hit Points by 20 percent and decreases its construction time by one third.

The placement of your houses has little bearing on the daily activities of your Villagers. (No foot traffic between houses, resource sites, or other buildings is necessary.) Therefore, the only consideration in regard to house placement on the map should be military. Do not place your houses too close to your neighbors should they become unfriendly at some point.

Losing houses does not cause you to lose units, however. When a House is destroyed it merely decreases the total number of Units you can support. If you currently have more Units than your houses can support, you need to build new housing before you can add more units.

Houses occupy physical space and block movement, so do not build them across paths to your resource sites. (You never want to slow resource traffic for any reason.) By the same token, houses are inexpensive obstructions to build in front of enemy foot soldiers. If you have plenty of wood but are low on stone, consider building a solid row of houses instead of small walls. Houses have just under half the Hit Points of small walls, but they cover more tiles and can be built more cheaply.

TOOL AGE BUILDINGS

Now that you have advanced to the Tool Age, your buildings become more expensive. They also become more specialized and allow your tribe to begin developing into a serious civilization. Your military strength increases dramatically with the addition of an Archery Range and a Stable.

ARCHERY RANGE

BUILDING ATTRIBUTES	DETAILS
Age	Tool
Prerequisite Buildings	Town Center, Barracks
Construction Time	40 seconds (with one Villager)/ 27 seconds (with one Villager and *Architecture*)
Construction Procedure	build a Tool Age Town Center, build a Barracks, then build an Archery Range
Cost	150 RPs of wood
Hit Points	350 (420 with *Architecture*)
Size of Structure	3 × 3 (9 tiles)
Outward Range of Visibility	3 tiles

The Archery Range is one of two Tool Age military buildings that give you the ability to begin producing more effective military units. Before you can build one, however, you must already have completed a Barracks. As the name suggests, the Archery Range is the place where your tribe builds and trains its archers. In the game, archers are sometimes referred to as missile troops. In this context, missile means arrow, stone, or other projectile—don't think that you're building ICBM-toting soldiers!

Early Archers are only marginally more effective than Clubmen or Axemen. They inflict the same damage (3 Hit Points), but they can use their weapons to attack enemy troops from a distance. By investing in archery training, however, more advanced archers can be created. The first military Unit to become available at the Archery Range is referred to as a Bowman. The more advanced archers include the Improved Bowman, Composite Bowman, Chariot Archer, Elephant Archer, Horse Archer, and Heavy Horse Archer.

The Archery Range is also a prerequisite for building the Siege Workshop. For this reason alone, no civilization should go without one—having two is even better. These buildings are bargains even at 150 RPs of wood, and limiting yourself to only one Archery Range is an unnecessary liability. Researching *Architecture* increases this structure's Hit Points by 20 percent and decreases its construction time by one third.

Obviously, you want to build your Archery Ranges where they can be defended easily. These structures can absorb 350 Hit Points of damage making them no more resilient than most Stone Age buildings. They do have the ability to create archer units, however, and having a row of archers standing guard should be enough to discourage any would-be attacker.

FARM

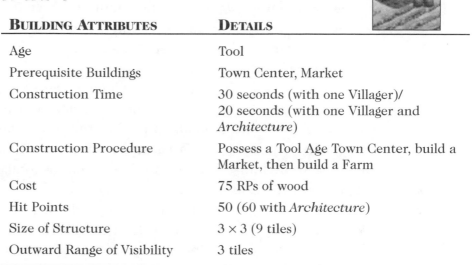

Building Attributes	Details
Age	Tool
Prerequisite Buildings	Town Center, Market
Construction Time	30 seconds (with one Villager)/ 20 seconds (with one Villager and *Architecture*)
Construction Procedure	Possess a Tool Age Town Center, build a Market, then build a Farm
Cost	75 RPs of wood
Hit Points	50 (60 with *Architecture*)
Size of Structure	3 × 3 (9 tiles)
Outward Range of Visibility	3 tiles

Although the Farm is not particularly glamorous, it is interesting to watch in operation. Before you can begin building farms, you must first construct a place where farmers can make their wares available—the Market. Once you build a Market, the option of building farms becomes available.

Farms are crucial to your civilization because they provide a steady supply of food when other sources begin to disappear. As the number of gazelle and other wild animals dwindle—and the ocean and rivers become fished out—the Farm represents a secure method for creating Units. Although farms are labor-intensive (they require farmers to harvest the resources), organized agriculture helps propel your tribe into the modern Ages.

Food resource points that farms produce must first be moved into storage, so build your Farms close to Granaries or Town Centers. Again, time spent moving food into storage should be minimized to make the most efficient use of these buildings.

Once a Farm is built, you can assign any number of Villagers (farmers) to work on it. No matter how many farmers are assigned, each Farm produces a total of 250 food points, after which it goes fallow. In other words, you could potentially have 25 farmers working a farm, each one making a single trip with ten food points, before the farmland is exhausted. (You will see the Farm begin to fade from view when this happens.)

Certain types of research can make your farms even more effective food-producing structures. Domestication, Irrigation, and Plow each add 75 resource points of food to the basic amount of food a Farm can produce. Thus, a Farm belonging to a civilization which has researched all three areas can produce a total of 475 RPs of food ($[3 \times 75] + 250 = 475$).

Farms can absorb 50 Hit Points of damage before they are destroyed. This Hit Point total distinguishes them as the weakest buildings in the game. Since Farms are not permanent structures to begin with, any enemy force that attacks one—instead of going after something else—is, in fact, doing you a favor. When a Farm is destroyed, all you really lose are the food resources that remain in the ground.

MARKET

Building Attributes	Details
Age	Tool
Prerequisite Buildings	Town Center, Granary
Construction Time	40 seconds (with one Villager)/27 seconds (with one Villager and *Architecture*)
Construction Procedure	Possess a Tool Age Town Center, build a Granary, then build a Market
Cost	150 RPs of wood
Hit Points	350 (420 with *Architecture*)
Size of Structure	3×3 (9 tiles)
Outward Range of Visibility	4 tiles

The Market is much more than just a place to buy and sell goods. It serves as a critical link in the development of your military and economic infrastructure. Frankly, new players are apt to gloss over its importance: It is easy to miss the connection between having a Market and being able to research such technologies as Woodworking, Artisanship, Craftsmanship, Stone Mining, Siegecraft, Gold Mining, Coinage, Domestication, the Plow, Irrigation, and the Wheel.

Wow! That's a lot of advancement tied up in this unimposing little building—maybe it should be renamed the Laboratory instead. In addition to being a veritable warehouse of knowledge, the Market initiates a path of construction that leads to the Farm, Government Center, and Temple. Again, beginners may overlook this "three-for-one." No other building opens up so many possibilities.

The Market costs 150 resource points of wood to build. It can sustain the same amount of damage as many of these buildings (350 Hit Points). Since foot traffic between the Market and other buildings or locations is unnecessary, the Market can be built anywhere on the map. Because of its importance, however, you may want to build it in an area that is easily defensible. A smart enemy makes a point of destroying a Market.

The best place to build a Market is next to your Town or Government Center. This way, any wall or towers you erect to defend these centers will be in a position to lend support to the Market. Researching *Architecture* increases this structure's Hit Points by 20 percent and decreases its construction time by one third. Keeping several archers nearby isn't a bad idea either.

SMALL WALL

Building Attributes	Details
Age	Tool
Prerequisite Buildings	Town Center, Granary
Construction Time	5 seconds (with one Villager)/ 3.3 seconds (with one Villager and *Architecture*)
Construction Procedure	possess a Tool Age Town Center, build a Granary, research Small Wall at the Granary, then build a Small Wall
Cost	5 RPs of stone
Hit Points	200 (240 with *Architecture*)
Size of Structure	1 × 1 (one section of Small Wall is equal to 1 tile)
Outward Range of Visibility	3 tiles

The Small Wall represents a modest section of a fixed rampart or field fortification. Each Small Wall is only one tile in length, but, at a cost of 5 RPs of stone, a row of Small Wall sections can be built quickly and cheaply. Although it is the weakest of all the wall sections in the game (200 Hit Points) with additional research, the Small Wall can be upgraded to Medium Wall and Fortification. By researching *Architecture*, the amount of damage a Small Wall structure can withstand is increased by 20 percent to 240 Hit Points. Its construction time is reduced by one-third as well.

One good thing about wall structures is that they are less susceptible to damage from normal weapons. Enemy military Units equipped with hand-to-hand weapons have their normal Hit Point damage reduced by 80 percent when they attack wall structures. Damage from Piercing Weapons is reduced even more. Siege Weapons also cause less damage to walls—on average only 75 percent of their normal attack damage.

Small Walls may be used as obstructions to block or channel enemy movement—they do not block enemy missile fire at all. Keep in mind that wall sections cannot distinguish friend from foe, so while you build your wall segments, be sure to leave an entrance and exit. These structures are most effective (and economical) when combined with natural terrain features. A thick forest or a water tile blocks movement just as well as a small wall.

Just how creative to be in building fixed fortifications depends entirely on you (and your access to stone supplies). Paranoid leaders like to build "Maginot lines," while others tend to shy away from permanent emplacements. Either way you go, the amount of effort you spend in building Small Walls should correspond in some way to the level of threat you are facing.

STABLE

Building Attributes	Details
Age	Tool
Prerequisite Buildings	Town Center, Barracks
Construction Time	40 seconds (with one Villager)/ 27 seconds (with one Villager and *Architecture*)
Construction Procedure	possess a Tool Age Town Center, build a Barracks, then build Stable
Cost	150 RPs of wood
Hit Points	350 (420 with *Architecture*)
Size of Structure	3 × 3 (9 tiles)
Outward Range of Visibility	3 tiles

The Stable is one of two Tool Age military buildings. This building, along with the Archery Range, gives you the ability to begin producing more effective military units. Before you can build a Stable, however, you first must build a Barracks. As the name suggests, the Stable is where you build and train your mounted troops. These Units include the Scout, Cavalry, Heavy Cavalry, Cataphract, Chariot, and War Elephant.

Since mounted troops move almost twice as fast as foot soldiers, Stables may be built further in the interior of your territory. You should place them in areas that are difficult to reach or are easily defensible by towers or archers. Station a couple archers nearby to discourage any half-hearted attacks.

You incur exactly the same building costs with a Stable as you do when you build an Archery Range. The Stable can absorb the same damage (350 Hit Points) as both the Archery Range and Barracks. Together, these buildings help you begin to raise an effective army. Researching *Architecture* increases the Stable's Hit Points by 20 percent and decreases its construction time by one third.

Because mounted troops are expensive to produce, it is usually necessary to build only one Stable. A single Stable should be sufficient to supply your army. If you find yourself in need of a second Stable (to replace losses or whatever), perhaps you should consider looking at why you are losing so many cavalry Units in the first place.

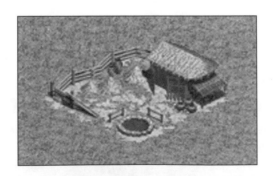

WATCH TOWER

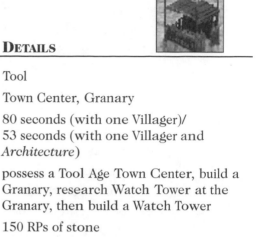

BUILDING ATTRIBUTES	DETAILS
Age	Tool
Prerequisite Buildings	Town Center, Granary
Construction Time	80 seconds (with one Villager)/ 53 seconds (with one Villager and *Architecture*)
Construction Procedure	possess a Tool Age Town Center, build a Granary, research Watch Tower at the Granary, then build a Watch Tower
Cost	150 RPs of stone
Hit Points	100 (120 with *Architecture*)
Size of Structure	2 × 2 (4 tiles)
Outward Range of Visibility	8 tiles
Missile Attack Damage	3 Hit Points (4 Hit Points with Alchemy)
Missile Range	5 tiles (+1 tile of range for each Artisanship, Craftsmanship, and Woodworking)
Rate of Fire	one missile every 1.5 seconds.

The Watch Tower is the weakest of all towers in the game, but it can be quickly upgraded into a more formidable structure. Towers are upgraded by conducting research at a Granary. The more advanced towers obtained through research include the Sentry Tower, Guard Tower, and Ballista Tower.

Certain types of research make Watch Towers more effective. Alchemy adds one Hit Point to its missile attack damage. Ballistics adds to accuracy, especially against moving targets. Artisanship, Craftsmanship, and Woodworking each add one tile of extra range to its missile fire. Researching *Architecture* increases this structure's Hit Points by 20 percent and decreases its construction time by one-third.

Watch Towers normally are used to protect stationary structures (such as buildings or resource sites) from attack. They are most effective when incorporated into existing wall defenses. Place the tower behind a section of wall in such a way that an attacking Unit will be unable to reach it. Missile fire from the tower, however, still reaches the attacker.

Watch Towers should be placed so that their fire can cover entrances, exits, and other breaches in your wall defenses. Multiple towers can usually generate enough missile fire to keep out all but the most determined raiders. Another good position for Watch Towers is near your Docks. Placing several Watch Towers on a section of coastline gives your fishing fleets a safe harbor should enemy vessels engage them in battle.

Another idea for placing Watch Towers is the concept of area denial. Consider building several Watch Towers, so that they have an interlocking field of fire over a resource site you wish to preserve or forest path you wish to keep clear of enemy units. In effect, you are denying the enemy free passage through the area. Deployed correctly, your towers can prohibit the movement of enemy units.

The drawback to building Watch Towers is their expense. A Watch Tower costs as much in terms of stone RPs as 30 sections of Small Walls. If you rely on towers as an integral part of your defenses, be prepared to mine a considerable amount of stone. One Watch Tower alone takes your miners 15 round trips to the quarry.

BRONZE AGE BUILDINGS

Bronze Age buildings expand on the infrastructure you have begun in the earlier two Ages, bringing some cultural depth and diversity to your civilization. The capabilities of your existing military Units continue to improve while new kinds of Units begin to appear. Matters of faith and religion also enter into the game with the addition of the Temple and Priests.

ACADEMY

BUILDING ATTRIBUTES	DETAILS
Age	Bronze
Prerequisite Buildings	Town Center, Barracks, Stable
Construction Time	60 seconds (with one Villager)/ 40 seconds (with one Villager and *Architecture*)
Construction Procedure	possess a Bronze Age Town Center, build a Barracks, build a Stable, then build an Academy
Cost	200 RPs of wood
Hit Points	350 (420 with *Architecture*)
Size of Structure	3 × 3 (9 tiles)
Outward Range of Visibility	5 tiles

The Academy is your civilization's equivalent of a Sandhurst or West Point. It is a place where the military is changed from a rabble militia into a professional fighting force. The training here produces the three most advanced infantry Units in the game—the Hoplite, Phalanx, and Centurion.

The Academy is a bargain at only 200 RPs of wood, only slightly more than the cost for a Barracks in the Stone Age. Researching *Architecture* increases its Hit Points by 20 percent and decreases its construction time by one-third.

Treat the Academy as you would the Barracks. The only difference between the two is the strength of the infantry Units they build. Your civilization only needs to build one Academy—guard it well!

Place the Academy in a secure location far from your frontier. Although this building can sustain the same damage as the Barracks, 350 Hit Points do not go as far in the Bronze Age. The elite Units at the Academy take longer to build, and, therefore, it takes longer to build a significant local fighting force.

The ideal defense would place a tower or two within missile range or to position a few excellent Bowmen nearby. In most cases, your armies consist of infantry—because they are relatively cheap to produce) backed by specialized Units like Elephants, Cavalry, or Siege Weapons. Do not jeopardize your supply of elite infantry by allowing your Academy to be destroyed.

BALLISTA TOWER

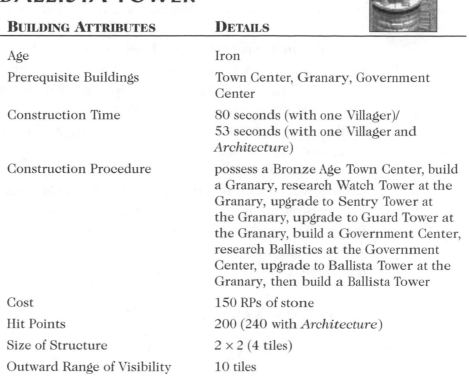

BUILDING ATTRIBUTES	DETAILS
Age	Iron
Prerequisite Buildings	Town Center, Granary, Government Center
Construction Time	80 seconds (with one Villager)/ 53 seconds (with one Villager and *Architecture*)
Construction Procedure	possess a Bronze Age Town Center, build a Granary, research Watch Tower at the Granary, upgrade to Sentry Tower at the Granary, upgrade to Guard Tower at the Granary, build a Government Center, research Ballistics at the Government Center, upgrade to Ballista Tower at the Granary, then build a Ballista Tower
Cost	150 RPs of stone
Hit Points	200 (240 with *Architecture*)
Size of Structure	2 × 2 (4 tiles)
Outward Range of Visibility	10 tiles
Missile Attack Damage	20 Hit Points (21 Hit Points with Alchemy)
Missile Range	7 tiles (+1 tile of range for each Artisanship, Craftsmanship, and Woodworking)
Rate of Fire	one missile every 3 seconds.

The Ballista Tower is the most advanced tower structure in the game. It has more attack strength and a further range than any of its predecessors. In fact, a Ballista Tower (which dishes out 20 Hit Points per volley) can eliminate most Units with only two or three shots.

Before you can upgrade your existing towers to Ballista Tower status, however, you first must research Ballistics. When you have researched Ballistics and paid the cost of the upgrade (at the Granary), all of your existing towers are upgraded instantly to Ballista Tower status.

Additional types of research can make the Ballista Tower even more effective. Alchemy adds one Hit Point to its missile attack damage. Artisanship, Craftsmanship, and Woodworking each add one tile of extra range to its missile fire. *Architecture* increases the Ballista Tower's Hit Points by 20 percent and decreases its construction time by one third.

Because these towers appear where you carefully placed your early towers (with lesser ranges), they automatically should have overlapping fields of fire. Any Unit caught in the crossfire of two Ballista Towers is as good as gone. Ballista Towers have only a few effective enemies—Siege Weapons whose range exceeds the tower's missile fire.

GOVERNMENT CENTER

BUILDING ATTRIBUTES	DETAILS
Age	Bronze
Prerequisite Buildings	Town Center, Granary, Market
Construction Time	60 seconds (with one Villager)/ 40 seconds (with one Villager and *Architecture*)
Construction Procedure	possess a Bronze Age Town Center, build a Granary, build a Market, then build a Government Center
Cost	175 RPs of wood
Hit Points	350 (420 with *Architecture*)
Size of Structure	3 × 3 (9 tiles)
Outward Range of Visibility	5 tiles

The Government Center is an extremely valuable building that every civilization needs. More than just the seat of government, this center of learning—like the Granary—allows you to begin research on numerous new technologies, including Writing, Architecture, Engineering, Aristocracy, Alchemy, and Ballistics.

One of the most important aspects of this building is that it allows your tribe to build additional Town Centers. These additional Town Centers give you the ability to increase your population quickly by creating many new Villagers simultaneously. In turn, this "population explosion" allows you to solidify your control over territories into which you have migrated.

The Government Center costs only 175 RPs of wood, although the research conducted here costs considerably more. The building can absorb 350 Hit Points of damage—equal to the Barracks, Stable, and other buildings. Researching *Architecture* increases this structure's Hit Points by 20 percent and decreases its construction time by one third.

Since foot traffic is not required for the building to operate, you can conceivably place it anywhere. It is a good idea, however, to locate the Government Center in a well-protected, permanently settled area. It may take some time to complete the research that this building makes available, so you will want to ensure its safety until you are finished with your research.

GUARD TOWER

Building Attributes	Details
Age	Bronze
Prerequisite Buildings	Town Center, Granary
Construction Time	5 seconds (with one Villager)/ 3.3 seconds (with one Villager and *Architecture*)
Construction Procedure	possess an Iron Age Town Center, build a Granary, research Watch Tower at the Granary, upgrade to Sentry Tower at the Granary, upgrade to Guard Tower at the Granary, then build a Guard Tower
Cost	150 RPs of stone
Hit Points	200 (240 with *Architecture*)
Size of Structure	2 × 2 (4 tiles)
Outward Range of Visibility	9 tiles
Missile Attack Damage	6 Hit Points (7 Hit Points with Alchemy)
Missile Range	7 tiles (+1 tile of range for each Artisanship, Craftsmanship, and Woodworking)
Rate of Fire	one missile every 1.5 seconds

Until now, towers were mainly nuisances—their value as defensive structures was primarily psychological. An enemy force that found itself under fire from a tower might be inclined to withdraw, as arrows whizzing by make the situation uncomfortable. Rarely did a force linger long enough in a tower's vicinity to suffer casualties.

All of that changes with the appearance of the Guard Tower. Its formidable missile fire inflicts a base of six Hit Points per volley. A Villager, for example, can only suffer 25 Hit Points of damage before he is killed. Thus, a Guard Tower can eliminate a Villager with five shots in less than eight seconds.

Certain kinds of research make the Guard Tower even more effective. Alchemy adds one Hit Point to its missile attack damage. Ballistics adds to the accuracy, especially against moving targets. Artisanship, Craftsmanship, and Woodworking each add one tile of extra range to its missile fire. *Architecture* increases the Guard Tower's Hit Points by 20 percent and decreases its construction time by one-third .

With more Hit Points, attack strength, and range than its predecessor, the Guard Tower is a structure to be reckoned with. When used with sections of a wall, the Guard Tower can make any attack a costly affair.

MEDIUM WALL

BUILDING ATTRIBUTES	DETAILS
Age	Bronze
Prerequisite Buildings	Town Center, Granary
Construction Time	5 seconds (with one Villager)/ 3.3 seconds (with one Villager and *Architecture*)
Construction Procedure	possess a Bronze Age Town Center, build a Granary, research Small Wall at the Granary, upgrade to Medium Wall at the Granary, then build a Medium Wall
Cost	5 RPs of stone
Hit Points	300 (360 with *Architecture*)
Size of Structure	1 × 1 (one section of medium wall is equal to 1 tile)
Outward Range of Visibility	3 tiles

The Medium Wall is a one-step upgrade from the Small Wall. All your existing Small Wall sections are transformed instantly into Medium Walls when you perform the necessary upgrade. At five RPs per each stone, the cost of these wall sections is negligible. You can afford to litter the map with walls if you desire to do so. It helps if you tie wall sections together to make them part of a cohesive defensive plan.

Medium Wall sections have 33 percent more Hit Points than the Small Walls do. Researching *Architecture* will further increase this structure's Hit Points by 20 percent. (*Architecture* also decreases construction time by one-third.)

As enemy Units become more lethal, walls are an excellent way to protect your civilization's important buildings. Wall structures are inherently less susceptible to damage from normal weapons. Enemy military Units equipped with hand-to-hand weaponry have their normal amount of Hit Point damage reduced by 80 percent when they attack wall structures. Damage from Piercing Weapons is reduced even more. Siege Weapons also cause less damage to walls—on average only 75 percent of their normal attack damage.

A ring of Medium Wall sections around your village slows attacking Units, but remember that missile-equipped troops can still fire direct missiles over wall sections. Be sure that your walls are set far enough away to keep these Units out of range of your buildings.

SENTRY TOWER

BUILDING ATTRIBUTES	DETAILS
Age	Bronze
Prerequisite Buildings	Town Center, Granary
Construction Time	80 seconds (with one Villager)/ 53 seconds (with one Villager and *Architecture*)
Construction Procedure	possess a Bronze Age Town Center, build a Granary, research Watch Tower at the Granary, upgrade to Sentry Tower at the Granary, then build a Sentry Tower
Cost	150 RPs of stone
Hit Points	150 (180 with *Architecture*)
Size of Structure	2 × 2 (4 tiles)
Outward Range of Visibility	9 tiles
Missile Attack Damage	4 Hit Points
Missile Range	6 tiles (+1 tile of range for each Artisanship, Craftsmanship, and Woodworking)
Rate of Fire	one missile every 1.5 seconds

The Sentry Tower is the next step up from the Watch Tower. All of your existing Watch Towers are upgraded immediately to Sentry Tower specs when you pay the prerequisite 50 food RPs. (The upgrade itself is performed at the Granary.)

Like the Watch Tower, the Sentry Tower can fire missiles at enemy Units (civilian, military, buildings, and boats). As you may guess, missile fire from the Sentry Tower has a longer range (six tiles) and inflicts greater damage (four Hit Points) than its predecessor. Although it costs the same to construct, a Sentry Tower can absorb 50 percent more damage than a Watch Tower.

Certain kinds of research make the Sentry Tower more effective. Alchemy adds one Hit Point to its missile attack damage.

Ballistics adds to accuracy, especially against moving targets. Artisanship, Craftsmanship, and Woodworking each add one tile of extra range to its missile fire. Researching *Architecture* increases the Sentry Tower's Hit Points by 20 percent and decreases its construction time by one-third.

Placement strategies for Sentry Towers mirror those for the Watch Towers—just remember that as towers become more powerful, their influence over the area within range of their missiles becomes more absolute.

SIEGE WORKSHOP

BUILDING ATTRIBUTES	DETAILS
Age	Bronze
Prerequisite Buildings	Town Center, Barracks, Archery Range
Construction Time	60 seconds (with one Villager)/ 40 seconds (with one Villager and *Architecture*)
Construction Procedure	possess a Bronze Age Town Center, build a Barracks, build an Archery Range, then build a Siege Workshop
Cost	200 RPs of wood
Hit Points	350 (420 with *Architecture*)
Size of Structure	3 × 3 (9 tiles)
Outward Range of Visibility	3 tiles

By now, chances are that your troops have encountered enemy fortifications on the map. Sending ground troops to tear down enemy walls and towers is time-consuming and can produce significant numbers in casualties. The Siege Workshop is the answer. With it, you can build Siege Weapons such as the Stone Thrower, Catapult, Heavy Catapult, Ballista, and Helepolis.

The Siege Workshop is inexpensive for a Bronze-Age expenditure. By now, you should have 150 Resource Points of wood just lying around in your stockpile. Like many other military buildings, the Siege Workshop can sustain 350 Hit Points of damage, though researching *Architecture* increases this total by 20 percent.

Since Siege Weapons are so costly, you probably can get by fairly well with one Siege Workshop. Be forewarned: These buildings are prime targets, especially if you are busy bombarding a neighboring tribe. You should count on a raiding party to come looking for the source of their woes.

Position your Siege Workshop in an area where it can be defended (either by multiple towers or a company of archers). Never expose it to unnecessary risk. Remember that this building elevates warfare to a new level of destruction—your neighbors (your enemies!) will not be happy that you have managed to build one.

TEMPLE

Building Attributes	Details
Age	Bronze
Prerequisite Buildings	Town Center, Granary, Market
Construction Time	60 seconds (with one Villager)/ 40 seconds (with one Villager and *Architecture*)
Construction Procedure	possess a Bronze Age Town Center, build a Granary, build a Market, then build a Temple
Cost	200 RPs of wood
Hit Points	350 (420 with *Architecture*)
Size of Structure	3 × 3 (9 tiles)
Outward Range of Visibility	3 tiles

Until now, spiritual matters have been largely ignored. It is assumed that your people follow local customs like worshipping sacred animals or barking at the moon—whatever. For better or worse, all this changes with a Temple and with the emergence of organized religion.

Although the Temple is a place of peace and goodwill, it is also a good addition to your military infrastructure. It allows you to create Priests, who are arguably the most powerful Units in the game, and it opens up numerous new areas for research. These new technologies (religions) include Polytheism, Mysticism, Astrology, Monotheism, Afterlife, Jihad, and Fanaticism.

As in real life, religion is very expensive. If you consider building a Temple, be sure to have plenty of gold at hand. You will find yourself having to pass the collection plate around many times to fund your Priests and theological research. Yes, this building can help answer your prayers for victory—but only if you back your devotion with good deeds (money!).

Treat the Temple as you would the Academy or Siege Workshop. These buildings become critical to any Iron Age war effort. Because Priests are so expensive, it is usually practical (or necessary) to build only one Temple. Researching *Architecture* increases this structure's Hit Points by 20 percent and decreases its construction time by one-third.

Place the Temple in a secure location near the center of your civilization. Even though Priests move slowly, it is important to keep your Temple well away from the frontier. Like the Siege Workshop, a Temple will be viewed by your neighbors with alarm. No one likes losing their Units to priestly conversion. You may just goad them into attacking you.

IRON AGE BUILDINGS

Having reached the Iron Age in one piece, we can safely assume that your tribe has built its share of fancy buildings. As long as you are doing so well, we should cover the final two structures in the game.

FORTIFICATION

BUILDING ATTRIBUTES	DETAILS
Age	Iron
Prerequisite Buildings	Town Center, Granary
Construction Time	5 seconds (with one Villager)/ 3.3 seconds (with one Villager and *Architecture*)
Construction Procedure	build a Town Center, build a Granary, research Small Wall at the Granary, upgrade to Medium Wall at the Granary, upgrade to Fortification at the Granary, then build a Fortification
Cost	5 RPs of stone
Hit Points	400 (480 with *Architecture*)
Size of Structure	1 × 1 (one section of fortification is equal to 1 tile)
Outward Range of Visibility	3 tiles

The Fortification is the strongest section of wall in the game. Although it costs the same in stone resources (5 RPs) as the other two wall sections, it can sustain 100 Hit Points of damage more than the Medium Wall and twice as many as the Small Wall. If your civilization has researched *Architecture*, the damage it can withstand is increased by an additional 20 percent (to 480 Hit Points). *Architecture* also reduces construction time by one third.

The Fortification can make your villages virtually impregnable. At 480 Hit Points per section, it takes something akin to a tactical nuke to destroy an appreciable amount of a fortification. They are inherently less susceptible to damage. Enemy military Units equipped with hand-to-hand weapons have their normal Hit Point damage reduced by 80 percent when they attack wall structures. Damage from piercing weapons is reduced even more. Siege weapons also cause less damage to walls—on average only 75 percent of their normal attack damage.

Chances are, however, that by the time players reach the Iron Age, fortifications are irrelevant. Your frontier will have expanded far beyond your original walls, and your strength should lie in your mobility. Even so, fortifications can provide a convenient place for retreat if the tide of battle shifts against you.

WONDER

BUILDING ATTRIBUTES	DETAILS
Age	Iron
Prerequisite Buildings	Town Center
Construction Time	210 seconds (with 20 Villagers)/ 140 seconds (with one Villager and *Architecture*)
Construction Procedure	possess an Iron Age Town Center, then build a Wonder
Cost	1,000 RPs of wood/ 1,000 RPs of stone/ 1,000 RPs of gold
Hit Points	500 (600 with *Architecture*)
Size of Structure	5 × 5 (10 tiles)
Outward Range of Visibility	2 tiles

Having reached the Iron Age, your tribe has managed to survive its most difficult period. Now that the people are well-fed, well-housed, and well-protected, the next step is to leave some lasting monument to their greatness—it is time to build a Wonder.

A Wonder is a massive structure—a civilization's crowning achievement—intended to last forever so that future generations can gaze upon it and reflect upon the splendor of its builder. The cost of building a Wonder is exorbitant (1,000 RPs each of wood, stone, and gold). But after all, isn't this the whole point? Researching *Architecture* increases this structure's Hit Points by 20 percent and decreases its construction time by one-third.

Beyond the resource cost, you also must factor in a considerable amount of labor. When you are ready to begin work on a Wonder, plan on using a work force of at least 10 to 15 Villagers. Even with 20 Villagers working on it constantly, it takes almost four minutes of game time to construct a Wonder—an eternity on this scale. *Architecture* is a must!

This lavish expenditure does more than just look pretty, however. Besides its aesthetic beauty, a Wonder usually triggers a scenario for victory. If you build a Wonder and can maintain it over the next two millennia, your civilization wins the game. It also adds considerably (100 points) to your final score.

Because your Wonder is likely to win the game for you (if you are the first to build one), a message is broadcast to other players indicating that you have started building one. It is safe to assume that, unless they want to lose the game, the other players will try to stop you.

Priests cannot convert these structures, so the only way to eliminate a Wonder is through direct attack. They are so beautiful that it almost seems a shame to destroy one. Wonders can withstand 500 Hit Points of damage before they come crashing down.

As a historical note, there are seven universally recognized Wonders of the ancient world. They are the pyramids of Egypt, the Temple of Artemis (Diana) at Ephesus, the Colossus of Rhodes, the mausoleum at Halicarnassus, the lighthouse on the island of Pharos, the Statue of Zeus (Jupiter) at Olympia, and the Hanging Gardens of Babylon. Only one of the original seven wonders, the Egyptian pyramids at Giza, can still be viewed today.

CHAPTER 5
The People

Buildings are necessary for advancing your civilization, but your people are the ones who do the real work. This chapter details each military and civilian Unit available to you in the game, and provides a detailed summary on each unit. Each recap follows the same format—a list of general Unit characteristics with a specific description for a particular unit. Because some terms in this chapter may not be familiar to you, an explanation of all the information fields used in the summaries is given below.

CHARACTER SUMMARY FORMAT

COMPOSITE	DESCRIPTION
Name	the name of the Unit
Age	the Age in which the Unit first becomes available
Prerequisite Buildings	buildings which contribute to the Unit's construction and which must be present before Unit development may begin
Construction Location	where Unit training is initiated and where the Unit appears after training
Construction Time	number of seconds (in real time) required to train the Unit once development has been initiated
Construction Procedure	sequential list of steps required to train the Unit
Production Cost	amount of stockpiled resources that must be expended to produce the Unit
Upgrade Cost	amount of stockpiled resources that must be expended to upgrade the Unit to the next Unit status

COMPOSITE	DESCRIPTION
Research Cost	amount of stockpiled resources that must be expended to research any required technologies
Training Cost	amount of stockpiled resources that must be expended to train each Unit
Hit Points	amount of damage (in Hit Points) the Unit can sustain before elimination from the map
Armor Rating	amount of damage (in Hit Points) subtracted from each enemy attack; certain armor is attack-specific (pierce)
Range of Visibility	visible area of the map (in tiles) around the Unit
Attack Damage	amount of combat damage (in Hit Points) the Unit inflicts each time its weapon strikes an enemy Unit or building
Attack Speed	how frequently the Unit inflicts damage in combat; that is, the number of seconds between each attack (given in real time)
Attack Range	distance (in tiles) over which the Unit can inflict damage; combat in adjacent tiles is considered hand-to-hand
Movement Speed	how fast the Unit moves (in tiles per second) on the map; speed is listed in real time

CIVILIANS

During the Stone and Tool ages, when you just begin to build your civilization and contact with your neighbors is minimal, civilians take precedence over military units. The key to survival—at least during these early, formative years—is proper task management of your civilian work force.

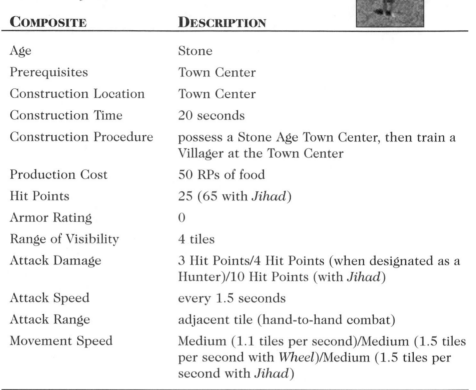

VILLAGERS

COMPOSITE	DESCRIPTION
Age	Stone
Prerequisites	Town Center
Construction Location	Town Center
Construction Time	20 seconds
Construction Procedure	possess a Stone Age Town Center, then train a Villager at the Town Center
Production Cost	50 RPs of food
Hit Points	25 (65 with *Jihad*)
Armor Rating	0
Range of Visibility	4 tiles
Attack Damage	3 Hit Points/4 Hit Points (when designated as a Hunter)/10 Hit Points (with *Jihad*)
Attack Speed	every 1.5 seconds
Attack Range	adjacent tile (hand-to-hand combat)
Movement Speed	Medium (1.1 tiles per second)/Medium (1.5 tiles per second with *Wheel*)/Medium (1.5 tiles per second with *Jihad*)

Villagers are the "worker bees" of your civilization. They assume different names depending on their assigned roles (Builder, Farmer, Fisherman, Forager, Hunter, Miner, Repairman). When Villagers act

as Builders, they are able to construct edifices as they become available. Construction times for buildings vary according to the building (see Chapter 4). This construction time can be reduced by up to 75 percent by assigning additional Villagers to the task. Damaged buildings can be repaired by your Villagers if they are assigned to the project as repairmen.

Villagers can be assigned to work as Farmers, harvesting food Resource Points from your farms. They also can acquire food Resource Points by acting as Fisherman, Foragers, and Hunters. As Miners, your Villagers can mine for Resource Points of gold and stone. Each Villager can carry 10 Resource Points of food, gold, stone, and wood per trip, and society benefits.

Certain kinds of Research improve your Villagers' performances. They are as follows:

- *Gold Mining* allows your gold miners to mine and carry an additional three RPs of gold.

- *Jihad* turns your Villagers into paramilitary fanatics. They receive increased attack strength, movement speed, and Hit Points.

- *Siegecraft* allows your stone miners to mine and carry an additional three RPs of stone (cumulative with other bonuses). It also enables your Villagers to inflict damage on walls and towers.

- *Stone Mining* allows your stone miners to mine and carry an additional three RPs of stone (cumulative with other bonuses).

- *Wheel* increases your Villagers' movement speed to 1.5 tiles per second.

PRIEST

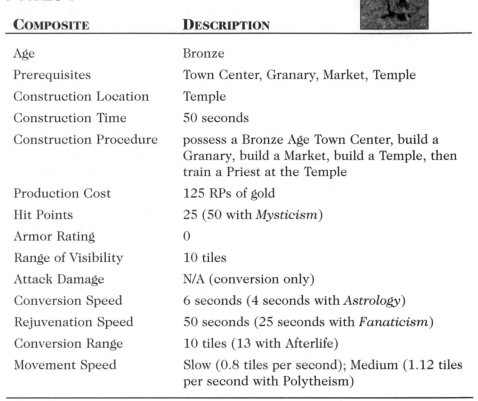

COMPOSITE	DESCRIPTION
Age	Bronze
Prerequisites	Town Center, Granary, Market, Temple
Construction Location	Temple
Construction Time	50 seconds
Construction Procedure	possess a Bronze Age Town Center, build a Granary, build a Market, build a Temple, then train a Priest at the Temple
Production Cost	125 RPs of gold
Hit Points	25 (50 with *Mysticism*)
Armor Rating	0
Range of Visibility	10 tiles
Attack Damage	N/A (conversion only)
Conversion Speed	6 seconds (4 seconds with *Astrology*)
Rejuvenation Speed	50 seconds (25 seconds with *Fanaticism*)
Conversion Range	10 tiles (13 with Afterlife)
Movement Speed	Slow (0.8 tiles per second); Medium (1.12 tiles per second with Polytheism)

Priests are more than just religious figures—they are an amalgam of benevolence and bloodlust. Priests can heal (remove damage from) friendly and allied Units at no cost in Resource Points. This useful feature keeps you from having to pay to train new Units from scratch. Injured Units can be removed from a fight, healed, and then sent back to battle as good as new.

In addition to this healing ability, Priests can "convert" enemy Units into friendly ones, an extremely effective form of attack.

Instead of eliminating enemy units, the alteration process causes them to join your tribe. After conversion, the "converted" Unit assumes your civilization's color.

Although the Priest moves slowly and carries no weapons or armor, his ability to "convert" enemy Units makes him one of the most dangerous Units on the map. Priests inspire hope in your allies and strike fear in the hearts of your enemies. They are prime targets on the battlefield and must be protected carefully by military units.

The following kinds of research improve your Priest's performance:

- *Afterlife* increases the conversion range attempts by 30 percent, raising it from 10 tiles to 13 tiles.
- *Astrology* increase likelihood to convert by 30 percent.
- *Fanaticism* cuts your Priest's rejuvenation time by 50 percent, lowering it from 50 seconds to 25 seconds.
- *Mysticism* doubles the damage your Priests can absorb, raising the amount from 25 Hit Points to 50 Hit Points.
- *Monotheism* allows your Priests direct conversion attempts at enemy Priests and buildings (except Town Centers, Walls, and Wonders).
- *Polytheism* increases the movement speed of your Priests by 40 percent, raising it from 0.8 tiles per second to 1.12 tiles per second.

PRIEST (BLIND LAME)

COMPOSITE	DESCRIPTION
Age	any
Prerequisites	N/A
Construction Location	N/A
Construction Time	initial scenario placement only
Hit Points	25
Armor Rating	0
Range of Visibility	N/A (blind)
Attack Damage	N/A (conversion only)
Conversion Speed	6 seconds
Conversion Range	adjacent tile only
Movement Speed	N/A (stationary figure)

The Blind Lame Priest appears in certain scenarios and is available to you in the Scenario Editor when you build your own scenarios. Because he is blind, he has no range of visibility. Because he is lame, he cannot move from the tile on which he is originally placed. He functions merely as a stationary source of healing for friendly forces. You must move your damaged Units adjacent to a Blind Lame Priest in order to heal them.

INFANTRY UNITS

Infantry Units are common foot soldiers—in modern-day wording, they would be referred to as "grunts." Units in this category include the Clubman, Axeman, Short Swordsman, Broad Swordsman, Long Swordsman, Legion, Hoplite, Phalanx, and Centurion. They likely will make up the bulk of your army because they can be built quickly and cheaply. Infantry Units move slowly and carry weapons that are good only in hand-to-hand combat. With advanced training and additional armor, however, infantry Units gradually evolve into more effective fighters.

CLUBMAN

COMPOSITE	DESCRIPTION
Age	Stone
Prerequisites	Barracks
Construction Location	Barracks
Construction Time	25 seconds
Construction Procedure	possess a Tool Age Town Center, build a Barracks, then train a Clubman at the Barracks
Training Cost	50 RPs of food
Hit Points	40
Armor Rating	0
Range of Visibility	4 tiles
Attack Damage	3 Hit Points
Attack Speed	every 1.5 seconds
Attack Range	adjacent tile (hand-to-hand combat)
Movement Speed	Medium (1.2 tiles per second)

The Clubman is the weakest of all the infantry Units. Unskilled, without arms, and unlikely to survive for long in battle, he attacks with the same weight as a Villager. One benefit to building these Units is the Clubman's ability to sustain damage. The Clubman can take 15 Hit Points of damage more than the average civilian can sustain. You will find yourself training Clubmen during the Stone Age because they are the only military Units available. Rather than train too many, save up your food resources to help you advance into the Tool Age. These Units automatically upgrade to Axemen when you reach the Tool Age and research the Battleaxe.

The following types of research improve your Clubman's performance:

- *Toolworking* increases the Clubman's attack damage by two Hit Points per attack.

- *Metalworking* increases the Clubman's attack damage by two Hit Points per attack.

- Metallurgy increases the Clubman's attack damage by three Hit Points per attack.

- *Leather Armor for Infantry* increases the Clubman's armor rating by two.

- *Scale Armor for Infantry* increases the Clubman's armor rating by two.

- *Chain Mail Armor for Infantry* increases the Clubman's armor rating by two.

- Bronze Shield increases the Clubman's armor rating by one against missile weapons, including the Ballista and Helepolis.

- *Iron Shield* increases the Clubman's armor rating by one against missile weapons, including the Ballista and Helepolis.

AXEMAN

COMPOSITE	DESCRIPTION
Age	Tool
Prerequisites	Town Center, Barracks
Construction Location	Barracks
Construction Time	25 seconds
Construction Procedure	possess a Tool Age Town Center, build a Barracks, upgrade to Battleaxe at the Barracks, then train an Axeman at the Barracks.

COMPOSITE	DESCRIPTION
Upgrade Cost	100 RPs of food
Training Cost	50 RPs of food
Hit Points	50
Armor Rating	0
Range of Visibility	4 tiles
Attack Damage	5 Hit Points
Attack Speed	every 1.5 seconds
Attack Range	adjacent tile (hand-to-hand combat)
Movement Speed	Medium (1.2 tiles per second)

Having reached the Tool Age, you can now spend 100 food Resource Points to upgrade your infantry to Axeman status. The Axeman only has a slightly greater attack strength than the Clubman, but he can withstand ten more Hit Points of damage. This extra staying-power gives your forces an early advantage. Axemen are upgraded and produced at the Barracks. Together with Clubmen, these Units make a distinct subclass of unskilled, barbarian infantry. The Axeman is the top Unit in this class.

The following kinds of research enhance your Axeman's performance:

- *Toolworking* increases the Axeman's attack damage by two Hit Points per attack.

- *Metalworking* increases the Axeman's attack damage by two Hit Points per attack.

- *Metallurgy* increases the Axeman's attack damage by three Hit Points per attack.

- *Leather Armor for Infantry* increases the Axeman's armor rating by two.

- *Scale Armor for Infantry* increases the Axeman's armor rating by two.
- *Chain Mail Armor for Infantry* increases the Axeman's armor rating by two.
- *Bronze Shield* increases the Axeman's armor rating by one against missile weapons, including the Ballista and Helepolis.
- *Iron Shield* increases the Axeman's armor rating by one against missile weapons, including the Ballista and Helepolis.

SHORT SWORDSMAN

COMPOSITE	DESCRIPTION
Age	Bronze
Prerequisites	Town Center, Barracks
Construction Location	Barracks
Construction Time	25 seconds
Construction Procedure	possess a Bronze Age Town Center, build a Barracks, upgrade to a Battleaxe at the Barracks, research Short Sword at the Barracks, then train a Short Swordsman at the Barracks
Research Cost	120 RPs of food, 50 RPs of gold
Training Cost	35 RPs of food, 15 RPs of gold
Hit Points	60
Armor Rating	1
Range of Visibility	4 tiles
Attack Damage	7 Hit Points
Attack Speed	every 1.5 seconds
Attack Range	adjacent tile (hand-to-hand combat)
Movement Speed	Medium (1.2 tiles per second)

The Short Swordsman is the first Unit in a brand new subclass of sword-bearing, partially armored infantry. The Short Swordsman can inflict greater damage than its predecessors and can withstand more damage as well. It requires that you research the Short Sword before you begin training these Units. Both the research and the training are conducted at the Barracks. Note that this Unit (like all Units in this subclass) requires you to expend gold resources as well as food.

Certain kinds of research improve your Short Swordman's performance. They are as follows:

- *Toolworking* increases the Short Swordsman's attack damage by two Hit Points per attack.

- *Metalworking* increases the Short Swordsman's attack damage by two Hit Points per attack.

- *Metallurgy* increases the Short Swordsman's attack damage by three Hit Points per attack.

- *Leather Armor for Infantry* increases the Short Swordsman's armor rating by two.

- *Scale Armor for Infantry* increases the Short Swordsman's armor rating by two.

- *Chain Mail Armor for Infantry* increases the Short Swordsman's armor rating by two.

- *Bronze Shield* increases the Short Swordsman's armor rating by one against missile weapons, including the Ballista and Helepolis.

- *Iron Shield* increases the Short Swordsman's armor rating by one against missile weapons, including the Ballista and Helepolis.

BROAD SWORDSMAN

COMPOSITE	DESCRIPTION
Age	Bronze
Prerequisites	Town Center, Barracks
Construction Location	Barracks
Construction Time	25 seconds
Construction Procedure	possess a Bronze Age Town Center, build a Barracks, upgrade the Battleaxe at the Barracks, research *Short Sword* at the Barracks, upgrade to a Broad Sword at the Barracks, train a Broad Swordsman at the Barracks.
Upgrade Cost	140 RPs of food, 50 RPs of gold
Training Cost	35 RPs of food, 15 RPs of gold
Hit Points	70
Armor Rating	1
Range of Visibility	4 tiles
Attack Damage	9 Hit Points
Attack Speed	every 1.5 seconds
Attack Range	adjacent tile (hand-to-hand combat)
Movement Speed	Medium (1.2 tiles per second)

The Broad Swordsman becomes available after you upgrade the Short Swordsman. Produced in the Barracks, the Broad Swordsman has more Hit Points and a slightly greater attack strength. Like the Short Swordsmen, these Units are the first in your army with armor protection, allowing them to engage and to defeat lesser troops in hand-to-hand combat even when outnumbered.

Certain kinds of research improve your performance as a Broad Swordsman. They are as follows:

 Toolworking increases the Broad Swordsman's attack damage by two Hit Points per attack.

- *Metalworking* increases the Broad Swordsman's attack damage by two Hit Points per attack.
- *Metallurgy* increases the Broad Swordsman's attack damage by three Hit Points per attack.
- *Leather Armor for Infantry* increases the Broad Swordsman's armor rating by two.
- *Scale Armor for Infantry* increases the Broad Swordsman's armor rating by two.
- *Chain Mail Armor for Infantry* increases the Broad Swordsman's armor rating by two.
- *Bronze Shield* increases the Broad Swordsman's armor rating by one against missile weapons, including the Ballista and Helepolis.
- *Iron Shield* increases the Broad Swordsman's armor rating by one against missile weapons, including the Ballista and Helepolis.

LONG SWORDSMAN

COMPOSITE	DESCRIPTION
Age	Iron
Prerequisite Buildings	Town Center, Barracks
Construction Location	Barracks
Construction Time	25 seconds
Construction Procedure	possess an Iron Age Town Center, build a Barracks, upgrade to a Battleaxe at the Barracks, research *Short Sword* at the Barracks, upgrade to a Broad Sword at the Barracks, upgrade to a Long Sword at the Barracks, then train a Long Swordsman at the Barracks
Upgrade Cost	160 RPs of food, 50 RPs of gold

COMPOSITE	DESCRIPTION
Training Cost	35 RPs of food, 15 RPs of gold
Hit Points	80
Armor Rating	2
Range of Visibility	4 tiles
Attack Damage	11 Hit Points
Attack Speed	every 1.5 seconds
Attack Range	adjacent tile (hand-to-hand combat)
Movement Speed	Medium (1.2 tiles per second)

The appearance of the Long Swordsman marks the end of this sub-class of infantry. The Long Swordsman is quite effective in hand-to-hand combat, inflicting a base of 11 Hit Points per attack. The increased armor rating gives this Unit additional protection. Coupled with an ability to absorb 80 Hit Points of damage, count on your Long Swordsman to have a lasting impact on the battlefield.

The following types of research improve your Long Swordsman's performance:

- *Toolworking* increases the Long Swordsman's attack damage by two Hit Points per attack.
- *Metalworking* increases the Long Swordsman's attack damage by two Hit Points per attack.
- *Metallurgy* increases the Long Swordsman's attack damage by three Hit Points per attack.
- *Leather Armor for Infantry* increases the Long Swordsman's armor rating by two.
- *Scale Armor for Infantry* increases the Long Swordsman's armor rating by two.
- *Chain Mail Armor for Infantry* increases the Long Swordsman's armor rating by two.

- *Bronze Shield* increases the Long Swordsman's armor rating by one against missile weapons, including the Ballista and Helepolis.

- *Iron Shield* increases the Long Swordsman's armor rating by one against missile weapons, including the Ballista and Helepolis.

LEGION

COMPOSITE	DESCRIPTION
Age	Iron
Prerequisite Buildings	Town Center, Barracks, Temple
Construction Location	Barracks
Construction Time	25 seconds
Construction Procedure	possess an Iron Age Town Center, build a Barracks, build a Temple, upgrade to a Battleaxe at the Barracks, research *Short Sword* at the Barracks, upgrade to a Broad Sword at the Barracks, upgrade to a Long Sword at the Barracks, research *Fanaticism* at the Temple, upgrade to a Legion at the Barracks, then train a Legion at the Barracks
Upgrade Cost	1,400 RPs of food, 600 RPs of gold
Research Cost of *Fanaticism*	150 RPs of gold
Training Cost	35 RPs of food, 15 RPs of gold
Hit Points	160
Armor Rating	2
Range of Visibility	4 tiles
Attack Damage	13 Hit Points
Attack Speed	every 1.5 seconds
Attack Range	adjacent tile (hand-to-hand combat)
Movement Speed	Medium (1.2 tiles per second)

Once your civilization reaches the Iron Age, a number of very strong infantry Units become available. Before you can upgrade your infantry to Legion status, however, you must research *Fanaticism*. Notice that the cost in food and gold resources is quite high. Carefully consider the proper timing in making this expenditure. Once the upgrade is made, however, Legionnaires are fantastic fighting Units. The Legion can withstand twice the damage of its predecessor. It is the top Unit in this subclass of infantry.

Certain types of research improve your Legion's performance. They are as follows:

- *Toolworking* increases the Legion's attack damage by two Hit Points per attack.
- *Metalworking* increases the Legion's attack damage by two Hit Points per attack.
- *Metallurgy* increases the Legion's attack damage by three Hit Points per attack.
- *Leather Armor for Infantry* increases the Legion's armor rating by two.
- *Scale Armor for Infantry* increases the Legion's armor rating by two.
- *Chain Mail Armor for Infantry* increases the Legion's armor rating by two.
- *Bronze Shield* increases the Legion's armor rating by one against missile weapons, including the Ballista and Helepolis.
- *Iron Shield* increases the Legion's armor rating by one against missile weapons, including the Ballista and Helepolis.

HOPLITE

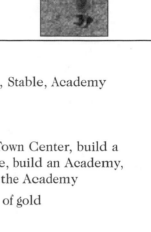

Composite	Description
Age	Bronze
Prerequisite Buildings	Town Center, Barracks, Stable, Academy
Construction Location	Academy
Construction Time	35 seconds
Construction Procedure	possess a Bronze Age Town Center, build a Barracks, build a Stable, build an Academy, then train a Hoplite at the Academy
Training Cost	60 RPs of food, 40 RPs of gold
Hit Points	120
Armor Rating	5
Range of Visibility	4 tiles
Attack Damage	17 Hit Points
Attack Speed	every 1.5 seconds
Attack Range	adjacent tile (hand-to-hand combat)
Movement Speed	Slow (0.9 tiles per second), Medium (1.12 tiles per second with *Aristocracy*)

The final subclass of infantry is the academy-trained professional. The Hoplite is the first of these elite soldiers to become available. It withstands less damage than the Long Swordsman but has a greater attack strength. The most significant benefit of the Hoplite is its high armor rating. A negative effect of all this armor is that the Hoplite moves more slowly than all other infantry units. This problem can be corrected somewhat by researching *Aristocracy*. The Hoplite costs 40 RPs of gold to train, and is much better than the Longsword.

The following kinds of research improve your Hoplite's performance:

- *Toolworking* increases the Hoplite's attack damage by two Hit Points per attack.
- *Metalworking* increases the Hoplite's attack damage by two Hit Points per attack.
- *Metallurgy* increases the Hoplite's attack damage by three Hit Points per attack.
- *Leather Armor for Infantry* increases the Hoplite's armor rating by two.
- *Scale Armor for Infantry* increases the Hoplite's armor rating by two.
- *Chain Mail Armor for Infantry* increases the Hoplite's armor rating by two.
- *Bronze Shield* increases the Hoplite's armor rating by one against missile weapons, including the Ballista and Helepolis.
- *Iron Shield* increases the Hoplite's armor rating by one against missile weapons, including the Ballista and Helepolis.
- *Aristocracy* increases the Hoplite's movement speed by 25 percent to 1.12 tiles per second.

PHALANX

COMPOSITE	DESCRIPTION
Age	Iron
Prerequisite Buildings	Town Center, Barracks, Stable, Academy
Construction Location	Academy
Construction Time	35 seconds

COMPOSITE	DESCRIPTION
Construction Procedure	possess an Iron Age Town Center, build a Barracks, build a Stable, build an Academy, upgrade to a Phalanx at the Academy, then train a Phalanx at the Academy
Upgrade Cost	300 RPs of food, 100 RPs of gold
Training Cost	60 RPs of food, 40 RPs of gold
Hit Points	120
Armor Rating	7
Range of Visibility	4 tiles
Attack Damage	20 Hit Points
Attack Speed	every 1.5 seconds
Attack Range	adjacent tile (hand-to-hand combat)
Movement Speed	Slow (0.9 tiles per second), Medium (1.12 tiles per second with *Aristocracy*)

More heavily armored than the Hoplite, the Phalanx (pronounced FAY-lanx) is the second of three academy-trained professional infantry units. It inflicts slightly greater attack damage, and, fortunately, its modest increase in ability costs you little. The upgrade cost of only 300 RPs of food and 100 RPs of gold should be pocket change to your civilization by now. Like the Hoplite, the Phalanx can easily crush any non-academy-trained enemy Units. The high armor rating, coupled with *Chain Mail* and *Iron Shield*, should make it nearly invincible.

Certain kinds of research improve the performance of a Phalanx. They are as follows:

- *Toolworking* increases the Phalanx's attack damage by two Hit Points per attack.
- *Metalworking* increases the Phalanx's attack damage by two Hit Points per attack.

- *Metallurgy* increases the Phalanx's attack damage by three Hit Points per attack.
- *Leather Armor for Infantry* increases the Phalanx's armor rating by two.
- *Scale Armor for Infantry* increases the Phalanx's armor rating by two.
- *Chain Mail Armor for Infantry* increases the Phalanx's armor rating by two.
- *Bronze Shield* increases the Phalanx's armor rating by one against missile weapons, including the Ballista and Helepolis.
- *Iron Shield* increases the Phalanx's armor rating by one against missile weapons, including the Ballista and Helepolis.
- *Aristocracy* increases the Hoplite's movement speed by 25 percent to 1.12 tiles per second.

CENTURION

COMPOSITE	DESCRIPTION
Age	Iron
Prerequisite Buildings	Town Center, Barracks, Stable, Government Center, Academy
Construction Location	Academy
Construction Time	35 seconds
Construction Procedure	possess an Iron Age Town Center, build a Barracks, build a Stable, build an Academy, upgrade to a Phalanx at the Academy, research *Aristocracy* at the Government Center, upgrade to a Centurion at the Academy, then train a Centurion at the Academy
Upgrade Cost	1,800 RPs of food, 700 RPs of Gold
Research Cost of *Aristocracy*	175 RPs of food, 150 RPs of gold

COMPOSITE	DESCRIPTION
Training Cost	60 RPs of food, 40 RPs of gold
Hit Points	160
Armor Rating	8
Attack Damage	30 Hit Points
Attack Speed	every 1.5 seconds
Attack Range	adjacent tile (hand-to-hand combat)
Movement Speed	Slow (0.9 per second)

The Centurion, the last academy-trained professional infantry unit, can inflict more damage and has greater armor protection than the Phalanx. Until now, researching *Aristocracy* was simply a good way to increase the speed of your Academy units—for the Centurion, it is a requirement. The high upgrade cost of the Centurion is prohibitive. Rather than spend your resources upgrading the Phalanx, use them to produce more Archers or Siege Weapons.

Certain kinds of research improve your Centurion's performance. They are as follows:

- *Aristocracy* is a requirement for producing the Centurion.
- *Toolworking* increases the Centurion's attack damage by two Hit Points per attack.
- *Metalworking* increases the Centurion's attack damage by two Hit Points per attack.
- *Metallurgy* increases the Centurion's attack damage by three Hit Points per attack.
- *Leather Armor for Infantry* increases the Centurion's armor rating by two.
- *Scale Armor for Infantry* increases the Centurion's armor rating by two.

- *Chain Mail Armor for Infantry* increases the Centurion's armor rating by two.
- *Bronze Shield* increases the Centurion's armor rating by one against missile weapons, including the Ballista and Helepolis.
- *Iron Shield* increases the Centurion's armor rating by one against missile weapons, including the Ballista and Helepolis.

ARCHER UNITS

Archer Units are considered missile Units because they shoot projectiles from a distance rather than engage in hand-to-hand combat. The damage they inflict on enemy troops is not as great as that of infantry Units, but Archers can attack outside of enemy reach. Archer Units include the Bowman, Improved Bowman, Composite Bowman, Chariot Archer, Elephant Archer, Horse Archer, and Heavy Horse Archer.

BOWMAN

COMPOSITE	DESCRIPTION
Age	Tool
Prerequisite Buildings	Town Center, Barracks, Archery Range
Construction Location	Archery Range
Construction Time	30 seconds
Construction Procedure	possess a Tool Age Town Center, build a Barracks, build an Archery Range, then train a Bowman at the Archery Range
Training Cost	40 RPs of food, 20 RPs of wood
Hit Points	35
Armor Rating	0

COMPOSITE	DESCRIPTION
Range of Visibility	7 tiles
Attack Damage	3 Hit Points
Attack Speed	every 1.5 seconds
Attack Range	5 tiles
Movement Speed	Medium (1.2 tiles per second)

The Bowman represents the first Unit that engages enemy Units from a distance. It becomes available after your tribe builds an Archery Range in the Tool Age. Trained at the Archery Range, the Bowman is only marginally effective. Its presence on the field of battle, even in the Tool Age, is mainly psychological. It inflicts the same damage as a Clubman but possesses fewer Hit Points.

The following research improves your Bowman's performance:

- *Alchemy* increases the Bowman's attack damage by one Hit Point per attack.

- *Ballistics* increases the Bowman's accuracy against moving targets.

- *Leather Armor for Archers* increases the Bowman's armor rating by two.

- *Scale Armor for Archers* increases the Bowman's armor rating by two.

- *Chain Mail Armor for Archers* increases the Bowman's armor rating by two.

- *Woodworking* increases the Bowman's range by one tile.

- *Artisanship* increases the Bowman's range by one tile.

- *Craftsmanship* increases the Bowman's range by one tile.

IMPROVED BOWMAN

COMPOSITE	DESCRIPTION
Age	Bronze
Prerequisite Building	Town Center, Barracks, Archery Range
Construction Location	Archery Range
Construction Time	30 seconds
Construction Procedure	possess a Bronze Town Center, build a Barracks, build an Archery Range, research *Improved Bow* at the Archery Range, then train an Improved Bowman at the Archery Range
Research Cost of *Improved Bow*	140 RPs of food, 80 RPs of wood
Training Cost	40 RPs of food, 20 RPs of gold
Hit Points	40
Armor Rating	0
Range of Visibility	8 tiles
Attack Damage	4 Hit Points
Attack Speed	every 1.5 seconds
Attack Range	6 tiles
Movement Speed	Medium (1.2 tiles per second)

The Improved Bowman is equivalent to the Axeman in terms of the damage it inflicts and equal to the Clubman in Hit Points. It has a range advantage of one tile and five additional Hit Points over its predecessor. You must research the *Improved Bow* before you can begin producing this Unit—it is not an upgrade from the Bowman.

Certain kinds of research improve your Improved Bowman's performance. They are as follows:

 Alchemy increases the Improved Bowman's attack damage by one Hit Point per attack.

- *Ballistics* increases the Improved Bowman's accuracy against moving targets.

- *Leather Armor for Archers* increases the Improved Bowman's armor rating by two.

- *Scale Armor for Archers* increases the Improved Bowman's armor rating by two.

- *Chain Mail Armor for Archers* increases the Improved Bowman's armor rating by two.

- *Woodworking* increases the Improved Bowman's range by one tile.

- *Artisanship* increases the Improved Bowman's range by one tile.

- *Craftsmanship* increases the Improved Bowman's range by one tile.

COMPOSITE BOWMAN

COMPOSITE	DESCRIPTION
Age	Bronze
Prerequisite Buildings	Town Center, Barracks, Archery Range
Construction Location	Archery Range
Construction Time	30 seconds
Construction Procedure	possess a Bronze Age Town Center, build a Barracks, build an Archery Range, research *Improved Bow* at the Archery Range, upgrade to a Composite Bow at the Archery Range, then train the Composite Bowman at the Archery Range
Upgrade Cost	180 RPs of food, 100 RPs of 100
Training Cost	40 food, 20 gold
Hit Points	45

COMPOSITE	DESCRIPTION
Armor Rating	0
Range of Visibility	9 tiles
Attack Damage	5 Hit Points
Attack Speed	Every 1.5 seconds
Attack Range	7 tiles
Movement Speed	Medium (1.2 tiles per second)

The Composite Bowman is the first truly effective archery Unit available. In numbers, this can be one of the most effective Units in the game, especially considering their relatively low cost. These Units lack the hitting power to eliminate other military Units. They do have a decent range of attack, however, and should be used primarily to snipe at enemy Villagers. The Composite Bowman is an upgrade from the Improved Bowman and is produced at the Archery Range.

Certain types of research improves the performance of your Composite Bowman. They are as follows:

- *Alchemy* increases the Composite Bowman's attack damage by one Hit Point per attack.
- *Ballistics* increases the Composite Bowman's accuracy against moving targets.
- *Leather Armor for Archers* increases the Composite Bowman's armor rating by two.
- *Scale Armor for Archers* increases the Composite Bowman's armor rating by two.
- *Chain Mail Armor for Archers* increases the Composite Bowman's armor rating by two.
- *Woodworking* increases the Composite Bowman's range by one tile.

● *Artisanship* increases the Composite Bowman's range by one tile.

● *Craftsmanship* increases the Composite Bowman's range by one tile.

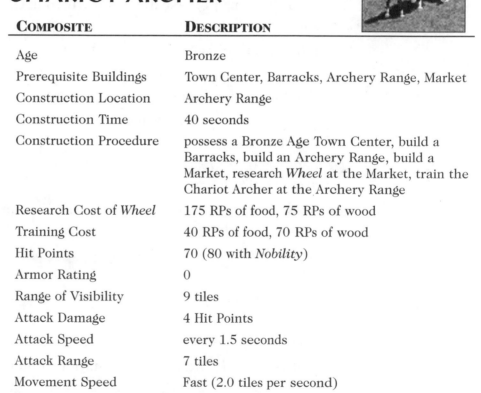

CHARIOT ARCHER

COMPOSITE	DESCRIPTION
Age	Bronze
Prerequisite Buildings	Town Center, Barracks, Archery Range, Market
Construction Location	Archery Range
Construction Time	40 seconds
Construction Procedure	possess a Bronze Age Town Center, build a Barracks, build an Archery Range, build a Market, research *Wheel* at the Market, train the Chariot Archer at the Archery Range
Research Cost of *Wheel*	175 RPs of food, 75 RPs of wood
Training Cost	40 RPs of food, 70 RPs of wood
Hit Points	70 (80 with *Nobility*)
Armor Rating	0
Range of Visibility	9 tiles
Attack Damage	4 Hit Points
Attack Speed	every 1.5 seconds
Attack Range	7 tiles
Movement Speed	Fast (2.0 tiles per second)

The Chariot Archer is a well-rounded and powerful addition to your army. It combines a good movement rate with a decent capacity to sustain damage. Though it lacks adequate attack strength for a Bronze Age Unit, it possesses some special attributes that make up for this deficiency. The Chariot Archer is quite effective against Priests. Its missile fire causes triple damage (12 Hit Points) against Priests, and Chariot Archers have an increased resistance to Priestly Conversion attempts. If you see that your enemy likes to build Priests, the Chariot Archer is the perfect countermeasure. Before you can produce Chariot Archers, you must first research the *Wheel*.

The following kinds of research improve your Chariot Archer's performance:

- *Wheel* is required for producing the Chariot Archer.
- *Alchemy* increases the Chariot Archer's attack damage by one Hit Point per attack.
- *Ballistics* increases the Chariot Archer's accuracy against moving targets.
- *Leather Armor for Archers* increases the Chariot Archer's armor rating by two.
- *Scale Armor for Archers* increases the Chariot Archer's armor rating by two.
- *Chain Mail Armor for Archers* increases the Chariot Archer's armor rating by two.
- *Woodworking* increases the Chariot Archer's range by one tile.
- *Artisanship* increases the Chariot Archer's range by one tile.
- *Craftsmanship* increases the Chariot Archer's range by one tile.
- *Nobility* increases the Chariot Archer's Hit Points by 15 percent from 70 to 80 Hit Points.

ELEPHANT ARCHER

COMPOSITE	DESCRIPTION
Age	Iron
Prerequisite Buildings	Town Center, Barracks, Archery Range
Construction Location	Archery Range
Construction Time	50 seconds
Construction Procedure	possess an Iron Age Town Center, build a Barracks, build an Archery Range, then build an Elephant Archer
Training Cost	180 RPs of food, 60 RPs of gold
Hit Points	600
Armor Rating	0
Range of Visibility	8 tiles
Attack Damage	5 Hit Points
Attack Speed	every 1.5 seconds
Attack Range	7 tiles
Movement Speed	Slow (0.9 tiles per second)

As you might imagine, the Elephant Archer is an incredibly strong Unit, combining the damage resistance of the Elephant with the attack strength (and range) of the Composite Bowman. This deadly combination makes for a moderately lethal attack platform with great staying power. Since the Elephant Archer lumbers along at a Slow rate of speed, perhaps the best defense against these Units is to stay out of their way, or to use Priests. Stopping these Units requires Siege Weaponry at the very least. Elephant Archers are trained at the Archery Range—they are not upgrades. If you can afford the food resources, they are fun Units to build.

Certain research improves your Elephant Archer's performance. They are as follows:

- *Alchemy* increases the Elephant Archer's attack damage by one Hit Point per attack.
- *Ballistics* increases the Elephant Archer's accuracy against moving targets.
- *Leather Armor for Archers* increases the Elephant Archer's armor rating by two.
- *Scale Armor for Archers* increases the Elephant Archer's armor rating by two.
- *Chain Mail Armor for Archers* increases the Elephant Archer's armor rating by two.
- *Woodworking* increases the Elephant Archer's range by one tile.
- *Artisanship* increases the Elephant Archer's range by one tile.
- *Craftsmanship* increases the Elephant Archer's range by one tile.

HORSE ARCHER

COMPOSITE	DESCRIPTION
Age	Iron
Prerequisite Buildings	Town Center, Barracks, Archery Range
Construction Location	Archery Range
Construction Time	50 seconds
Construction Procedure	possess an Iron Age Town Center, build a Barracks, build an Archery Range, then train the Horse Archer at the Archery Range
Training Cost	50 RPs of food, 70 RPs of gold

COMPOSITE	DESCRIPTION
Hit Points	60 (69 with *Nobility*)
Armor Rating	0
Range of Visibility	6 tiles
Attack Damage	7 Hit Points
Attack Speed	every 1.5 seconds
Attack Range	7 tiles
Movement Speed	Fast (2.2 tiles per second)

By the time your civilization reaches the Iron Age, battlefield mobility will be the key to victory. The Horse Archer is an extremely fast Unit with modest striking power. It has armor that increases its armor rating by two—including projectiles fired by naval vessels, towers, the Ballista, and the Helepolis. For all its positive features, the Horse Archer can sustain only one-tenth of the damage of an Elephant Archer. These Units are strong but fragile. If you train Horse Archers, use them judiciously.

The following kinds of research improve your Horse Archer's performance:

- *Alchemy* increases the Horse Archer's attack damage by one Hit Point per attack.

- *Ballistics* increases the Horse Archer's accuracy against moving targets.

- *Woodworking* increases the Horse Archer's range by one tile.

- *Leather Armor for Archers* increases the Horse Archer's armor rating by two.

- *Scale Armor for Archers* increases the Horse Archer's armor rating by two.

- *Chain Mail Armor for Archers* increases the Horse Archer's armor rating by two.

- *Artisanship* increases the Horse Archer's range by one tile.
- *Craftsmanship* increases the Horse Archer's range by one tile.
- *Nobility* increases the Horse Archer's Hit Points by 15 percent from 60 to 69 Hit Points.

HEAVY HORSE ARCHER

COMPOSITE	DESCRIPTION
Age	Iron
Prerequisite Buildings	Town Center, Barracks, Storage Pit, Archery Range
Construction Location	Archery Range
Construction Time	60 seconds
Construction Procedure	possess an Iron Age Town Center, build a Barracks, build an Archery Range, research *Chain Mail for Archers* at the Storage Pit, upgrade to a Heavy Horse Archer at the Archery Range, then build the Heavy Horse Archer at the Archery Range
Upgrade Cost	1,750 RPs of food, 800 RPs of gold
Research Cost of *Chain Mail for Archers*	150 RPs of food, 100 RPs of gold
Training Cost	50 RPs of food, 70 RPs of gold
Hit Points	90
Armor Rating	0
Range of Visibility	9 tiles
Attack Damage	8 Hit Points
Attack Speed	every 1.5 seconds
Attack Range	7 tiles
Movement Speed	Fast (2.5 tiles per second)

The Heavy Horse Archer is an upgraded Horse Archer. It possesses only a slightly greater attack strength than the Horse Archer but can withstand a whopping 50 percent more damage. Like the Horse Archer, it has armor that gives a +2 defense against missile weaponry—including missiles from naval vessels, towers, Ballista, and Helepolis. Before you can train the Heavy Horse Archer, you must research *Chain Mail for Archers* at the Storage Pit. The Heavy Horse Archer is the top Archer Unit in the game and comes with the price tag to prove it.

Research improves your Heavy Horse Archer's performance. They are as follows:

- *Chain Mail Armor for Archers* is a requirement for producing Heavy Horse Archer units.
- *Alchemy* increases the Heavy Horse Archer's attack damage by one Hit Point per attack.
- *Ballistics* increases the Heavy Horse Archer's accuracy against moving targets.
- *Woodworking* increases the Heavy Horse Archer's range by one tile.
- *Artisanship* increases the Heavy Horse Archer's range by one tile.
- *Craftsmanship* increases the Heavy Horse Archer's range by one tile.
- *Nobility* increases the Heavy Horse Archer's Hit Points by 15 percent from 90 to 103 Hit Points.

CAVALRY UNITS

The introduction of cavalry Units gives your army a measure of battlefield mobility. Cavalry can be used to scout an enemy's civilization or to investigate new areas on the map. These Units lack the high attack strength of infantry Units, but they are fast and able to withstand considerable damage. On average, at least 25 percent of your army should consist of these mounted troops.

SCOUT

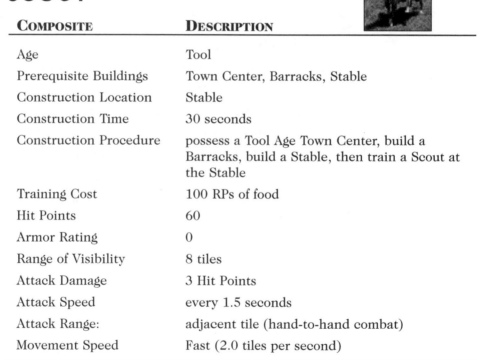

COMPOSITE	DESCRIPTION
Age	Tool
Prerequisite Buildings	Town Center, Barracks, Stable
Construction Location	Stable
Construction Time	30 seconds
Construction Procedure	possess a Tool Age Town Center, build a Barracks, build a Stable, then train a Scout at the Stable
Training Cost	100 RPs of food
Hit Points	60
Armor Rating	0
Range of Visibility	8 tiles
Attack Damage	3 Hit Points
Attack Speed	every 1.5 seconds
Attack Range:	adjacent tile (hand-to-hand combat)
Movement Speed	Fast (2.0 tiles per second)

The Scout is less of a cavalry Unit and more of a simple Villager on horseback. Though laughably weak, it is the first mounted Unit to appear in the game. Scouts are better used as explorers, not fighters. Their range of visibility and movement speed allows them to reveal large areas of the map quickly. You are wise to train only a few of these Units. It is better to spend the Resource Points on leading your tribe into the Bronze Age than on food Resource Points for a cadre of Scouts.

Certain types of research improve your Scout's performance. They are as follows:

- *Toolworking* increases the Scout's attack damage by two Hit Points per attack.
- *Metalworking* increases the Scout's attack damage by three Hit Points per attack.
- *Metallurgy* increases the Scout's attack damage by three Hit Points per attack.
- *Leather Armor for Cavalry* increases the Scout's armor rating by two.
- *Scale Armor for Cavalry* increases the Scout's armor rating by two.
- *Chain Mail Armor for Cavalry* increases the Scout's armor rating by two.
- *Nobility* increases the Scout's Hit Points by 15 percent from 60 to 69 Hit Points.

CHARIOT

COMPOSITE	DESCRIPTION
Age	Bronze
Prerequisite Buildings	Town Center, Barracks, Stable
Construction Location	Stable
Construction Time	40 seconds

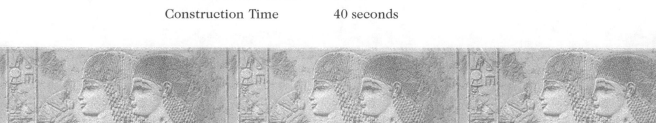

COMPOSITE	DESCRIPTION
Construction Procedure	possess a Bronze Age Town Center, build a Barracks, build a Stable, then build a Chariot at the Stable
Research Cost of *Wheel*	175 RPs of food, 75 RPs of wood
Training Cost	40 RPs of food, 60 RPs of wood
Hit Points	100
Armor Rating	0
Range of Visibility	4 tiles
Attack Damage	7 Hit Points
Attack Speed	every 1.5 seconds
Attack Range	adjacent tile (hand-to-hand combat)
Movement Speed	Fast (2.0 tiles per second)

For a Bronze Age military Unit, the Chariot is somewhat weak. The fast-moving, damage-resistant Chariot has attack strength only equal to that of the Short Swordsman. Like the Chariot Archer, Chariots possess the same special abilities. Their attacks cause triple damage (21 Hit Points) against Priests, and they have an increased resistance to Priestly Conversion attempts. Unlike the Chariot Archer, however, the Chariot must engage the enemy in hand-to-hand combat. Before you can begin training Chariot Units, you must first research the *Wheel*. These Units are trained at the Stable.

The following kinds of research improve your Chariot's performance:

- *Toolworking* increases the Chariot's attack damage by two Hit Points per attack.

- *Metalworking* increases the Chariot's attack damage by three Hit Points per attack.

- *Metallurgy* increases the Chariot's attack damage by three Hit Points per attack.
- *Leather Armor for Cavalry* increases the Chariot's armor rating by two.
- *Scale Armor for Cavalry* increases the Chariot's armor rating by two.
- *Chain Mail Armor for Cavalry* increases the Chariot's armor rating by two.
- *Nobility* increases the Chariot's Hit Points by 15 percent from 100 to 115 Hit Points.

CAVALRY

COMPOSITE	DESCRIPTION
Age	Bronze
Prerequisite Buildings	Town Center, Barracks, Stable
Construction Location	Stable
Construction Time	40 seconds
Construction Procedure	possess a Bronze Age Town Center, build a Barracks, build a Stable, upgrade to a Cavalry at the Stable, then build a Cavalry at the Stable
Training Cost	70 RPs of food, 80 RPs of gold
Hit Points	150
Armor Rating	0
Range of Visibility	4 tiles
Attack Damage	8 Hit Points (+5 Hit Points vs. infantry Units)
Attack Speed	every 1.5 seconds
Attack Range	adjacent tile (hand-to-hand combat)
Movement Speed	Fast (2.0 tiles per second)

The Cavalry Unit is the first truly effective mounted Unit in this class. It is particularly deadly when used against infantry Units. The +5 attack damage bonus given to Cavalry Units against infantry is due to their ability to charge and intimidate unmounted troops. The Cavalry is fast and can absorb significant damage; however, at 80 RPs of gold each, they are very expensive to train. Cavalry can be upgraded to Heavy Cavalry. You can train and upgrade these Units at the Stable.

Certain types of research improve your Cavalry's performance. They are as follows:

- *Toolworking* increases the Cavalry's attack damage by two Hit Points per attack.
- *Metalworking* increases the Cavalry's attack damage by three Hit Points per attack.
- *Metallurgy* increases the Cavalry's attack damage by three Hit Points per attack.
- *Leather Armor for Cavalry* increases the Cavalry's armor rating by two.
- *Scale Armor for Cavalry* increases the Cavalry's armor rating by two.
- *Chain Mail Armor for Cavalry* increases the Cavalry's armor rating by two.
- *Nobility* increases the Cavalry's Hit Points by 15 percent from 150 to 173 Hit Points.

HEAVY CAVALRY

COMPOSITE	DESCRIPTION
Age	Iron
Prerequisite Buildings	Town Center, Barracks, Stable
Construction Location	Stable
Construction Time	40 seconds
Construction Procedure	possess an Iron Age Town Center, build a Barracks, build a Stable, upgrade to a Heavy Cavalry at the Stable, then build a Heavy Cavalry at the Stable
Upgrade Cost	350 RPs of food, 125 RPs of gold
Training Cost	70 RPs of food, 80 RPs of gold
Hit Points	150
Armor Rating	1 (2 vs. missile weapons)
Range of Visibility	4 tiles
Attack Damage	10 Hit Points (+5 Hit Points vs. infantry units)
Attack Speed	every 1.5 seconds
Attack Range	adjacent tile (hand-to-hand combat)
Movement Speed	Fast (2.0 tiles per second)

Like its predecessor, Heavy Cavalry is a fast-moving, hard-hitting addition to your army. It receives the same +5 attack damage bonus as Cavalry against enemy infantry Units and can withstand the same amount of damage. Heavy Cavalry sports more armor than Cavalry and receives an additional point of armor rating (pierce) when attacked by missile weapons—including ships, towers, the Ballista, and the Helepolis. Though expensive, the additional armor and increased attack strength make Heavy Cavalry Units worthwhile.

The following kinds of research improve your Heavy Cavalry's performance:

- *Toolworking* increases the Heavy Cavalry's attack damage by two Hit Points per attack.

- *Metalworking* increases the Heavy Cavalry's attack damage by three Hit Points per attack.

- *Metallurgy* increases the Heavy Cavalry's attack damage by three Hit Points per attack.

- *Leather Armor for Cavalry* increases the Heavy Cavalry's armor rating by two.

- *Scale Armor for Cavalry* increases the Heavy Cavalry's armor rating by two.

- *Chain Mail Armor for Cavalry* increases the Heavy Cavalry's armor rating by two.

- *Nobility* increases the Heavy Cavalry's Hit Points by 15 percent from 150 to 173 Hit Points.

CATAPHRACT

COMPOSITE	DESCRIPTION
Age	Iron
Prerequisite Buildings	Town Center, Barracks, Stable
Construction Location	Stable
Construction Time	50 seconds
Construction Procedure	possess an Iron Age Town Center, build a Barracks, build a Stable, upgrade to a Heavy Cavalry at the Stable, research *Metallurgy* at the Storage Pit, upgrade to a Cataphract at the Stable, then build a Cataphract at the Stable
Upgrade Cost	2,000 RPs of food, 850 RPs of gold

COMPOSITE	DESCRIPTION
Research Cost of Metallurgy	300 RPs of food, 180 RPs of gold
Training Cost	70 RPs of food, 80 RPs of gold
Hit Points	180
Armor Rating	3 (4 vs. missile weapons)
Range of Visibility	4 tiles
Attack Damage	12 Hit Points (+5 Hit Points vs. infantry units)
Attack Speed	every 1.5 seconds
Attack Range	adjacent tile (hand-to-hand combat)
Movement Speed	Fast (2.0 tiles per second)

The Cataphract is a special type of heavily armored cavalry unit. Like all cavalry units, it is fast, especially considering its high armor rating. Before you can begin training Cataphract units, you must first research Metallurgy. (You are forgiven if you begin to think of the Cataphract as a modern-day tank.) The Cataphract receives the same +5 infantry attack bonus as Heavy Cavalry plus the additional point of armor rating (pierce) when attacked by missile weapons—including ships, towers, the Ballista, and the Helepolis. The Cataphract is the top cavalry Unit in the game.

Certain types of research improve your Cataphract's performance. They are as follows:

- *Toolworking* increases the Cataphract's attack damage by two Hit Points per attack.

- *Metalworking* increases the Cataphract's attack damage by three Hit Points per attack.

- *Metallurgy* is a requirement to begin training Cataphract units. It increases the Cataphract's attack damage by three Hit Points per attack.

- *Leather Armor for Cavalry* increases the Cataphract's armor rating by two.
- *Scale Armor for Cavalry* increases the Cataphract's armor rating by two.
- *Chain Mail Armor for Cavalry* increases the Cataphract's armor rating by two.
- *Nobility* increases the Cataphract's Hit Points by 15 percent from 180 to 207 Hit Points.

WAR ELEPHANT

COMPOSITE	DESCRIPTION
Age	Iron
Prerequisite Buildings	Town Center, Barracks, Stable
Construction Location	Stable
Construction Time	50 seconds
Construction Procedure	possess an Iron Age Town Center, build a Barracks, build a Stable, then build a War Elephant at the Stable
Training Cost	170 RPs of food, 40 RPs of gold
Hit Points	600
Armor Rating	0
Range of Visibility	5 tiles
Attack Damage	15 Hit Points trample damage (inflicted on all adjacent units)
Attack Speed	every 1.5 seconds
Attack Range	adjacent tile (hand-to-hand combat)
Movement Speed	Slow (0.9 tiles per second)

What would a game about ancient warfare be without a few good elephants? Besides the fun you have moving them around on the map, War Elephants are an awesome force to be reckoned with. Very few Units can withstand a pounding from these pachyderms. The War Elephant moves slowly, but that's because nothing on the battlefield can force it to move fast! A few of these monsters can go a long way—every army should have at least a couple.

Research improves the performance of your War Elephant. The forms of helpful research are as follows:

- *Leather Armor for Cavalry* increases the War Elephant's armor rating by two.
- *Scale Armor for Cavalry* increases the War Elephant's armor rating by two.
- *Chain Mail Armor for Cavalry* increases the War Elephant's armor rating by two.

SIEGE WEAPONS

Siege Weapons are the answer to field fortifications. These early artillery pieces cause a fantastic amount of damage, but they move slowly and require serious protection. They are easily destroyed by counter fire. Siege weapons are expensive; if you consider building these units, be prepared to spend lots of gold and wood resources. Units in this category include the Stone Thrower, Catapult, Heavy Catapult, Ballista, and Helepolis.

STONE THROWER

COMPOSITE	DESCRIPTION
Age	Bronze
Prerequisite Buildings	Town Center, Barracks, Archery Range, Siege Workshop
Construction Location	Siege Workshop
Construction Time	60 seconds
Construction Procedure	possess a Bronze Age Town Center, then build a Barracks, build an Archery Range, build a Siege Workshop, then build a Stone Thrower at the Siege Workshop
Construction Cost	180 RPs of wood, 80 RPs of gold
Hit Points	75
Armor Rating	0
Range of Visibility	12 tiles
Attack Damage	50 Hit Points
Attack Speed	every 5 seconds
Minimum Attack Range	2 tiles
Maximum Attack Range	10 tiles
Damage radius (Small)	1 tile (1 x 1 tile area)
Movement Speed	Slow (0.8 tiles per second)

The Stone Thrower is the first siege engine (weapon) to appear on the battlefield. As the name suggests, it hurls large stones over great distances. Note that this Unit has a minimum range as well as a maximum range. Its projectiles cause serious damage to wall structures and other stationary objects. The Stone Thrower is less effective against troops, however, because they can usually move out of the way before the projectile strikes them. Like all siege weapons, the Stone Thrower is fragile and best kept away from enemy missile weapons. These Units are built and upgraded at the Siege Workshop.

The following kinds of research improve your Stone Thrower's performance:

- *Alchemy* increases the Stone Thrower's attack damage by one Hit Point per attack.
- *Ballistics* increases the Stone Thrower's accuracy against moving targets.
- *Engineering* increases the Stone Thrower's range by two tiles.

CATAPULT

COMPOSITE	DESCRIPTION
Age	Iron
Prerequisite Buildings	Town Center, Barracks, Archery Range, Siege Workshop
Construction Location	Siege Workshop
Construction Time	60 seconds
Construction Procedure	possess an Iron Age Town Center, build a Barracks, build an Archery Range, build a Siege Workshop, upgrade to a Catapult at the Siege Workshop, then build a Catapult at the Siege Workshop
Upgrade Cost	300 RPs of food, 250 RPs of wood
Construction Cost	180 RPs of wood, 80 RPs of gold
Hit Points	75
Armor Rating	0
Range of Visibility	14 tiles
Attack Damage	60 Hit Points

COMPOSITE	DESCRIPTION
Attack Speed	every 5 seconds
Minimum Attack Range	2 tiles
Maximum Attack Range	12 tiles
Damage radius (Medium)	4 tiles (2 x 2 area)
Movement Speed	Slow (0.8 tiles per second)

The Catapult represents a significant improvement over the Stone Thrower. Not only does the Catapult have a greater range, but the area affected by its projectile is four times as large. This increased effect has the potential of causing tremendous damage to densely packed enemy troops. Like the Stone Thrower, these Units are generally employed against stationary objects; they are less effective against fast naval vessels or mounted troops. Like all Siege Weapons, the Catapult is fragile and should steer clear of missile-equipped enemy Units. They are built and upgraded at the Siege Workshop.

Certain kinds of research improve your Catapult's performance. They are as follows:

- *Alchemy* increases the Catapult's attack damage by one Hit Point per attack.
- *Ballistics* increases the Catapult's accuracy against moving targets.
- *Engineering* increases the Catapult's range by two tiles.

HEAVY CATAPULT

COMPOSITE	DESCRIPTION
Age	Iron
Prerequisite Buildings	Town Center, Barracks, Market, Archery Range, Siege Workshop
Construction Location	Siege Workshop
Construction Time	60 seconds
Construction Procedure	possess an Iron Age Town Center, build a Barracks, build an Archery Range, build a Siege Workshop, upgrade to a Catapult at the Siege Workshop, research *Siegecraft* at the Market, upgrade to a Heavy Catapult at the Siege Workshop, then build a Heavy Catapult at the Siege Workshop
Upgrade Cost	1,800 RPs of food, 900 RPs of wood
Research Cost of *Siegecraft*	190 RPs of food, 100 RPs of stone
Construction Cost	180 RPs of wood, 80 RPs of gold
Hit Points	150
Armor Rating	0
Range of Visibility	16 tiles
Attack Damage	60 Hit Points
Attack Speed	Every 5 seconds
Minimum Attack Range	2 tiles
Maximum Attack Range	13 tiles
Damage radius (Large)	9 tiles (3 x 3 area)
Movement Speed	Slow (0.8 tiles per second)

The Heavy Catapult is the top Unit in this category of stone-hurling siege engines. It has a greater range than its predecessors and causes damage in an area over twice as large (nine tiles). The Unit itself can withstand twice as much damage as the Catapult. The Heavy Catapult is an impressive addition to your army. Your neighbors will take notice if you have constructed one. One or two of these Units can smash a civilization (or a Wonder) in no time at all. The cost of these Units can be equally devastating. A considerable amount of food and wood is needed just to pay for the upgrade. Think how many gazelle your people will have to hunt to acquire 1,800 RPs of food.

The following types of research improve your Heavy Catapult's performance:

- *Siegecraft* is a prerequisite technology for constructing the Heavy Catapult.
- *Alchemy* increases the Heavy Catapult's attack damage by one Hit Point per attack.
- *Ballistics* increases the Heavy Catapult's accuracy against moving targets.
- *Engineering* increases the Heavy Catapult's range by two tiles.

BALLISTA

COMPOSITE	DESCRIPTION
Age	Iron
Prerequisite Buildings	Town Center, Barracks, Archery Range, Siege Workshop
Construction Location	Siege Workshop
Construction Time	50 seconds

COMPOSITE	DESCRIPTION
Construction Procedure	possess an Iron Age Town Center, build a Barracks, build an Archery Range, build a Siege Workshop, then build a Ballista at the Siege Workshop
Construction Cost	100 RPs of wood, 80 RPs of gold
Hit Points	55
Armor Rating	0
Range of Visibility	11 tiles
Attack Damage	40 Hit Points
Attack Speed	every 3 seconds
Minimum Attack Range	3 tiles
Maximum Attack Range	9 tiles
Movement Speed	Slow (0.8 tiles per second)

Although the Ballista appears in the same section as the Catapults and Stone-Throwers, it would be equally accurate to include it with the list of missile-firing Archers. Instead of heaving a large stone, the Ballista fires a bolt resembling a huge arrow. Consequently, it has a higher rate of fire but does less damage. The Ballista is a fragile piece of machinery, able to absorb only 55 Hit Points. Two shots from some other Siege Weapon are more than enough to destroy it.

Certain kinds of research improve the performance of the Ballista. They are as follows:

- *Alchemy* increases the Ballista's attack damage by one Hit Point per attack.
- *Ballistics* increases the Ballista's accuracy against moving targets.
- *Engineering* increases the Ballista's range by two tiles.

HELEPOLIS

COMPOSITE	DESCRIPTION
Age	Iron
Prerequisite Buildings	Town Center, Barracks, Market, Archery Range, Siege Workshop
Construction Location	Siege Workshop
Construction Time	50 seconds
Construction Procedure	possess an Iron Age Town Center, build a Barracks, build an Archery Range, build a Market, build a Siege Workshop, research *Craftsmanship* at the Market, upgrade to a Helepolis at the Siege Workshop, then build a Helepolis at the Siege Workshop
Upgrade Cost	1,500 RPs of food, 1,000 RPs of wood
Research Cost of *Craftsmanship*	240 RPs of food, 200 RPs of wood
Construction Cost	100 RPs of wood, 80 RPs of gold
Hit Points	55
Armor Rating	0
Range of Visibility	12 tiles
Attack Damage	40 Hit Points
Attack Speed	every 1.5 seconds
Minimum Attack Range	3 tiles
Maximum Attack Range	10 tiles
Movement Speed	Slow (0.8 tiles per second)

The Helepolis or "city killer" is well named. This fast-firing siege engine is remarkably destructive. It throws out bolts of 40-point damage at a rate of two bolts every three seconds. Like the Ballista, however, it is fragile and should not be employed in the vicinity of enemy catapults. Because its maximum range is only 10 tiles,

enemy Siege Weapons can attack your Helepolis out of range. The Helepolis moves so slowly that it will not surprise an attentive enemy. A good trick is to move these Units by sea—out of enemy view—then disembark with them near the intended target.

Research improves your Helepolis's performance. The forms of research for the Helepolis are as follows:

- *Craftsmanship* is a prerequisite technology for building Helepolis units.
- *Alchemy* increases the Helepolis's attack damage by one Hit Point per attack.
- *Ballistics* increases the Helepolis's accuracy against moving targets.
- *Engineering* increases the Helepolis's range by two tiles.

NAVAL VESSELS

Naval vessels fall into four main categories—fishing vessels (food-generating), merchant shipping (trade-generating), transport vessels (water transport of land units), and warships (military).

FISHING VESSELS

Fishing vessels are extremely important to your tribe's Stone and Tool Age development. Once built, they haul significant amounts of food, freeing your Villagers to perform other tasks such as chopping wood, mining, or constructing buildings. If nothing else, fishing boats expand your knowledge of the world by revealing new areas of the map.

Fishing Boat

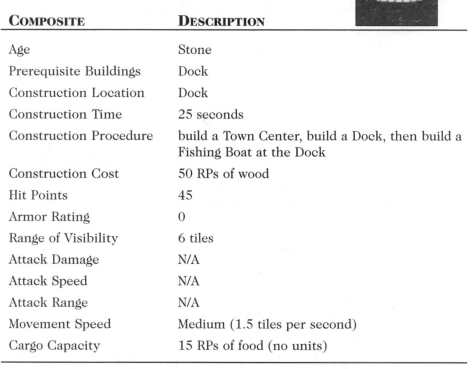

COMPOSITE	DESCRIPTION
Age	Stone
Prerequisite Buildings	Dock
Construction Location	Dock
Construction Time	25 seconds
Construction Procedure	build a Town Center, build a Dock, then build a Fishing Boat at the Dock
Construction Cost	50 RPs of wood
Hit Points	45
Armor Rating	0
Range of Visibility	6 tiles
Attack Damage	N/A
Attack Speed	N/A
Attack Range	N/A
Movement Speed	Medium (1.5 tiles per second)
Cargo Capacity	15 RPs of food (no units)

Fishing Boats play an essential role in the early development of your tribe. They gather large amounts of food and free your Villagers to perform other more important tasks. Each Fishing Boat can carry up to 15 Resource Points of food per trip. The food is not placed into your tribe's stockpile until the Fishing Boat returns to the Dock. Like all naval vessels, the Fishing Boat has twice the normal resistance to Priestly Conversion attempts.

Fishing Ship

COMPOSITE	DESCRIPTION
Age	Bronze
Prerequisite Buildings	Dock
Construction Location	Dock
Construction Time	20 seconds
Construction Procedure	possess a Bronze Age Town Center, build a Dock, upgrade to a Fishing Ship at the Dock, then build a Fishing Ship at the Dock.
Upgrade Cost	50 RPs of food, 100 RPs of wood
Construction Cost	50 RPs of wood
Hit Points	75
Armor Rating	0
Range of Visibility	4 tiles
Attack Damage	N/A
Attack Speed	N/A
Attack Range	N/A
Movement Speed	Fast (2.2 tiles per second)
Cargo Capacity	20 RPs of food (no units)

The Fishing Ship—an improved version of the Fishing Boat—is faster and has a greater capacity for cargo than its predecessor. For the same amount of wood, you can construct Fishing Ships rather than boats. These vessels can sustain more damage before sinking. There is no down side to these vessels. Be sure to upgrade your Fishing Boats as soon as you enter the Bronze Age. Like all naval vessels, Fishing Ships have twice the normal resistance to Priestly Conversion attempts.

MERCHANT VESSELS

Trading Boats allow you to conduct friendly economic contact with other civilizations. Your trading partners pay you in gold for food, wood, or stone resources. In multiplayer games, this free-trade model establishes a pattern of diplomatic goodwill that you can exploit later.

Trade Boat

COMPOSITE	DESCRIPTION
Age	Stone
Prerequisite Buildings	Dock
Construction Location	Dock
Construction Time	35 seconds
Construction Procedure	possess a Stone Age Town Center, build a Dock, then build a Trade Boat at the Dock
Construction Cost	100 RPs of wood
Hit Points	200
Armor Rating	0
Range of Visibility	4 tiles
Attack Damage	N/A
Attack Speed	N/A
Attack Range	N/A
Movement Speed	Fast (2.0 tiles per second)
Cargo Capacity	20 Resource Points (no units)

The Trade Boat is a rudimentary Merchant Vessel that becomes immediately available once you build a Dock. It carries up to 20 Resource Points of food, wood, or stone. The Trade Boat loads these resources at the Dock and, then, transports them to another Dock. The amount of gold you receive from this trade depends on the

distance between the two Docks. These Units pay for themselves after just a few trips.

Merchant Ship

COMPOSITE	DESCRIPTION
Age	Bronze
Prerequisite Buildings	Dock
Construction Location	Dock
Construction Time	25 seconds
Construction Procedure	possess a Stone Age Town Center, build a Dock, upgrade to a Merchant Ship at the Dock, then build a Merchant Ship at the Dock
Upgrade Cost	200 RPs of food, 75 RPs of wood
Construction Cost	100 RPs of wood
Hit Points	250
Armor Rating	0
Range of Visibility	4 tiles
Attack Damage	N/A
Attack Speed	N/A
Attack Range	N/A
Movement Speed	Fast (2.5 tiles per second)
Cargo Capacity	20 Resource Points (no units)

The Merchant Ship is an improved version of the Trading Boat. Though it has the same cargo capacity as its predecessor, the Merchant Ship moves faster and can withstand 25 percent more damage. Whether this increase is worth the cost of the upgrade depends on the volume of trade in which you expect to engage. In most cases, your civilization can get by on Trading Boats alone. The cost of producing merchant shipping is usually an unnecessary expense.

TRANSPORT VESSELS

Transport vessels allow you to move your land Units across water to conduct D-Day-like amphibious assaults and to explore new territories. These vessels are crucial to your navy. Though sturdy, transports are unarmed and require serious protection from warships.

Raft

COMPOSITE	DESCRIPTION
Age	any
Prerequisite Buildings	N/A
Construction Location	N/A
Construction Time	N/A
Construction Procedure	initial scenario placement only
Construction Cost	N/A
Hit Points	40
Armor Rating	0
Range of Visibility	4 tiles
Attack Damage	N/A
Attack Speed	N/A
Attack Range	N/A
Movement Speed	Slow (0.8 tiles per second)
Cargo Capacity	1 ground unit

You cannot build a Raft during the course of a game. The Raft only appears in certain scenarios and is available to you in the Scenario Builder. This Unit moves slowly and has a cargo capacity of one unit. Like all naval vessels, the Raft has twice the normal resistance to Priestly conversion attempts.

Light Transport

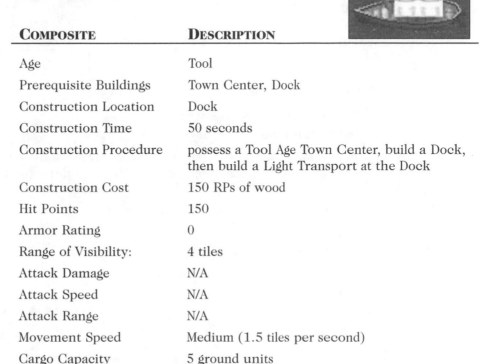

COMPOSITE	DESCRIPTION
Age	Tool
Prerequisite Buildings	Town Center, Dock
Construction Location	Dock
Construction Time	50 seconds
Construction Procedure	possess a Tool Age Town Center, build a Dock, then build a Light Transport at the Dock
Construction Cost	150 RPs of wood
Hit Points	150
Armor Rating	0
Range of Visibility:	4 tiles
Attack Damage	N/A
Attack Speed	N/A
Attack Range	N/A
Movement Speed	Medium (1.5 tiles per second)
Cargo Capacity	5 ground units

Eventually, water transport plays an important part in your civilization's expansion. The Light Transport is the first transport vessel available. It can load, transport, and unload up to five units, allowing them to cross bodies of water. Like all naval vessels, the Light Transport has twice the normal resistance to Priestly conversion attempts.

Heavy Transport

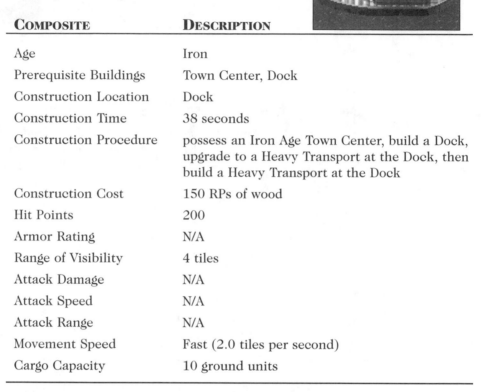

COMPOSITE	DESCRIPTION
Age	Iron
Prerequisite Buildings	Town Center, Dock
Construction Location	Dock
Construction Time	38 seconds
Construction Procedure	possess an Iron Age Town Center, build a Dock, upgrade to a Heavy Transport at the Dock, then build a Heavy Transport at the Dock
Construction Cost	150 RPs of wood
Hit Points	200
Armor Rating	N/A
Range of Visibility	4 tiles
Attack Damage	N/A
Attack Speed	N/A
Attack Range	N/A
Movement Speed	Fast (2.0 tiles per second)
Cargo Capacity	10 ground units

The Heavy Transport is faster and can sustain more damage than the Light Transport. It carries exactly twice the number of land Units as its predecessor. Because Heavy Transports can carry so much cargo, a few probably will suffice. (In fact, the Light Transport is capable of handling most of your transport needs during the course of a game.) Protect your transports—losing a Heavy Transport loaded with 10 land Units may cost you the game. Like all naval vessels, the Heavy Transport has twice the normal resistance to Priestly Conversion attempts.

WARSHIPS

Warships, of course, allow you to engage your enemies in naval combat. As your civilization expands into new areas, it undoubtedly will discover bodies of water that block your progress. Warships are necessary if you want to conduct military operations to continue your civilization's expansion.

Scout Ship

COMPOSITE	DESCRIPTION
Age	Tool
Prerequisite Buildings	Town Center, Dock
Construction Location	Dock
Construction Time	40 seconds
Construction Procedure	possess a Tool Age Town Center, build a Dock, then build a Scout Ship at the Dock
Construction Cost	135 RPs of wood
Hit Points	120
Armor Rating	0
Range of Visibility	7 tiles
Attack Damage	5 Hit Points
Attack Speed	every 2 seconds
Attack Range	5 tiles
Movement Speed	Fast (2.0 tiles per second)

Certain kinds of research improve your Scout Ship's performance. They are as follows:

- *Alchemy* increases the Scout Ship's attack damage by one Hit Point per attack.

- *Ballistics* increases the Scout Ship's accuracy against moving targets.

- *Woodworking* increases the Scout Ship's range by one tile.

- *Artisanship* increases the Scout Ship's range by one tile.

- *Craftsmanship* increases the Scout Ship's range by one tile.

War Galley

COMPOSITE	DESCRIPTION
Age	Bronze
Prerequisite Buildings	Town Center, Dock
Construction Location	Dock
Construction Time	30 seconds
Construction Procedure	possess a Bronze Age Town Center, build a Dock, upgrade to a War Galley at the Dock, then build a War Galley at the Dock
Upgrade Cost	150 RPs of food, 75 RPs of wood
Construction Cost	135 RPs of wood
Hit Points	160
Armor Rating	0
Range of Visibility	8 tiles
Attack Damage	8 Hit Points
Attack Speed	every 2 seconds
Attack Range	6 tiles
Movement Speed	Fast (2.0 tiles per second)

The War Galley is the first practical warship to become available. The Scout Ship is nice, but the War Galley is more equipped to hold its own in combat. It inflicts greater damage, has a great range, and withstands more enemy fire than the Scout Ship can. By the time you reach the Bronze Age, the War Galley is somewhat obsolete, however. Fortunately, at 135 RPs of wood, you can afford to build numerous War Galleys. Be prepared to upgrade your navy to Trireme status as soon as you reach the Iron Age. Like all naval vessels, the War Galley has twice the normal resistance to Priestly conversion attempts.

The following kinds of research improve your War Galley's performance:

- *Alchemy* increases the War Galley's attack damage by one Hit Point per attack.
- *Ballistics* increases the War Galley's accuracy against moving targets.
- *Woodworking* increases the War Galley's range by one tile.
- *Artisanship* increases the War Galley's range by one tile.
- *Craftsmanship* increases the War Galley's range by one tile.

Trireme

COMPOSITE	DESCRIPTION
Age	Iron
Prerequisite Buildings	Town Center, Dock
Construction Location	Dock
Construction Time	30 seconds

COMPOSITE	DESCRIPTION
Construction Procedure	possess an Iron Age Town Center, build a Dock, upgrade to a War Galley at the Dock, upgrade to a Trireme at the Dock, then build a Trireme at the Dock
Upgrade Cost	250 RPs of food, 100 RPs of wood
Construction Cost	135 RPs of wood
Hit Points	200
Armor Rating	0
Range of Visibility	9 tiles
Attack Damage	12 Hit Points
Attack Speed	every 2 seconds
Attack Range	7 tiles
Movement Speed	Fast (2.2 tiles per second)

The Trireme is the standard warship in the game. It is the strongest of all pre-catapult-equipped vessels. Fast and able to withstand a considerable amount of damage, these vessels should be used to escort (protect) your transports through unfriendly water. The Trireme carries a quick-firing Ballista. What this weapon lacks in striking power, it makes up for in frequency. Like all naval vessels, the Trireme has twice the normal resistance to Priestly Conversion attempts.

The following kinds of research improve the performance of the Trireme:

- *Alchemy* increases the Trireme's attack damage by one Hit Point per attack.
- *Ballistics* increases the Trireme's accuracy against moving targets.
- *Woodworking* increases the Trireme's range by one tile.

- *Artisanship* increases the Trireme's range by one tile.
- *Craftsmanship* increases the Trireme's range by one tile.

Catapult Trireme

COMPOSITE	DESCRIPTION
Age	Iron
Prerequisite Buildings	Town Center, Dock
Construction Location	Dock
Construction Time	45 seconds
Construction Procedure	possess an Iron Age Town Center, build a Dock, upgrade to a War Galley at the Dock, upgrade to a Trireme at the Dock, research *Catapult Trireme* at the Dock, build a Catapult Trireme at the Dock.
Research Cost of *Catapult Trireme*	300 RPs of food, 100 RPs of wood
Construction Cost	135 RPs of wood, 75 RPs of gold
Hit Points	120
Armor Rating	0
Range of Visibility	11 tiles
Attack Damage	35 Hit Points
Attack Speed	every 5 seconds
Attack Range	9 tiles
Damage Radius (Small)	1 tiles (1 x 1 area)
Movement Speed	Fast (2.0 tiles per second)

The Catapult Trireme is a new type of warship. It has fewer Hit Points and a slower rate of fire than a Trireme; however, it has much

greater attack strength. As you may guess, this vessel is armed with a Catapult (an area weapon), which can be devastating to structures and Units alike. These warships should be gathered together in small fleets and then used to blockade an enemy coast or clear enemy ships from a body of water. They should not be used to escort friendly transports. Like all naval vessels, the Catapult Trireme has twice the normal resistance to Priestly conversion attempts.

Certain research improves your Catapult Trireme's performance. They are as follows:

- *Alchemy* increases the Catapult Trireme's attack damage by one Hit Point per attack.
- *Ballistics* increases the Catapult Trireme's accuracy against moving targets.
- *Engineering* increases the Catapult Trireme's range by two tiles.

Juggernaught

COMPOSITE	DESCRIPTION
Age	Iron
Prerequisite Buildings	Town Center, Dock, Government Center
Construction Location	Dock
Construction Time	45 seconds
Construction Procedure	possess an Iron Age Town Center, build a Dock, upgrade to a War Galley at the Dock, upgrade to Trireme at the Dock, research *Catapult Trireme* at the Dock, build a Government Center, research *Engineering* at the Government Center, upgrade to a Juggernaught at the Dock, then build a Juggernaught at the Dock.

COMPOSITE	DESCRIPTION
Upgrade Cost	2,000 RPs of food, 900 RPs of wood
Research Cost of *Engineering*	200 of food, 100 wood
Construction Cost	135 RPs of wood, 75 RPs of gold
Hit Points	200
Armor Rating	0
Range of Visibility	12 tiles
Attack Damage	35 Hit Points
Attack Speed	every 5 seconds
Attack Range	10 tiles
Damage Radius (Medium)	4 tiles (2 x 2 area)
Movement Speed	Fast (2.0 tiles per second)

The Juggernaught is the top military warship in the game. You must research *Engineering*, however, before you can begin to build them. This vessel is equipped with a strong catapult, which fires at map locations and at particular units. If you reach a point where you can build these vessels, you are probably close to winning. A handful of these Iron Age battleships is all it takes to ravage any tribe foolish enough to build its villages near the coast. Like all naval vessels, the Juggernaught has twice the normal resistance to Priestly Conversion attempts.

The following research assists your Juggernaught's performance:

- *Engineering* is a requirement for constructing the Juggernaught.
- *Alchemy* increases the Juggernaught's attack damage by one Hit Point per attack.
- *Ballistics* increases the Juggernaught's accuracy against moving targets.
- *Woodworking* increases the Juggernaught's range by one tile.

- *Artisanship* increases the Juggernaught's range by one tile.
- *Craftsmanship* increases the Juggernaught's range by one tile.

Flying Dutchman

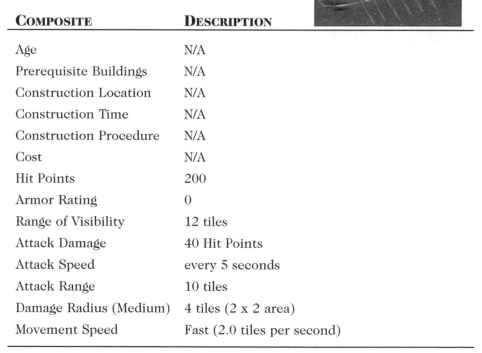

COMPOSITE	DESCRIPTION
Age	N/A
Prerequisite Buildings	N/A
Construction Location	N/A
Construction Time	N/A
Construction Procedure	N/A
Cost	N/A
Hit Points	200
Armor Rating	0
Range of Visibility	12 tiles
Attack Damage	40 Hit Points
Attack Speed	every 5 seconds
Attack Range	10 tiles
Damage Radius (Medium)	4 tiles (2 x 2 area)
Movement Speed	Fast (2.0 tiles per second)

The Flying Dutchman is a special naval vessel that only appears in certain scenarios. (It is available to you as an option in the Scenario Builder.) It acts as a Juggernaught in all respects, except that its catapult causes five additional points of damage per attack. Like all naval vessels, the Flying Dutchman has twice the normal resistance to Priestly Conversion attempts. It can also move on land.

HEROES

Within every people, there are exceptional individuals who emerge and stand apart from the rest. Ancient history is full of examples. In *Age of Empires*, these individuals appear in certain campaign scenarios. They also are made available to you via the Scenario Editor. Known as Heroes, they are notable for their intelligence, strength, bravery, and fighting skill.

ALEXANDER

COMPOSITE	DESCRIPTION
Hero's Unit	Heavy Cavalry
Hit Points	400
Armor Rating	1
Range of Visibility	5 tiles
Attack Damage	22 Hit Points
Attack Range	adjacent tile (hand-to-hand combat)

AMON RA

COMPOSITE	DESCRIPTION
Hero's Unit	Priest
Hit Points:	150
Range of Visibility	14 tiles
Armor Rating	0
Attack Damage	N/A (conversion only)
Attack Range	12 tiles

CORLIS

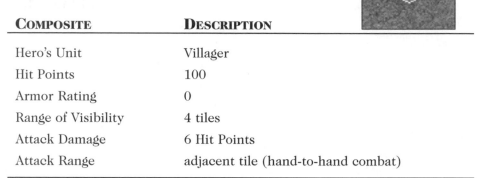

COMPOSITE	DESCRIPTION
Hero's Unit	Villager
Hit Points	100
Armor Rating	0
Range of Visibility	4 tiles
Attack Damage	6 Hit Points
Attack Range	adjacent tile (hand-to-hand combat)

HECTOR

COMPOSITE	DESCRIPTION
Hero's Unit	Heavy Cavalry
Hit Points	350
Armor Rating	3 (Armor and Bronze Shield)
Range of Visibility	5 tiles
Attack Damage	25 Hit Points
Attack Range	adjacent tile (hand-to-hand combat)

HERISFON

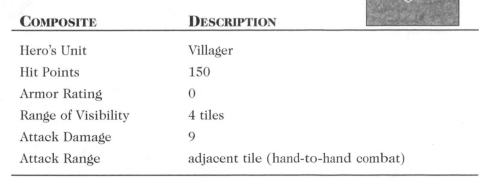

COMPOSITE	DESCRIPTION
Hero's Unit	Villager
Hit Points	150
Armor Rating	0
Range of Visibility	4 tiles
Attack Damage	9
Attack Range	adjacent tile (hand-to-hand combat)

JASON

COMPOSITE	DESCRIPTION
Hero's Unit	Short Swordsman
Hit Points	180
Armor Rating	0
Range of Visibility	4 tiles
Attack Damage	20 Hit Points
Attack Range	adjacent tile (hand-to-hand combat)

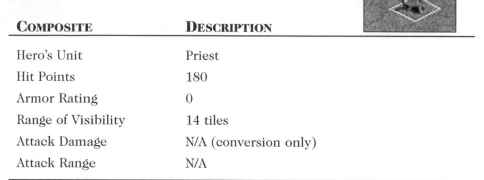

MOR HAVOC

COMPOSITE	DESCRIPTION
Hero's Unit	Priest
Hit Points	180
Armor Rating	0
Range of Visibility	14 tiles
Attack Damage	N/A (conversion only)
Attack Range	N/A

PERSEUS

COMPOSITE	DESCRIPTION
Hero's Unit	Composite Bowman
Hit Points	100
Armor Rating	3
Range of Visibility	11 tiles
Attack Damage	10 Hit Points
Attack Range	7 tiles

TIBERIUS

COMPOSITE	DESCRIPTION
Hero's Unit	Chariot
Hit Points	250
Armor Rating	0
Range of Visibility	5 tiles
Attack Damage	15 Hit Points
Attack Range	adjacent tile (hand-to-hand combat)

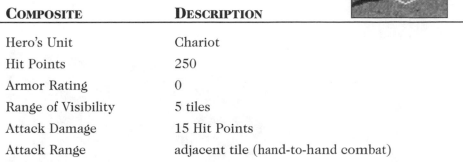

XERXES

COMPOSITE	DESCRIPTION
Hero's Unit	Short Swordsman
Hit Points	200
Armor Rating	3
Range of Visibility	5 tiles
Attack Damage	20 Hit Points
Attack Range	adjacent tile (hand-to-hand combat)

CHAPTER 6

General Play Tips and Hints

This chapter is a broad overview of certain aspects of the game. Unlike some strategy games, *Age of Empires* is far too dynamic to be won consistently with the same tactics and strategies. The best anyone can hope to do is to use the information presented here as a basis for further development of his or her own ideas. With this in mind, look at this chapter as a collection of general play hints and common sense tips.

GATHERING RESOURCES

At the beginning of each game, the map represents a prehistoric world in all its pristine beauty. Unspoiled by human exploitation, this idyllic place of natural wonders burgeons with birds in the air and with fish in the sea. The fragrance of exotic flowers wafts in the crisp, clean air, and wildlife abounds.

Okay—here's where we come in.

For your people to advance as a civilization, they must stockpile four different resources—food, gold, stone, and wood. This section details some of the techniques you can use to collect and manage these resources.

FOOD

Food is needed to build Units and structures and to research different technologies. Without it, you cannot build additional Villagers to increase your working population or build structures to advance into the next Age. After all, people must eat, right?

As a general rule, you should never allow your stockpile of food to fall below 50 RPs. If some disaster befalls your civilization—if you lose all of your Villagers—without at least 50 RPs of food to build another Villager—you are history. Of course, some kind soul may take pity on you and lend you some food—but don't count on it.

There are four ways to acquire food resources: hunting, fishing, foraging, and farming. All of these methods involve Villagers (and boats, in the case of fishing) moving to the site of the food resource, performing one of the actions above, and then returning to the appropriate place to transfer the resources they have collected into the inventory (stockpile).

Hunting

The process of using Villagers to convert wild animals into Food Resource Points is known as hunting; the Villagers are designated as Hunters. Initially, wild animals are plentiful and scattered throughout the map. As more and more humans appear (and eat), animal numbers begin to dwindle. By the time your civilization reaches the Bronze Age, wild animals are usually scarce; by the Iron Age, they are usually gone altogether. Meat from game animals should make up part of your people's diet, and there are steps you can take to ensure that you always have a steady supply.

As your Villagers explore the map, they will discover lone animals (like a Lion or an Alligator) or herds of animals (like Elephants and Gazelles). If disturbed, some animals attack, while others flee. In general, animals like the Gazelle tend to flee in a direction away from the perceived threat. You can use this instinctive reflex to your benefit.

Say, for example, you spot a herd of Gazelles on top of a steep incline. Naturally, you do not want to kill the animals up there because your Villagers would have to walk up the hill every time you needed to get a fresh load of meat. (Walking uphill slows a Unit's movement rate, too.) The trick is to spook the animals, so they flee and run down the hill. They are much easier to catch at lower elevations.

Another interesting trick is the Cattle Drive. A Cattle Drive is the term for the cooperative efforts of several Villagers to round up a herd of Gazelles and then drive them (by virtue of their flee reflex) toward a particular location. The purpose of organizing a Cattle Drive is twofold. First, you want to move the herd to a more convenient location before slaughtering the animals. Obviously, you want to kill them as close to a Storage Pit or Town Center as possible. This procedure minimizes the transit time between moving the food resources from the animal's carcass and placing it in your stockpile.

The second reason for organizing a Cattle Drive is to deny the food to other players. A Cattle Drive lets you take animals from their natural habitat and move them to a new location, preferably one that is more readily defensible. It is not unheard of that a player might even build a "Gazelle pen" out of sections of Small Wall. (Hunting Gazelles gives you an opportunity to be a bit creative. It's just another reason why *Age of Empires* is such a great game!)

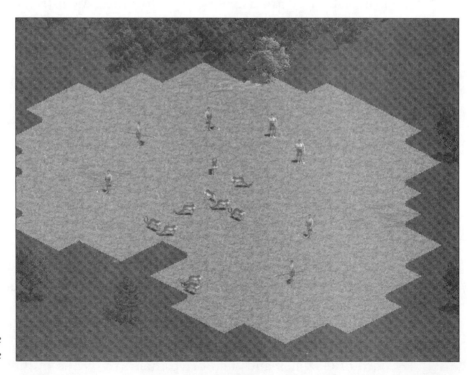

The Cattle Drive

Only Gazelles allow themselves to be "driven." Other animals are a little nastier. They attack and sometimes kill a hapless Villager, turning the Villager into food instead. When you hunt, it is always better to create a Hunting Party by hunting in pairs (or even as a trio). Not only does a Hunting Party bring down a Gazelle more quickly, but it can defend itself more effectively should a member of the party be attacked.

TABLE 6-1

"Game" Animals	Attack Damage	Hit Points	Food Generated (in RPs)
Gazelle	0	8	150
Alligator	4	20	100
Tame Lion	3	20	100
Lion	4	20	100
Elephant	9	45	300
Lion King	10	40	100
Elephant King	14	60	300

This table lists all the animals in *Age of Empires* that may be hunted and converted into food. Notice that some animals fight back. The amount of damage they inflict per round of attack is listed in the "Attack Damage" column. The Hit Points it takes to bring the animal down before butchering it are listed in the Hit Points column.

As you can see by the table, some animals can cause considerable damage to Villagers. The Elephant, for example, attacks with the strength of a Broad Swordsman and can trample Villagers adjacent to it. Definitely eat the Elephants.

Lions, on the other hand, attack without provocation or warning. You can trigger an attack just by venturing too close. Don't mess with Lions. Send a bunch of Villagers to kill them. A Lion only produces 100 RPs of food, so is it worth losing a Villager (one that you built at a cost of 50 RPs) to a Lion? Lions also chase after and attack nearby Gazelles. Be sure that your "Cattle Drives" keep a respectful distance.

Fishing

Fishing is one of the more practical ways of acquiring large supplies of food. You can assign Villagers as Fishermen to spear fish in coastal tiles, but this is not the most productive way to go about it. The really big fish are in the sea, and the only way to get to them is by building fishing vessels. In addition, all fishing sites are equal. As you can see on the table below, they all produce exactly 250 RPs of food.

TABLE 6-2 Fish of the Sea

TYPE	FOOD GENERATED (IN RPS)
Salmon	250
Shore-Fish	250
Tuna	250
Whale	250

Creating a fleet of fishing vessels frees your Villagers to perform other tasks, such as building structures and exploring the countryside. While you must expend food RPs to create new Villagers—the very resource you are stockpiling to reach the next Age—fishing vessels are constructed from wood RPs.

Fishing vessels are faster than Villagers (even Yamato Villagers), which means they can reach fishing sites and return with the day's catch more frequently. Not only are they faster, but fishing vessels can carry more too. A Fishing Boat carries 50 percent more food (15 RPs) than a Villager; the Fishing Ship carries twice as much (20 RPs).

Eventually, all the choice fishing spots will be fished out. You will see this begin to happen near the end of the Bronze Age. This means that you will have to send your boats farther from your coastal waters to fish. It also means that your fishing fleet has to operate without the protection of nearby Docks or without nearby repair facilities in the form of friendly Villagers.

All this comes at a time when the enemy has had ample time to assemble a fleet of warships. Recognize that your dependence on fishing vessels has made them into an economic target of opportunity. Count on an attack against them at some point in the game. By sinking your fishing vessels, the enemy effectively cuts off your food supply.

Fishing vessels deposit their food RPs into inventory upon returning to the nearest Dock. After they have been unloaded, fishing vessels automatically turn around and return for more fish. When a site becomes fished out (i.e., there are no food RPs remaining at that particular location), the fishing vessel simply remains there. You must keep an eye on your fishing vessels, so that you can direct them to a new site manually. Otherwise, they remain idle at the fished-out location indefinitely. Villagers can fish along the shore for coastal fish. (No boats are needed for this.)

Foraging

Foraging, like hunting, is an activity undertaken by Villagers as a means of gathering food. The process is basically the same, except that berry bushes do not attack your Villagers or try to run away. Each berry bush is a separate foraging location that contains 150 RPs of food. Villagers sent to gather berries are designated as Foragers. This distinction is important because, as Foragers, these Villagers inflict one less Hit Point of damage if they are attacked.

The most important thing to keep in mind when you forage is the distance between the foraging site and your Granary or Town

Center. The further your Villagers have to travel to place food into inventory, the longer it takes to start on another trip. It is almost always a good idea to construct a Granary directly next to a grove of berry bushes.

Farming

Farming becomes an option after you reach the Tool Age. Before you can begin to construct Farms, however, you first must build a Market. Farms produce a steady supply of food throughout the game even as the productivity of other methods of collecting food begins to wane.

Each Farm produces a total of 250 RPs of food with some exceptions. Persian Farms produce only 175 RPs (a 30 percent reduction) and Minoan Farms produce 310 RPs (a 24 percent increase). Research can make everyone's Farms more effective, however.

On the Farm

Domestication, Irrigation, and Plow each add 75 additional Resource Points to the total Farm output of each Farm.

Having additional Villagers does not increase the amount of food your Farms produce, only the speed at which you harvest the food. Minimizing the transit time between your Farms and your Granary (or Town Center) is the most efficient use of your people-power. Generally, your Villagers have more important things to do than to toil in the fields. You only want two farmers per field if it's a long way from the Granary or Town Center.

GOLD AND STONE MINING

Mining is a fairly straightforward process. Your Villagers are designated as Miners when they are asked to recover RPs of gold or stone. They proceed to the mining site and automatically mine to their transportation limit (usually 10 RPs). The gold or stone is transported back to a Storage Pit or to the Town Center (whichever is closer), where the resources are added into inventory. The process is repeated until the resource site is depleted of its resources. (Each stone mine contains a total of 250 RPs of stone. Each gold mine contains a total of 400 RPs of gold.)

Certain civilizations have intrinsic mining advantages of which you should be aware. Babylonian stone Miners can mine and carry 30 percent more stone, for example, while Egyptian gold Miners can mine and carry 20 percent more gold.

The secret to productive mining is a combination of researching the appropriate technologies and minimizing the transit time between your mines and your Storage Pit (or Town Center). *Stone Mining* and *Siegecraft* each increase the Stone Mining ability of your Villagers by 30 percent. *Gold Mining* and *Coinage* add 30 percent and 25 percent, respectively, to your Villagers' Gold Mining ability.

WOOD (WOODCUTTING)

Like mining, woodcutting is a simple process of moving Villagers to the resources, having them load up with wood RPs, and then having them return to a Storage Pit or Town Center to place the resources into inventory. Three things affect your woodcutting ability: (1) your civilization's attributes, (2) technological research, and (3) the round-trip distance between the wood site and the storage area.

While no civilization receives any specific woodcutting benefits, Villagers from Assyria and Yamato move at a 30 percent higher rate of speed. This significantly impacts the time it takes to perform the resource-to-stockpile circuit.

Woodworking, Artisanship, and *Craftsmanship* all increase your Villagers' woodcutting abilities by allowing them to carry more wood and to cut it at a faster rate. Each technology adds two RPs to your Villagers' capacity to carry wood.

Once again, the farther your Villagers have to walk, the longer it takes them to complete the task. Examine the table below. It clearly shows how distance can affect the speed at which resources are entered into inventory.

Table 6-3 Gathering Wood: Distance and Time

DISTANCE TRAVELED (IN TILES)	TIME FOR COMPLETE CIRCUIT (IN SECONDS)
5	25
10	33
15	41
20	49

As you can see, a Villager walking at normal speed will take 41 seconds to make a complete circuit between a grove of trees located 15 tiles away from the nearest Stockpile repository. Although these time differences seem insignificant at first glance, consider how long it would take a Villager to gather 100 Resource Points at the different distances.

Simple math tells you that it takes 250 seconds of game time to collect 100 Resource Points from a site five tiles away. The same Villager requires a stunning 490 seconds (or over eight minutes of game time) to collect 100 Resource Points from a site that is 20 tiles away.

MOVEMENT AND EXPLORATION

Part of what makes *Age of Empires* such a fascinating game is that it involves exploring the unknown, just as real-life civilizations have had to do. Assuming that you play most of your games with the Reveal Map option turned off, this section details general tactics you can use to help your movement about the map.

As each game begins, you are given a map of the world. It is a cold, dark, and scary place. Nothing is revealed to you except what your Units can see with their own eyes—*and that ain't much*. Your mission is to take a primitive group of people and overcome their fear of the unknown. You must explore this world, exploit its resources, and in the process, build a thriving civilization.

REVEALING THE MAP

As each Unit moves around the map, it "lights up" a zone of tiles. Anything within this zone—be it building, terrain, or Unit—is instantly revealed. For this reason, the zone is referred to as the Unit's Range of Visibility. They range from a mere four tiles for Villager Units to a maximum of 16 tiles for the Heavy Catapult. (A summary of all the Units and their Range of Visibility are contained in Chapter 5 of this guide. Buildings have Ranges of Visibility also. You can find a list of their ranges in Chapter 4.)

Obviously, the greater a Unit's Range of Visibility (ROV), the faster it can scout areas of the map. With its 16-tile range, the Heavy Catapult seems, at first, to be an excellent choice. But, would you really send a Catapult Unit on a reconnaissance mission? Of course not. For one thing, Catapult Units are far too important to spend time wandering the countryside. Besides that, they cost too much.

Beyond a Unit's ROV, its movement speed is another important factor. Fast-moving Units can quickly reveal vast areas on the map even though they may not see as far. The Scout, for example, is a mounted Unit with an ROV of eight (8) tiles. It has twice the range of a Villager. It moves at a rate of two tiles per second, allowing the Scout to cover considerable ground. As far as cost is concerned, the Scout may be a little expensive (100 RPs of food) for a Tool Age Unit, but it pays for itself in time saved exploring the map.

UNCOVERING RESOURCES

Distributed throughout the world map are natural resources you need to advance your civilization. There are forests to provide you with wood, deposits of stone and gold to discover, and a variety of food resources to hunt or gather. But before you can add these resources to your Stockpile, you must go into the world and find them.

The more quickly you discover the resources, the sooner you can begin processing them. But just because you may be the first to find a particular resource does not mean that you can lay undisputed claim to them. Chances are that other civilizations will stumble upon the site sooner or later. When this happens, you may find yourself standing shoulder-to-shoulder with a neighboring tribe's Villagers and depleting the same resources.

One tactic that seems to work reasonably well is to explore areas of the map far from your initial Town Center starting point.

This way you deplete resources located far from home first. You begin to work back toward your Town Center later in the game as resources begin to diminish. Not only should you husband your nearby resources for later, you should begin the game by depleting resources that are closer to the other players.

COMBAT

"Can't we all just get along?" The answer, unfortunately, is a resounding "No." Conflict is part of human existence. You can try to win the game through peaceful means, but chances are that your neighbors are not going to let you win without a fight. It is possible, of course, but highly unlikely. With human nature being what it is, combat between civilizations will be part of almost every game.

KNOW THY ENEMY

One of the first rules of warfare is *"know thy enemy."* Unless you play with the *Full Tech Tree* option turned on, every civilization is different from the others. A civilization's army usually reflects these differences. The Yamato, for example, tend to field large armies of mounted warriors, while the Greeks concentrate on building slow-moving, heavily armored foot soldiers.

Your strategy should take into account the relative strengths and weaknesses of these different civilizations. For example, the Hittites have a particular fondness for building walls and towers. If you discover them next to you in a multiplayer game, you should count on building lots of siege weapons, as the Hittites prefer to fight from behind their stone fortifications. To beat them, you have to hammer them from the air into the ground.

MOBILE OR STATIC WARFARE

There are basically two predominant kinds of warfare in *Age of Empires*—(1) fast-moving mobile warfare with mounted armies and (2) static warfare with Siege Weaponry and heavy infantry Units. Within these two main types of warfare, there are many variations, but for the most part, you can categorize every campaign as either mobile or static. Recognizing the type of campaign you are fighting is the first step in deciding which tactics to use and which Units to build.

Certain civilizations have a proclivity towards mobile warfare. The Yamato is one civilization that leans toward a fast-moving game. Egypt (with its Chariots) and Persia (with its Horse Archers and Heavy Cavalry) also engage in this kind of campaign. To combat these civilizations effectively, you must make them fight by your rules, not theirs. First—using a combination of walls, towers and natural terrain—you must slow these civilizations down, so that their speed is no longer a factor. Then, once you have deprived them of their mobility, subject them to concentrated missile fire.

GENERAL COMMENTS ON MAJOR UNIT TYPES

Military Units can be grouped into five different categories—infantry, cavalry, Archers, Siege Weaponry, and warships. Each Unit category has its own general set of strengths and weaknesses.

Infantry Units

- Slow-moving
- Armor bonuses (both pierce and bash armor)
- High attack strength

- Medium Hit Points
- Relatively inexpensive
- Hand-to-hand combat only

Cavalry Units

- Fast-moving
- No armor bonus (except for Heavy Cavalry and Cataphract)
- Expensive to build (requires lots of gold)
- Medium attack strength
- Charge bonus vs. infantry
- High Hit Points
- Hand-to-hand combat only

Archer Units

- Foot Archers (move as infantry)
- Mounted Archers (very fast)
- Low Hit Points
- Research armor
- Missile-firing (attacks from a distance)

Siege Weaponry

- Cause massive damage (area effects)
- Slow rate of fire
- Very slow-moving

- Fragile—lacks Hit Points
- Conspicuous on battlefield
- Expensive to produce
- Can't live without 'em

Naval Vessels

- Act like waterborne Siege Weapons
- Fast-moving
- Lots of Hit Points
- Resistant to conversion
- Missile-firing (area effects)
- Can carry Units for amphibious landing (transports only)

SCORCHED EARTH TACTICS

Scorched Earth is the name given to a particularly nasty style of warfare, in which one deliberately spoils the enemy's territory to render it worthless. This tactic is employed when you are not strong enough to defeat an opponent outright, but you still want to teach him a lesson. You can employ this tactic as often as the situation presents itself.

Villagers that kill wildlife butcher the animals for food. Military Units, on the other hand, remove any wildlife they kill from the game; in this case, the animal may not be used for food. By raiding your neighbor's territory (with military Units) and killing the area animals, you, in effect, lay waste to the land. It prevents your enemy from using the animals as a source of food. After you kill the animals, you can simply withdraw from the area, leaving the enemy nothing but Scorched Earth.

KILL ZONES

One advanced tactic to use against aggressive neighbors is the creation of Kill Zones. A Kill Zone is an area that traps enemy Units and subjects them to concentrated missile fire. Usually, you want to protect your structures by surrounding them with walls and towers. But since you cannot completely enclose your structures with walls, there will always be a way for enemy Units to enter.

You can use this opening to your benefit, however. You can create a Kill Zone simply by placing your walls and towers in strategic locations. As the illustration shows, walls have been positioned, so that enemy Units must pass a gauntlet of fire from multiple towers for an extended period of time. Enemy Units cannot simply enter your fortifications in a hurry—they must spend time in a maze-like entryway with shots flying at them the entire time.

The Kill Zone

HUNTERS VS. OTHER VILLAGER DESIGNATIONS

When your Villagers are designated as Hunters, they inflict four Hit Points of damage per attack. When your Villagers are building, repairing, or out picking berries, they only inflict three Hit Points of damage. Obviously, when your Villagers come under attack from enemy Units, it behooves you to be able to inflict more damage. Therefore, when your Villagers are about to be attacked, quickly re-designate them as Hunters (even if they do not hunt).

USING TERRAIN FEATURES

The best and cheapest way to protect your people is to incorporate terrain features into your overall defensive plan. This means that you need to make good use of impassable terrain to prevent enemy movement, set up natural Choke-points to restrict enemy movement, or take to the high ground to impede enemy progress.

IMPASSABLE TERRAIN

Certain parts of your map contain terrain features that block Unit movement. These "impassable" terrain features include water, forests, and cliffs. Knowing the location of these physical features and tying them into your manmade defenses can make a strong position even stronger.

Except for shallows, land Units cannot pass through tiles with water. The only way land Units can cross water obstacles is to ferry across the water on a transport vessel.

Tiles with trees are also impassable. Unlike the water tiles, however, trees can be cut down by Villagers. Not only is wood from the tile entered into your Stockpile, but the tile is rendered passable. For this reason, be careful when you rely on forests to block enemy

movement. A smart enemy commander will have a nearby Villager or two chop a passage for his troops.

Unlike forests, cliffs are a permanent part of the landscape. No Unit may move across a cliff—ever. Because of their impassability, cliffs are an excellent terrain feature to which to anchor a section of wall.

CHOKE POINTS

Choke points are specific locations on the map that tend to channel or restrict movement. For example, forests are impassable areas. A break in a forest that allows passage is considered a Choke-point. A narrow waterway (or Strait) also can be considered a Choke-point.

Choke-points are valuable defensive terrain features. You can block passage by erecting walls, or you can choose to guard a particular Choke-point with towers. When you explore the map, be sure to look for these natural Choke-points.

In the illustration below, the player has found a sheltered harbor for his Dock. Naval vessels wishing to enter or exit the harbor must pass under the watchful eye of two Sentry Towers.

A Sheltered Harbor

TAKE AND HOLD THE HIGH GROUND

"Always take and hold the high ground." This axiom has been with us since the dawn of warfare. It is a commonly accepted principle that whoever holds the high ground will ultimately win the battle. In *Age of Empires*, elevation comes into play in a number of different ways.

First, the obvious: your Units move more slowly uphill and faster downhill. Strategically, this loss of speed is a serious issue, especially if your Units are moving uphill to attack missile Units. The longer it takes your troops to reach the top, the more damage they will sustain from enemy missile fire. Having your troops storm a hill under fire is not the smartest move you could make as a commander.

Always try to build your structures on high ground—never in valleys. If you build your structures in a valley, you are betting that you will be able to hold the surrounding hills for the rest of the game. Don't risk the lives of your people on a bet like that. Every time you build a structure at the bottom of a hill or at the foot of a cliff, an image of the settlements beneath the Golan Heights should flash through your mind.

Every time a Unit is attacked from a higher elevation, there is a 25 percent chance that the damage it suffers will be tripled. For example, a Legion Unit is attacking a Short Swordsman on a lower elevation. The Legion normally inflicts 13 Hit Points per attack, but since its attack is downhill, there is a 25 percent chance it will inflict 39 Hit Points on any given round of combat.

This elevation benefit also extends to missile Units and Siege Weapons. Place a Ballista Unit on a high point of ground. Given its range of nine tiles, the Ballista will hold a commanding position over an expansive area. Factor in the elevation bonus, and you can see just how important holding the high ground can be.

VICTORY CONDITIONS (WAYS TO WIN)

As much fun as *Age of Empires* is to play, sooner or later someone has to win. It may as well be you. In keeping with its dynamic nature, there are a number of different ways to win this game.

STANDARD VICTORY CONDITIONS

The Standard Victory conditions allow for several different types of "wins." Each player can pursue his or her own victory condition. In other words, one player can try to win by capturing all the Artifacts, while another civilization may look for a Conquest victory.

A civilization may win using one of the following four "standard" strategies:

- *Conquest*—the first player to eliminate all the other players wins the game. This means eliminating all Units and buildings belonging to other players, except for wall structures.

- *Ruins*—the first player to control all the Ruins on the map and to hold them for 2,000 years wins the game.

- *Artifacts*—the first player to control all the Artifacts on the map and to hold them for 2,000 years wins the game.

- *Wonders*—the first player to build a Wonder and to succeed at defending it for 2,000 years wins the game.

NON-STANDARD VICTORY CONDITIONS

If you ever get bored with the Standard Victory Conditions, you can choose a victory condition from the following set of non-Standard Victory Conditions:

- *Conquest*—a player *must* eliminate all the other players in order to win the game. This Victory Condition is essentially the same as the one in the Conquest in the Standard Victory Conditions set, except that players are now restricted to this method of victory.

- *Score*—all players compete to be the first player to achieve a pre-designated score.

- *Time Limit*—all players compete to have the highest score within a given time limit.

SCENARIO BUILDER VICTORY CONDITIONS

If two sets of Victory Conditions still are not enough, *Age of Empires* goes further and provides you with even more Victory Conditions in the Scenario Builder. You can create incredibly complex interrelationships between players by assigning them Victory Conditions from the following list of Individual Victory Conditions:

- *Bring Object to Object*—a player must bring a predetermined object adjacent to another predetermined object to win the game.

- *Bring Object to Area*—a player must bring a predetermined object to a predetermined destination to win the game.

- *Create # of Objects*—a player must create a predetermined number of predetermined objects to win the game.

- *Destroy # of Objects*—a player must destroy a predetermined number of predetermined objects of a specified player to win the game.

- *Destroy Specific Object*—a player must destroy a specific object belonging to a predetermined player to win the game.

- *Destroy all Objects*—a player must destroy all predetermined objects belonging to a specified player to win the game.

- *Destroy Player*—a player must destroy a specified player to win the game.

- *Capture Object*—a player must capture a specified object to win the game.

- *Gold Stockpile*—a player must have a preset amount of gold in inventory to win the game.

- *Food Stockpile*—a player must have a preset amount of food in inventory to win the game.

- *Wood Stockpile*—a player must have a preset amount of wood in inventory to win the game

- *Stone Stockpile*—a player must have a preset amount of stone in inventory to win the game.

- *Population*—a player must have a preset amount of military and civilian Units to win the game.

- *Age*—a player must reach a predetermined Age to win the game.

- *Exploration*—a player must explore a predetermined percentage of the map to win the game.

- *Other Attributes*—a player must achieve a preset number of attributes to win the game. These attributes include Razings, Conversions, Kill Ratio, Military Population, Technologies, Kills, and Villager Population.

- *Technologies*—a player must research and produce a predetermined technology to win the game.

END OF GAME
ACHIEVEMENT SUMMARY

At the end of each game—whether you win or lose—your overall performance is rated on the Achievements Summary screen. This performance rating is broken into a number of different categories—Military, Economy, Religion, Technology, Survival, and Wonder. The score from each category is combined to produce your Total Score for the game.

MILITARY

The military score reflects your ability as a military leader. Your score is determined according to the following factors:

- *Kills*—1/2 point for each enemy destroyed Unit
- *Razings*—1 point per building destroyed
- *Losses*—Number of friendly Units destroyed (you lose one point per Unit eliminated)
- *Kills/Losses*—Number of kills to # of losses (value must be positive)
- *Largest Army* (Most military Units and towers)—25-point bonus

ECONOMY

The economy score reflects how well you ran your civilization's economy. Your score is determined according to the following factors:

- *Gold Collected* (from mining and trade)—1/100 of value (you get one point for every 100 gold RPs)

- *Villager High*—1 point per Villager, trade, transport, and fishing Units

- *Villager Bonus*—25-point bonus (Villagers, trade, transport, and fishing Units)

- *Exploration*—1 point for every 3 percent of the map explored

- *Largest area explored*—25-point bonus

- *Tribute Given*—1/60 of value (every 60 you give in Tribute, you get one point)

RELIGION

The religion score reflects how devoted you were to your particular deities and beliefs. Your score is determined according to the following factors:

- *Conversions*—2 points per conversion

- *Most conversions*—25-point bonus

- *Ruins*—10 points per controlled Ruin

- *Artifacts*—10 points per controlled Artifact

- *Temples*—3 points per Temple built

- *All Artifacts/Ruins* (control of all Ruins or Artifacts)—50-point bonus

TECHNOLOGY

The technology score reflects how technologically advanced your civilization became. Your score is determined according to the following factors:

- *Technologies*—2 points per technology researched
- *Most Technologies* (researched)—50-point bonus
- *Bronze Age First* (First civilization to reach the Bronze Age)—25-point bonus
- *Iron Age First* (First civilization to reach the Iron Age)—25-point bonus

SURVIVAL

Did you survive until the end of the game? If so, great! This is all the thanks you get. If you were eliminated from the game or if you resigned, 100 points are deducted from your score.

- *Survival (Yes)*—0 points
- *Survival (No)*—100-point deduction

WONDER

Did you build and hold a Wonder? If so, how many? You are awarded 100 points for each Wonder you build during the course of the game.

- *Wonder*—100 points per Wonder

MULTIPLAYER STRATEGIES

Because they involve human players instead of artificial intelligence, multiplayer games are both exciting and unpredictable. Instead of dealing with civilizations run by programmed sets of instructions, you now have to deal with the creativity (and the limitations) of the human mind.

In multiplayer games you suddenly have to become a diplomat as well as a military and economic visionary. When great oratory fails you, part of good diplomacy involves spreading a little money around through trade or Tribute. Trade and Tribute are two ways of establishing good relations with other players—right before you attack them. The following section examines some of the finer points of multiplayer gaming.

TRADE RELATIONS

Not only is trading with your neighbors a way to establish good relations, it is also a quick method of introducing large amounts of gold into the game. Trade can only be conducted between Docks and between different civilizations. (You cannot conduct trade between two of your own Docks.) The two civilizations do not need to be allied to one another to conduct trade. They can even be designated as enemies.

Basically, the trade model rewards you with gold in exchange for your food, stone, and wood. Up to 20 Resource Points are loaded aboard a Trading vessel at one of your Docks. (You obviously must have the resources in inventory before they can be loaded.) Your

Trade is conducted over water only

trade vessel sails to another player's Dock and unloads these resources.

In exchange for your goods, the vessel returns to your Dock loaded with gold. The trade has no effect, however, on the other player's Stockpile of resources. No food, wood, or stone is added to the other player's inventory; no gold is deducted. In essence, the gold is simply created out of thin air and introduced into the game. The amount of gold you receive depends entirely on the distance between the two Docks.

The table below indicates the amount of gold you receive per "distance" traveled. The maximum amount of gold you can receive for a single trip is seventy-five (75) RPs, regardless of distance.

TABLE 6-4 The Profitability of Trade

Distance Between Docks (in tiles)	Gold Received for Trade (in RPs)
0–10	5
11–20	10
21–30	15
31–40	20
41–50	25
51–60	30
61–70	35
71–80	40
81–90	45
91–100	50
101–110	55
111–120	60
121–130	65
131–140	70
141+	75

TRIBUTE

Trade is one way to acquire gold outside of the normal means of gathering resources; receiving Tribute is another. Tribute is different from trade. A Tribute is a donation of resources from one civilization to another. It can involve gold, but it can also involve food, wood, or stone.

The mechanics of paying a Tribute are simple. First, you must build a Market. Once this is completed, you may begin to pay Tribute to other players and to receive Tribute from them in return. The amount of resources involved in a Tribute is set using the Diplomacy pull-down menu (which is accessible at any time in the game). Simply note the amount you wish to send in the appropriate player-column.

Until your civilization has researched *Coinage*, there is a 25-percent tax placed on this transaction. For example, if you wish to send a fellow player a Tribute of 100 RPs of wood, the total amount of wood deducted from your Stockpile is 125 RPs.

Tribute is an excellent way to win friends and influence people (including your enemies). Players are free to place whatever conditions they like on the transfer of resources. Of course, no one can be forced to pay a Tribute involuntarily, but a few coins in the right person's pocket just may keep him from sacking one of your structures. By the same token, no one is forced to adhere to any of the bargains involved in a Tribute. *"Ya pays yer money, ya takes yer chances."*

DIPLOMACY

Diplomacy is the art of saying "nice doggie" while looking for a big rock. In many ways, this statement characterizes players' attitudes toward each other. No one wants to be attacked and eliminated from the game, so it is in everyone's interest to remain friendly. Ultimately, there can be only one winner (or allied team of winners), so friendly relations cannot last forever.

In Single Player games, diplomacy is not important. Your computer opponents will do whatever they want, no matter how obsequious you become. (You cannot impress artificial intelligence no matter how well you smooch butt.) Multiplayer games are a different story. Here, you deal with the gamut of human emotions; everything from fear to rage to jealousy.

Since your motivation is to win the game, count on your fellow players to do whatever they feel is necessary to win. As with most things in life, there are no points for second place. (Well . . . literally, that's not quite true. Everyone in a multiplayer game receives a point score regardless of how and where he finishes. So let's rephrase the statement to read—there is no satisfaction in second place.) Remember, you want to win, *and so does everyone else.*

Since this is the case, your diplomatic efforts must be seen in light of mutual benefit. No one, out of misplaced altruism, will make a deal with you to lessen his chance of winning the game, whether perceived or based on "fact." You must convince the other players that the deal you propose is in their best long-term interest. Failing at that, you should at least persuade them that the deal is a *quid pro quo*—something for everyone. For example, you should not say to another player, *"How about attacking the Greeks for me—they're giving me troubles."* The other player is likely to ask, *"What's in it for me?"* But you could say; *"How about repairing my boats for me, I'll pay you a Tribute of 50 gold."*

Diplomacy takes on added importance in multiplayer games because more than one player can win the game. Multiplayer games allow for "team wins," which—in today's terminology—would be referred to as a Coalition victory. In order to become a partner in a Coalition, you must declare yourself as an Ally with the other members of the Coalition. Now, as a member of the Coalition, you can pursue a joint victory.

Being a member of a coalition presents problems of its own, and—of course—the victory isn't as sweet as having it all to

yourself. As Napoleon once said, "I'd rather fight a coalition than be part of one." Still, sharing a victory with others sure beats the heck out of losing. Bear in mind that there is nothing to prevent members of a Coalition from changing their position toward you at any time. You may be assisting them by conducting joint military operations one moment and be declared an enemy the next. Watch out!

DIRTY TRICKS

The following list of cheat codes is by no means exhaustive. There are all kinds of cheats and "Easter Eggs" hidden throughout this game. To active a cheat, simply access the Chat bar (even in a Single Player game) and type in the desired cheat. Although I am not at liberty to repeat all of the Top Secret codes, here is a partial list:

- *PEPPERONI PIZZA*—instantly adds 1,000 RPs of food to your Stockpile.

- *COINAGE*—instantly adds 1,000 RPs of gold to your Stockpile.

- *WOODSTOCK*—instantly adds 1,000 RPs of wood to your Stockpile.

- *QUARRY*—instantly adds 1,000 RPs of stone to your Stockpile.

- *STEROIDS*—turns on Quick Build; structures are completed at an accelerated pace.

- *DIEDIEDIE*—instantly destroys all enemy buildings and Units.

- *HARI KARI*—instantly destroys all of your buildings and Units.

- *HOME RUN*—instantly credits you with a scenario victory.

- *RESIGN*—instantly causes you to resign from the game.

CHAPTER 7

Scenario
Hints and Tips

Age of Empires comes with four campaigns consisting of 36 exciting scenarios. It also features a number of multiplayer games for four or eight players. This chapter summarizes each campaign and multiplayer game scenario. Each summary details a set of helpful hints and tips.

Bear in mind, however, that the strategies outlined in this chapter represent only *one* way to win. Because of the numerous options and the dissimilar nature of individual games, it's nearly impossible to devise a "one strategy fits all" solution. Undoubtedly, you will develop your own techniques for victory as you become more familiar with the game.

As such, use this chapter's scenario summaries as *guidelines only*. They have been developed with the game settings set to the *moderate* difficulty level—a middle-of-the-road setting that is neither too easy nor too difficult. Harder difficulty settings will alter your games dramatically and may even invalidate some strategies presented here.

THE CAMPAIGN GAMES

Each campaign highlights one of the four civilization groups. By the time you have finished playing all the scenarios in all the campaigns, you will have become intimately familiar with each group. Playing these campaign games also gives you valuable experience that you can use when you finally build your own campaigns and scenarios.

ASCENT OF EGYPT (LEARNING CAMPAIGN)

This campaign is a collection of extremely helpful tutorials featuring the Egyptian group of civilizations. These scenarios begin in

8000 BCE (Before Common Era) and continue until 1250 BCE. You should play these games first. I know, I know . . . many of you will say, "Hey, I'm an experienced gamer. I don't need to waste my time playing tutorials." Well, even though this is a learning campaign, the action can still get pretty hot. Tutorial games gradually introduce you to new game concepts, so that—by the time you're finished with all of them—you'll be an expert at *Age of Empires*.

Hunting (8000 BCE)

Objective: Create seven Villagers.

Scenario Instructions: The Ice Age has passed; plants and wildlife are plentiful thanks to the improved climate. Although the technology of your tribe is still primitive, your hunting skills are excellent. Establish a small village on this Nile delta and grow your tribe to seven people.

Resources: Wood—50 RPs, Food—30 RPs, Gold—0 RPs, Stone—0 RPs

This scenario gives you some practical experience in your tribe's hunting activities. Luckily, there are several Gazelles nearby; each one is worth 150 RPs of food. These animals provide your fledgling civilization with an ample supply of food for some time to come.

You start this scenario with one Villager, a Town Center, and 30 food RPs in your stockpile—an inadequate amount of food to create a second Villager right away. Have your Villager begin by hunting. Select the Villager (left click on the Villager Unit) and then choose an animal for him to slaughter (right click on the animal). You may have more than one Villager hunting the same animal.

To expedite the process of hunting for food resources, herd the animals close to your Town Center—or Storage Pit if you have one—before you kill them. This strategy reduces the time it takes to transport and store food RPs in your inventory.

Each time you have acquired 50 or more food RPs, create a new Villager. When you have four Villagers, you have reached your population's support limit. You must build a House before you can support any more Villagers. Use 50 wood RPs in your inventory to build a House, increasing your support limit to eight Villagers—more than enough to win this scenario.

Foraging (7000 BCE)

Objective: Build a Storage Pit, a Granary, and a Dock.

Scenario Instructions: Hunting has been good along the Nile for hundreds of years, but growing numbers of Hunters have depleted the wild game. Edible plants are alternative food sources that can supplement or complement hunting. Hunters have reported berry bushes across the river to the east. Find these storage sites and collect food from them. Establish a significant village in this area by building a Granary, Storage Pit, and Dock.

Resources: Wood—0 RPs, Food—0 RPs, Gold—0 RPs, Stone—0 RPs

You begin this scenario with three Villagers and a Town Center, but with no resources whatsoever. Unlike the previous scenario, food is not a problem. In this scenario, you must "create" buildings, not Villagers; therefore, collecting wood is your primary concern. Since you have no wood when you begin the scenario, you must immediately start chopping down trees. An excellent grove of trees lies just west of your Town Center. Your other two Villagers can collect berries from the berry bushes to the east.

Directions on how to chop wood and forage for food are included in the onscreen scenario instructions. This simple procedure resembles the mouse-clicking process in the previous scenario, in which you have your Villagers hunt for animals.

Before you build any of the structures you need for a win, you

should build a House first. Together with the Town Center, a House allows your civilization to support up to eight Villagers. Once the House is complete, begin to produce Villagers up to a level that your food supply can maintain. Five or six Villagers is all you really need. Use these Villagers to chop more wood. It costs 340 wood RPs to build the three structures you need to win (excluding the cost of the House, which brings the total to 390).

Discoveries (6500 BCE)

Objective: Find the five Discoveries before the Libyans do.

Scenario Instructions: Hunter-gatherers in the Nile delta and along the river have begun encountering other cultures located to the south up the Nile, to the west along the Mediterranean coast, and to the northeast into the Sinai and beyond. Parties of explorers are searching the borderlands. You have been sent into a region to the west toward people called the Libyans. According to legend, there are several sacred sites in the area near your campsite. The sacred sites are known as Discoveries and can be recognized by the figure of a white horse etched into the ground. Find the five Discoveries before the encroaching Libyans.

Resources: Wood—15 RPs, Food—90 RPs, Gold—0 RPs, Stone—0 RPs

As the scenario instructions indicate, you encounter a hostile tribe—the Libyans—at some point during the scenario. Fortunately, the Libyans are not too strong. Their Town Center is located on a plateau to your northeast. Cliffs block direct access to this town, but you can reach the Libyan stronghold by first moving to the east and then finding the passage to the north.

Your objective in this scenario is to find the five sacred sites before the Libyans. When you find a Discovery, the site is automatically marked with a double-pole flag. You will see the colored flag appear magically.

Both wood and food (in the form of berry bushes and Gazelles) are plentiful in this scenario. You should begin producing Villagers right from the start. As your population increases, have a few Villagers explore the countryside. Remember that you are racing to beat the Libyans—don't dawdle!

The nearest Discovery lies just a short distance to the west of your Town Center past a grove of trees. Watch out for the Lion standing near the first Discovery. Far to the north of your Town Center lies a second Discovery. Again, watch out for the nearby Lion. A third Discovery lies just south of the berry bushes to your east; the fourth lies atop the plateau, dangerously close to the Libyan Town Center; the fifth and final Discovery rests far from your Town Center in the northeast corner of the map.

For protection, you should group a number of Villagers together. (The onscreen scenario instructions explain how to "group" your Units.) This way, if Libyans or wild animals attack your Villagers, they will be relatively safer in groups than if they were by themselves. In this scenario, three or four Villagers can make short work of a Lion or an enemy soldier.

Discoveries remind us of the cave paintings found in Lascaux, France.

Dawn of a New Age (6000 BCE)

Objective: Advance to the Tool Age.

Scenario Instructions: Exploration and contact with other cultures have brought new ideas to Egypt. You are learning new skills, including new technologies for fishing. Advance your culture to the Tool Age to gain access to even better skills and capabilities.

Resources: Wood—0 RPs, Food—0 RPs, Gold—0 RPs, Stone—0 RPs

You begin this scenario with three Villagers and a Town Center—but again, without resources in your inventory. Your objective is to advance to the Tool Age, meaning that you must build at least two Stone-Age structures and stockpile at least 500 food RPs. There's no time limit associated with this scenario, but in later games you do receive points for reaching a new age before other players.

You should put two of your three Villagers to work chopping wood immediately. A school of fish is conveniently located along the coast just a few steps from your Town Center. Have your third Villager begin spear-fishing from the shoreline. (The noble sight of this Villager carrying a huge fish back to town is a sight worth seeing.)

Once your Villagers are actively gathering resources, your next step is to increase your civilization's support capacity by building a House. Your only food source in this scenario comes from fishing; therefore, as soon as you have 100 wood RPs, build a Dock. After the Dock, build two or more fishing vessels and have your Villagers fish. The more Fishing Boats you build, the faster you will reach the necessary 500 food RPs.

While you wait to accumulate food, have your Villagers begin to construct a Granary or Storage Pit, giving you the two Stone-Age buildings you need to advance. Once you have stockpiled your food, select your Town Center and press the Advance to Tool Age button. When the progress meter reaches 100 percent, you win.

Skirmish (5500 BCE)

Objective: Destroy the Enemy Tribe.

Scenario Instructions: With new technologies for obtaining food, populations along the Nile have been growing for many generations. Neighboring tribes are moving toward conflicts as they strive to control good food lands, stone tool sites, and defensive positions. Recently, raiding parties from Upper Egypt (up river but to the south) have been coming down the river. Food gatherers nearby have spotted one such party. Intercept and destroy these invaders before they infiltrate your village sites and stores of food.

Resources: Wood—0 RPs, Food—0 RPs, Gold—0 RPs, Stone—0 RPs

This scenario is an early lesson in how battle groups are formed and combat is resolved. You start the scenario with four Axemen and three Bowmen. Your mission is to eliminate the half-dozen or so enemy warriors located in the map's northeast corner. The exact number of enemy Units you face depends on the difficulty setting. When set to the easiest level, you only need to kill four enemy Units—two Axemen and two Bowmen.

Because there are no Villagers in this scenario, you do not need to collect resources. By the same token, you cannot replace any losses—what you see is what you get! Separate your Axemen and Bowmen into two battle groups. Slowly move your men eastward, carefully scouting the terrain ahead.

The enemy Units are dispersed widely among the cliffs and ravines. This works to your advantage as this dispersal prevents the enemy from ganging up on your men. You should always attack with numerical superiority. Don't let the enemy Archers shoot down on your troops from above, as there is a 25-percent possibility that the difference in elevation will triple the damage your men sustain.

Your Axemen should move quickly to engage enemy Units in

close combat, while your Archers remain at a distance. Never let enemy Units engage your Archers in hand-to-hand combat—they are not designed to withstand this kind of attack. Carefully explore the map's eastern section for enemy troops. When the last one is eliminated, you win.

Farming (5000 BCE)

Objective: Control the Ruin and stockpile 800 food Resource Points.

Scenario Instructions: Invaders of Egypt have been stopped, at least temporarily, but migrants and traders continue to enter the region. Those from Mesopotamia have brought the techniques of farming and herding to the Nile region. The future of Egypt depends on making use of the great natural advantages of the Nile Valley, primarily through agriculture. Food surpluses are the basis for the increasing population, the economic power, and the achievement of civilization. Beware of the encroaching Nubians from the north.

Resources: Wood—100 RPs, Food—100 RPs, Gold—100 RPs, Stone—100 RPs

As the name suggests, this scenario is a lesson on the value of farming. Wildlife and foraging sites are scarce, fishing sites nearly nonexistent. Your objective is to stockpile 800 food RPs. This normally would not be too difficult, except that an aggressive enemy tribe occupies a strong position across the river to the northwest.

You begin the game with three Clubmen, three Villagers, a Barracks, and a Tool-Age Town Center. Use the 100 food RPs currently in your inventory to build two more Villagers and then put everyone to work chopping wood. You will need lots of wood in a short period of time. Build a Market as quickly as you can, so that you can start building Farms.

In terms of the military, you should first upgrade your existing

Clubmen to Axemen. This upgrade requires 100 food RPs, but in return, you increase the strength of your foot soldiers. You also will want to build an Archery Range to begin producing Bowmen. Once you have built a force of about ten Axemen and Bowmen, you are strong enough to move against the enemy tribe across the river.

Chances are, however, that the enemy comes to you first. Two shallow river crossings provide the enemy with immediate access to the other side of the river, and the river crossing to the north of your village is practically a highway for enemy Units. Expect the main attack from this direction, but be aware of the other crossing to the south. You can use this shoal to ford the river with greater safety but with a greater distance to travel in order to reach the enemy village.

To win this scenario, you need to control the Ruin that lies close to the southern shallow crossing. While the enemy is preoccupied with the northern crossing, take the opportunity to sneak a few Units to the Ruin to capture it.

The enemy is not particularly strong, and if you hurry, you can begin your assault on its town before it can fortify its position. Ultimately, this scenario consists of attacking the enemy village and having ample Villagers on the Farms to stockpile the necessary 800 food RPs. Defeat or neutralize the enemy, control the Ruin, and stockpile food—that's all you do to win this one.

Trade (2000 BCE)

Objective: Stockpile 1,000 gold and 1,000 stone Resource Points.

Scenario Instructions: Now that you have mastered the techniques of farming along the river, your civilization is among the fastest-growing and most advanced in the world. Your increasing wealth makes it possible to trade abroad. The Pharaoh requests that you take advantage of your position near the coast to help gather resources for a wondrous new temple he is planning.

Your contribution is 1,000 gold and 1,000 stone. Gold can be obtained by Trading with the Minoans, Canaanites, or Libyans, who are all likely to be antagonistic. Stone can be found nearby.

Resources: Wood—200 RPs, Food—200 RPs, Gold—0 RPs, Stone—200 RPs

In this scenario, your objective is to stockpile 1,000 gold RPs and 1,000 stone RPs to hand over to the Pharaoh. There are insufficient mines on the map to produce this much gold, so Trading is necessary. None of the other three tribes is particularly friendly, but be especially wary of the Minoans.

You begin this scenario with three Villagers and a quaint Tool-Age village already in place. It's a good thing, too, because the Libyans (yellow player) shortly will come to call. Since trade is conducted over water, you want to begin work on a Dock as soon as possible. Your neighbors will contest your control over the waterways early, so count on building many scout vessels.

Several Stone Mines are located to the east of your village beyond the forest and near the northeastern edge of the map. Send several Villagers there to explore, and be sure to have enough wood to build a Storage Pit next to the Stone Mines. You cannot mine all the stone you need from these mines, however. Prepare to go out and find some more.

The only place to find more stone is the tiny Minoan island located along the middle of the southwestern edge of the map. The Minoans have stationed a number of siege weapons on the island, so it is best to delay your attack until you have naval vessels to take them out. Once established on the island, build a Storage Pit and mine the stone.

There are no Gold Mines anywhere on the map. You must trade to get enough gold to win the scenario. Your best Trading partner is the Canaanite (red) civilization. Use your naval vessels to scout the central area of the map, where you will find a Canaanite Dock. Create at least three Trade Boats or merchant vessels and begin Trading

wood or food for Canaanite gold. Once you reach a total of 1,000 gold RPs, you win.

Crusade (1900 BCE)

Objective: Capture (convert) the Ballista and bring it to your Town Center.

Scenario Instructions: The great new temple has had a powerful effect on the people of Egypt. Priests are revitalized in their fervor and are spreading the word up river and along the coast. You are leading a new settlement in the west near Libya, where raiders have been harassing Egyptian towns. These raiders possess a powerful new weapon called a Ballista. Capture (convert) the Ballista and bring it to your Town Center.

Resources: Wood—100 RPs, Food—100 RPs, Gold—0 RPs, Stone—0 RPs

This scenario introduces you to the marvelous technique of using Priests to convert enemy Units. Your objective is fairly simple. You need to steal a Ballista from an enemy force to your southwest. If the Ballista is destroyed, you lose. You start this scenario with one Priest and without any gold resources to build more.

The fact that you have only one Priest complicates your task. The Ballista makes short work of a Priest if they go head-to-head. (A Priest usually cannot convert a Ballista before the weapon kills him.) Because of this precarious situation, you cannot just march your Priest south and convert the weapon very quickly.

Unfortunately, gold is too scarce in this scenario with only one small gold mine to the south of your Town Center. Sending Villagers to mine for gold likely would trigger an enemy attack, so be careful. If you can mine gold without attack, do so because you do not have anyone to trade with during this scenario. Use the gold to either build more Priests or to improve the one you have.

As an alternative, you can forget about mining the gold and build a force of conventional military Units. The trick here is to protect the Priest, while moving him close enough to the Ballista to convert it. The best way to accomplish this feat with a military is to distract the Ballista, making it fire at other targets. You may lose a few Units in the process, but . . . so what? Your objective here is to provide your Priest with enough time to convert the Ballista, and that's all you really need to be concerned with.

River Outpost (1700 BCE)

Objective: Locate the large Nile River island. Build a Town Center and two Guard Towers on the island.

Scenario Instructions: The power of our armies and religion has stabilized our frontiers for the time being. The Nubians to the south remain a threat, however, although subduing them is too expensive to consider. As an alternative, the Pharaoh has ordered that a river outpost be placed on a strategic Nile River island to discourage Nubian raiders from coming down river. Locate the large island in the center of the river to the north and build a Town Center and two Guard Towers there.

Resources: Wood—400 RPs, Food—400 RPs, Gold—0 RPs, Stone—0 RPs

This scenario requires that you master the art of amphibious operations. Your objective is to land on a large island and defeat the enemy there. Luckily, you begin the scenario surrounded by a wealth of resources in the Bronze Age. You eventually need to create a force of approximately 10 Villagers just to keep up with your civilization's voracious appetite for resources. (In order to build the Guard Towers, you must advance to the Iron Age at a cost of 1,000 food RPs and 800 gold RPs.)

Immediately put your Villagers to work chopping wood. You need to build several Docks (to build ships), a Market (to build Farms), and an Archery Range (to produce missile troops). Early enemy interference depends on the difficulty setting, but count on a Nubian invasion from the north at some point during the game.

It is unnecessary to develop a huge land army in this scenario even though this opportunity is very tempting. Essentially, you need only to fend off minor attacks from the north, while you build a strong naval presence. Your main effort should be directed towards building and upgrading a fleet of Triremes.

Because you need to build a second Town Center on the island to win, you must first build a Government Center. One or two Temples are not absolutely necessary, but—hey, it can't hurt. Having one or two Priests around to convert enemy Units can be a real blessing.

The island in question lies to the west of your Town Center in the middle of the Nile, which divides the map into two sides. Numerous enemy towers are situated on the island; you must deal with these towers before you can land any ground Units. Your navy comes into play here. A half-dozen Triremes, in this instance, will work quite well. Concentrate the naval vessels' fire on one tower at a time. This way, you systematically destroy the island defenses with little losses.

Besides the towers, several Lions and Alligators must also be killed because of the danger they pose to your Villagers. After you have eliminated the animal foes, it is safe to land your Villagers. (You can use your naval vessels to kill the animals.) You must build a Town Center on the island as part of the victory conditions. Shift your Villagers' production to this new Town Center and then put them to work building a Storage Pit and mining stone. In order to win this scenario, you must also build two Guard Towers on the island—an easy task once you have acquired the necessary 300 stone RPs.

Naval Battle (1650 BCE)

Objective: Recover a stolen Artifact and take it to your Town Center.

Scenario Instructions: The Nile forts have brought peace to the south for many generations, but the Libyans have once more become a problem. They have been raiding your coasts and intercepting Trading ships heading for the Nile delta. They recently captured an important ship belonging to the Pharaoh and carried off a treasured Artifact sent to him by the kings of Canaan. Build a naval base in this area off the coast and attack the Libyan raiders at their home port. Recover the stolen Artifact and return it to your Town Center.

Resources: Wood—200 RPs, Food—200 RPs, Gold—200 RPs, Stone—200 RPs

Now that you have some experience in conducting amphibious operations, this scenario tests your ability to wage a full-scale war at sea. You must cross an expanse of water to land a large army in Libyan territory. Reinforcing this army is difficult because of the distance involved. Nevertheless, once this army has landed, it must attack and defeat a strong enemy force to retake the stolen Artifact.

You begin the scenario in a functioning Bronze-Age village complete with all the necessary amenities. An abundant food supply and a wood source are nearby. Enemy warships from the north begin to attack your coast soon after the game begins. As time elapses, the enemy begins to send transports in an attempt to land an invasion force.

You should approach this scenario in three separate stages. Stage one is defensive, and requires you to stabilize the current situation by stopping these raids and sinking the transports. A scarcity of stone prevents you from fortifying your coastline completely; however, there is enough available stone to build a few walls and towers near your village. You must build a powerful navy. Start

by chopping all the wood you can and by upgrading your Triremes as soon as possible—that is, upgrade them right away!

Stage two requires you to put your navy to sea. Your objective is to control all movement over water by destroying enemy Docks and by sinking any enemy vessel you discover or encounter. Remember, use your ships *en masse*, instead of committing them to battle piecemeal.

Stage three involves loading your transports on your naval vessels to conduct a D-Day type invasion off the Libyan coast. You will discover that the Libyans have fortified their coast with towers and have placed the Artifact within a walled section of their village. (The village is located near the map's northern corner.) If your army is large enough—and if you can reinforce it regularly with fresh troops—neither the towers nor the Libyan cavalry will be able to stop you from taking back what is rightfully yours.

A Wonder of the World (1625 BCE)

Objective: Build a Wonder.

Scenario Instructions: The Pharaoh has decreed that a great monument be built to celebrate our recent victories over the Libyans. This monument gives most of the credit to the Pharaoh of course, but he cannot help with the construction costs or raw materials of this Wonder at this time. You are required to build this monument at your own expense. Gather the materials where you can. The Minoans are friendly and may be of help through trade. Beware of the Canaanites who may try to undermine such trade.

Resources: Wood—100 RPs, Food—100 RPs, Gold—100 RPs, Stone—100 RPs

This scenario familiarizes you with an alternate way of winning the game—building a Wonder. This scenario differs somewhat from the usual way of winning with a Wonder; you normally build a

Wonder and then defend it for 2,000 game years to win the game. A Wonder is often a signal to your enemies that you are close to winning. It gives them 2,000 years to do something about it!

In this scenario, the Canaanites, advanced tribespeople with a village on an island in the western corner of the map, are very aggressive. Not only do they seek to undermine your trade with the Minoans, but they want to destroy your civilization altogether. Expect them to begin landing powerful forces—including siege weapons—along your coastline quite early in the game.

The best way to deal with the Canaanite threat is to intercept their transports before they land. To do this, you must build a powerful navy and blockade the Canaanite coast. Have your Villagers immediately chop wood for ships. Upgrade your warships as soon as possible. You need to build War Galleys in order to deal with the Canaanite scouting vessels that seem to appear out of nowhere.

Gold is in short supply. As the scenario instructions point out, you can obtain gold by Trading wood or food with the Minoan Docks located in the center of the southeast edge of the map. To expedite the process, have several Trading Boats plying the water between the Minoans and your own Docks. You need almost 2,000 gold RPs to advance to the Iron Age to build your Wonder.

A large deposit of gold lies at the base of some cliffs on the Canaanite island. To mine this gold, however, you first will probably have to defeat the Canaanites first. Whether it is worth the effort is entirely up to you. Trading with the Minoans is slower, but infinitely safer.

There is enough stone on the map to build your Wonder, but you must explore a bit to find it. One Stone Mine is located along the map's northwestern edge directly across from a shallow river crossing to the west of your Town Center. An even larger deposit of stone is located on a deserted island in the far eastern corner of the map. From these two sites, you should find enough stone to build your Wonder.

Siege in Canaan (1450 BCE)

Objective: Destroy the Canaanite Government Center.

Scenario Instructions: Our glorious new monument to the Pharaoh is the envy of everyone and marks Egypt as the greatest civilization in the world. With this major project completed, the Pharaoh wishes to turn his attention to the Canaanites, who have been a thorn in Egypt's side for generations. They have foolishly resisted becoming part of greater Egypt for too long. You are to take their largest city under siege and destroy their Government Center. This assault is intended to bring them to heel. The smaller Canaanite cities must surrender to you once their mightiest citadel has fallen.

Resources: Wood—200 RPs, Food—200 RPs, Gold—200 RPs, Stone—20 RPs

You should consider this final scenario of the learning campaign as Graduation Day. The objective is to destroy the Canaanite Government Center located in the northern corner of the map. Unfortunately, the building is situated on a fortified mountain top and is well protected by Canaanite archers. You must put everything you have learned so far into good use during the end of this campaign

This scenario is long, so get comfortable. You start with a Stone-Age Town Center, a Barracks, and four Houses. You also have three Villagers and an army of three Archers and three Clubmen—a considerable force this early in the game.

A narrow river bisects the map from west to east with only a single shallow river crossing. As a result, all land movement is channeled through this one crossing point. You want to fortify this position to keep enemy troops from transversing, while you preserve it as a future launching point for your invasion.

The first step in winning this scenario should be to clear out all enemy Units from *your* side of the river (the south section of the

map). Begin by eliminating the enemy troops and towers on the bluffs just to the west of your Town Center. Be sure to guard the river crossing with multiple towers, so that enemy Units north of the river are prevented from interfering. The area on your side of the river can be easily cleared—just avoid the potential triple damage caused by elevated missile shots.

Once your side of the river is secure, you should begin to amass your army. Priests and siege weapons should be well represented in this army, too. The ability to convert enemy Units (and buildings) comes in handy. Ranged fire is also important because of the numerous enemy towers you must deal with along the way. Invest heavily in siege weaponry, some of the few Units that have a greater range than the Canaanite towers.

The Canaanite Government Center is difficult to reach. Your army must pass through several natural Choke-points, which the Canaanites cleverly guard with towers. Take your time—this is a siege, after all. Move the maximum number of missile-firing Units into position and then attack each tower systematically. Although the Canaanite village is fortified, an opening in the wall gives your troops easy access to the Government Center.

GLORY OF GREECE

The Glory of Greece campaign features exploration and combat in the Aegean and eastern Mediterranean. This campaign demonstrates the value of a small, yet well-trained professional army. Like the previous learning campaign, the Glory of Greece scenarios are patterned after historical events. Here you can relive the epic conflicts that shaped the development of the Western world. The scenarios begin in 2000 BCE and continue until 331 BCE.

Land Grab (2000 BCE)

Objective: Destroy all Dorian Farms and establish five Farms.

Scenario Instructions: The Ice Age is over, and food is plentiful. To survive and grow in an increasingly hostile world, however, your tribe must take possession of good forage lands. There are three other tribes in this area already. The Dorians are the strongest tribe. Build five Farms to establish your presence in the valley while destroying all Dorian Farms to weaken your most powerful neighbor. It may be necessary to eliminate the Ionians or Tirynians first to obtain a foothold in this area.

Resources: Wood—200 RPs, Food—400 RPs, Gold—0 RPs, Stone—200 RPs

For most of you, this scenario will be your first campaign scenario out of the learning campaign. Now that school is over, welcome to the real world. This scenario can be difficult because time is not on your side. The Dorians (the red) to the north attack early and often. Your objective is to destroy their Farms while you build five of your own.

You start this scenario with four Villagers and six Clubmen. You need to establish a village immediately by building a Town Center. You also need to build some Houses and a Barracks, all of which require a considerable amount of wood—so get chopping!

The Tirynians, the yellow player to the east, are considerably weaker than the Dorians; you may want to take care of them first. Build a Dock on the lake to the east of your starting position and begin fishing. Three Fishing Boats are adequate to deplete the lake's stock of fish. Use this food resource to build a squad of Clubmen. If the Dorians leave you alone, send your clubmen into the Tirynian village to sack it. There are excellent foraging sites and ample Gazelles nearby.

The Dorians, however, probably will not leave you alone. Expect to see increasing numbers of Dorian Clubmen paying you visits. In time, these Clubmen will be upgraded to Axemen, and then you

really have real a problem. The best way to deal with the Dorian threat early on is to build walls and Watch Towers. Seal your northern border to hold the Dorians at bay, while you subjugate the Tirynians. At least this defensive line gives you time to build a strong army of your own.

Advance to the Tool Age as fast as you possibly can. You want to upgrade your own Clubmen before tackling the Dorians. If you suspect that the Dorians have not yet upgraded their own Clubmen, you may want to go on the offensive. An army of 10 to 15 Axemen should prove decisive. Destroy the Dorian Farms, and, once this has been accomplished, you only need five of your own Farms to win the scenario.

Citadel (1500 BCE)

Objective: Capture the Ruins and establish two Sentry Towers beside the Ruins.

Scenario Instructions: Greece is now largely settled, and growth is possible mainly at the expense of neighbors. The Thebans are beginning to expand and covet the lands that you now control. They must not be allowed to continue. Gain control of this region by capturing the ancient Ruins close to the nearby Theban town. Build two Sentry towers adjacent to the Ruins to ensure your control.

Resources: Wood—400 RPs, Food—400 RPs, Gold—200 RPs, Stone—400 RPs

With a good supply of resources in your inventory and a large village infrastructure (i.e., many buildings), your civilization is in a strong position at the start of the scenario. The challenge that faces you will tax your skills and quickly deplete your resources. Your objective is to capture one very well-guarded Theban Ruin and to build two Sentry Towers nearby.

The Thebans are far too strong to be approached directly. In

fact, for a large part of this scenario, they come after you—not vice versa. The indirect route, however, requires that you execute an island-hopping campaign, capturing Gold and Stone Mines as you go. Before you set off on this amphibious campaign, you must secure your own village by fortifying your northern flank.

There is a shallow river crossing to the northeast of your Town Center. This crossing is a major thoroughfare for enemy troops. At the game's beginning, you have just enough stone to wall it off and, perhaps, to build a tower. Unless you seal off this border, Theban troops will harass your village continuously, and your own campaign will fail.

Once the northern flank has been secured, begin your invasion. Start by building several Docks on the shore to the west of your Town Center. Build a few warships and transport vessels. Assemble a large contingent of ground troops with a few Villagers, and move them to the uninhabited island directly to the west.

Use this island as a staging area for the rest of your campaign. On the opposite side of this island, shallow crossings connect to the mainland. Continue moving northward using your warships to protect your army's right flank. Gold and stone are in short supply, so exploit the mines you uncover along the way.

Wait until you have amassed an overwhelming number of strong ground Units before you begin your assault on the Theban village. Once again, the preferred method of attack is to unleash one massive wave of troops, rather than attack the town with individual or paired Units. Priests and siege weapons should figure prominently in your offensive.

Eliminate the Theban towers and Priests first, and *then* move in to complete their annihilation. With the Theban army out of the way and many of their structures aflame, it is simply a matter of locating the Ruin and building the two towers necessary to win this scenario.

Ionian Expansion (1400 BCE)

Objective: Establish a Government Center on Ionia inside the flagged region *or* find three Ruins.

Scenario Instructions: The Athenians have pushed back their neighbors and have one of the stronger places in Greece. The crops of Athens are now falling short of the demand for food, however. The city-state is in danger of falling into anarchy if new food sources are not found and if the population is not reduced. The ruling council is embarking upon on a bold plan to move people overseas to establish colonies. You are directed to establish a foothold on the eastern side of the Aegean sea by placing a colony in Ionia. The Phrygians think Ionia is their land, but they are too weak to hold it. Establish a colony across the sea by locating the flagged area on the far land mass and building a Government Center within it. Alternatively, take possession of the three Ruins in Asia. Take the initiative now before food reserves are gone or the Phrygians get ideas about colonizing Greece.

Resources: Wood—0 RPs, Food—400 RPs, Gold—400 RPs, Stone—400 RPs

This scenario requires that you exercise control over an expanse of ocean. You need to build several Docks, many warships, and some transports. Gold is ultimately the key to winning this scenario. By far, the largest supply of gold lies scattered in some uninhabited islands to the north of the Lydian enclave. Once you control the waterways, transport some Villagers to the largest of these islands, build a Storage Pit, and exploit the nearby Gold Mines.

The flagged region referred to in the Objective above is centered along the northeast edge of the map. Impassable cliffs surround three sides of this region, which is guarded by Ionian towers, as well. You can reach the flagged region only by moving overland and approaching it from the southeast. Unfortunately, an Ionian stronghold of considerable size rests to the southeast of the flagged region.

You will gain access to the flagged region only after you have done away with the Ionians.

Luckily, your civilization begins this scenario with excellent position and with a relatively large inventory of resources. Use your wood to build Docks along your northern and western coastlines. Abundant fishing sites just wait to be discovered. The main reason for building Docks, however, is to create a powerful navy.

The Ionians attack you throughout this scenario. At first, you occasionally spot their scout vessels offshore, but this means that transports with ground troops are not far behind. Obviously, you want to engage the Ionian vessels at sea away from your coast. Even on the lower difficulty levels, these frequent raids will annoy you. Only one boat load of Ionian troops needs to land to disrupt and interrupt your plans.

Although you must use large amounts of wood to build Docks and warships, you will prevail eventually if you keep at it. Now, it is your chance to turn the tables on the Ionians. Begin raiding their coastline for a change. Send your warships after Ionian Docks and coastal tower defenses. When the time is right, load your transports with ground troops and carry out an amphibious assault on the Ionian mainland.

Land your troops in the northeast corner of the map—far from, and to the southeast of, the Ionian stronghold. Your invasion force should include several Villagers. Put these people to work building a Town Center. Once the Town Center is in place, start producing more Villagers. You want to create a small village quickly to use as a base of operations.

Use the gold you discover on the tiny islands to fund a general assault on the Ionian stronghold. This attack should be spearheaded by Academy Units and Priests with fire support from multiple Catapults. Your warships should be on hand to protect the left

flank of your advance as you move into the flagged region. Build your Government Center inside this region to complete the victory conditions as described above.

You can also win this scenario by uncovering three Ruins, which are scattered throughout the map, but winning the game this way is not very satisfying. It is not as much fun as winning the game by conquest. Besides, after suffering from Ionian raids all game long, you'll look forward to a little pay-back.

Trojan War (1250 BCE)

Objective: Kill Hector and capture Priam's Treasure.

Scenario Instructions: Greek expansion overseas has brought the Greeks into contact with other cultures that pose both opportunities and dangers. The beautiful Helen has been stolen by Paris and taken back to his home city of Troy. Paris is the son of Priam, king of Troy. To restore the honor of the Myceneans, take revenge on the City of Troy by killing Hector, its Hero, and capturing the treasure of Priam. Troy is far across the sea, and taking the city requires an invasion of the Trojan homeland. The Trojan navy must be neutralized first.

Resources: Wood—300 RPs, Food—300 RPs, Gold—300 RPs, Stone—300 RPs

This is one of the more imaginative scenarios in the game. Your objective is to kill Hector (a hero character) and then break into Troy to nab the loot. Since your civilization is prevented from advancing to the Iron Age, some of your strongest Units are unavailable. Use your Alexander Hero Unit selectively. He is powerful but not invincible. Always have one or two Priests nearby to heal his wounds if necessary.

Once again, the key to victory lies in controlling the open seas. In order to win, you must cross the Mediterranean and take the

fight to the enemy. Knowing this, the Trojans will attempt to conduct raids and landings along your coast right from the scenario's beginning. Although your civilization starts in a good position with many Villagers and access to vast resources, it comes to naught if you lose the naval battle.

Begin by building several Docks. You want to protect these structures with Watch Towers. Fortunately, you begin the game with enough wood and stone to accomplish this task. Any extra stone should be used to build shoreline fortifications to prevent the enemy from setting foot on land. Walls and towers are crucial to preserving your village's integrity. Hector is smart, and the Trojans will land if you give them an opportunity—they are not content to wait around and let you enter Troy.

The most valuable piece of land on the map is an island located to the southeast of your village. This island has numerous Gold Mines that will finance your campaign. You cannot win this scenario without building lots of high-end Units at, of course, high-end prices. One word of caution is in order: On this island, there are numerous Lion kings, who are not so much interested in guarding the gold as they are in a quick snack. Use your warships to kill these animals before you have your Villagers disembark.

The city of Troy is located in the eastern corner of the map, but Trojan territory extends the full length of the map's southeast edge. Trojan cavalry Units expect you to land and actively patrol the region. Your best bet is to land as far south of Troy as possible. When you finally do land, land a strong force. The Trojans will come to meet you rather than remain behind their city walls. Be ready to fight.

Transporting Units from your mainland is time-consuming. Be sure to include a couple of Villagers in your invasion force. Have them build a Temple, an Academy, and one or two Siege Workshops on Trojan soil. Hector and his Cavalry will not let you get

This scene from the Trojan War depicts Troy's downfall. Hector has been killed, and the walls are coming down.

away with this unnoticed. Use your Priests to convert as many Trojans as possible, and have plenty of infantry Units on hand to tie up their attack.

Once you have won the battle outside the walls, amass your siege weapons and begin eliminating the towers that encircle the city. Enter the city from the south, and search for Priam's treasure (represented by the Artifact). Take the Artifact to a safe location. If you have managed to reach the Artifact, Hector probably is already dead. (Hector is a Heavy Cavalry Hero Unit in this scenario.)

Hector must be killed to win the scenario. If a Priest converts Hector, you will be unable to finish the game in regular fashion. If you did convert him, have several of your Catapults aim their fire at a particular piece of ground. Walk Hector back and forth through this fire until he is dead.

I'll Be Back (1200 BCE)

Objective: Capture the Artifact and destroy the Temple.

Scenario Instructions: After helping the Minoans capture a powerful artifact, you discover that they plan to use it to dominate the world. Led by a group called the "Seven Yellow Old Men," the Minoans plan to kill you and your men. Hopelessly outnumbered, your only chance is to flee. Run like the wind, and don't stop until you find Allies. Return to Crete and make the Minoans pay. Beware—the Minoans have Allies, too. Destroy the Temple of the Seven Yellow Old Men and take back the Artifact to hold it safe.

Resources: Wood—0 RPs, Food—0 RPs, Gold—0 RPs, Stone—0 RPs

In this outstanding scenario, your forces have been betrayed and are very nearly trapped within the Minoan fortress. You must fight your way free, quickly descend from the mountain, and then board a few transport vessels to escape. Initially, you lose a substantial number of your men—it's unavoidable—but as long as one of your Units escapes, you have a chance to win this scenario.

Your salvation lies in the southern corner of the map, where your Allies have a walled village. Inside this village is a tremendous army which is more than willing to assist you in destroying the Minoan Temple and in recovering your Artifact. Before you can employ this army, however, you first must reach it.

The scenario's first stage involves getting your men away from the Seven Yellow Old Men. Have them board the waiting transports to make a clean get-away. Your transports need to cross this body of water quickly. Minoan War Galleys also sail these waters, and may be in a position to intercept this move. Use your warships to escort your transports.

The transports are more valuable than they may first appear. You need to ensure that at least one of your transports survives. You will use these same vessels to return to the island later. If they are

all destroyed, you have no way to cross the water to recapture the Artifact. Once the transports drop your men off, move them to some safe, inconspicuous location and keep them there.

The next step involves moving your surviving men overland to reach the allied village to the south. The heavily forested terrain offers many well-worn paths that you may take. The reason these paths are well-worn is that enemy uses them, too. Protective towers and siege weapons have been positioned at regular intervals. Avoid coming in contact with enemy Units if possible. Your main concern here is to reach your Allies, not to battle the enemy.

The lone transport in the southern part of the map is crucial. You need it to ferry your men across another body of water that separates your Allies' village from the mainland. Once your men reach the village, the full extent of your Allies' army is revealed to you.

Retracing your steps, perhaps, is the best method for returning to the Minoan fortress. Exploring the central land mass just forces you to fight more towers—and for no good reason. You may be tempted to use your Priests to convert the nearby Ballistas. Don't. You will find that your Priests are killed far more frequently than Ballistas are converted from one side to the other.

Once you have made your way across the land mass, begin ferrying your ground troops back to the Minoan island. This may take some time, especially if you only have one transport remaining. From here, it's an uphill battle—literally. Use your missile-equipped troops to occupy the Minoan towers, while your Priests and infantry Units begin to march up the path.

The Seven Yellow Old Men convert some of your troops. But never fear—your own Priests can wage a religious "war" with the Seven. Mass your missile troops, and kill the Minoan Priests as soon as they appear. The level of difficulty for this final confrontation depends on the number of Units you have managed to keep alive. Destroy the Temple and recapture your Artifact.

Siege of Athens (431 BCE)

Objective: Capture the enemy Artifacts.

Scenario Instructions: Over the past 500 years, the Greeks have grown strong at home and overseas. Their interference in Persian affairs attracted two Persian invasions, but these were turned back. Now the Greeks are squabbling at home over dividing up the spoils of their Mediterranean trade. Sparta and Athens are fighting for dominance. The Spartan army is approaching Athens and is too powerful to be met in open combat. Defend the walls to delay them while the Athenian army is reinforced. Its farmland is outside the walls, unfortunately, so your food sources are probably lost. Use the Athenian advantage at sea to obtain food and trade overseas. The Spartans are thought to have no naval power, but that may change. When your armies have been strengthened, engage the Spartan army and drive it from your lands. The Spartans have brought a large baggage train of supplies. If that can be captured, they will be forced to fall back.

Resources: Wood—100 RPs, Food—100 RPs, Gold—100 RPs, Stone—100 RPs

The scenario begins with a massive ground assault from the southwest on your city, Athens. Even if you manage to stop the attack, your city is under siege. Since you have access to the sea, however, you can continue to trade with other civilizations. To win this scenario, you must lift the siege by defeating the Spartans and then recover the four Artifacts, which represent the Spartan baggage train.

At the very beginning of the game, you should adopt a "retreat to win" strategy. You cannot hope to hold your initial position, so pull your Villagers behind the protection of your city walls. The Ballista Towers that encircle your city are formidable. On easier difficulty settings, your towers are more than enough to break up any ground attack. In fact, your city is never really under any great threat.

Throughout history, Athens was famous for the strength of its walls. The Spartan army doesn't stand a chance of entering the city.

You must maintain your superiority at sea. As long as you can keep the Spartans from blockading your Docks, your merchant vessels and transports have free reign to explore the map. Maintaining safe trade routes is extremely important, as you need to generate a fair amount of gold (through trade) before you can even take on the Spartans.

In fact, the Spartans can be defeated fairly easily in open combat, too. Like you, they have a Grecian-style army that relies on heavily armed professional soldiers. Expect to see many Hoplites and Phalanxes, but few Archers. Siege weapons also figure prominently. Besides the normal combat Units, the Spartans have several Heroes. These "superman" Units are easily overlooked in the heat of battle, but they can inflict considerable damage.

Before you set out to capture the Artifacts (located along the map's southwestern edge), be sure that your infantry Units have the benefit of all technology related to hand-to-hand combat,

defensive armor, *and* shield bonuses. Even though you are the one under siege, you have the stronger army, provided that you keep your sea lanes clear and open.

Xenophon's March (401 BCE)

Objective: Capture the Artifact and escort it to your Government Center.

Scenario Instructions: The Peloponnesian War has ended, and you are part of a group of Greek soldiers hired originally to support Cyrus the Younger in his bid to claim the Persian throne. Cyrus has just been killed during the battle of Cunaxa; however, your contingent of mercenaries is isolated deep within the Persian empire. While the main Persian army is not a threat, having been defeated at Cunaxa, there is a long and dangerous journey ahead before you can return to Greece. The decision has been made to strike out for the Black Sea. That is the least dangerous land route to a good sea port, and a rich treasure there can substitute for the uncollected spoils and pay. Capture the Artifact held in the coastal city, build a transport there, and carry the Artifact to the friendly building in the northern corner of the map.

Resources: Wood—120 RPs, Food—0 RPs, Gold—0 RPs, Stone—0 RPs

This Iron Age scenario lets you recreate Xenophon's famous "March to the Sea." The map portrays a long, treacherous route with narrow canyon and difficult terrain. This scenario is among the best in the game visually.

You begin this scenario with a homesick contingent of Villagers, Priests, and military Units. In order to return home, you must advance along a narrow route full of wild animals, enemy ambushes, and fortified positions. This is not a timed scenario, so don't be in a hurry. A steady, methodical advance is your best bet.

As always, your Priest is extremely valuable. You only have one Priest in this scenario and cannot produce any more—protect him at all costs. Having him convert enemy Units is a quick way to boost your small band of travelers. You also will want to protect your two Ballista Units. These Units, the lone Priest and the Ballistas, represent your army's only weapons with range. Everyone else must close with the enemy and engage in hand-to-hand combat.

The relatively easy first leg of your journey ends at a small enemy village situated on the bank of a narrow river. Have your Villagers build a Storage Pit near the village with the 120 wood RPs you already have in your inventory. After the Storage Pit, put them to work chopping wood. You must build a Dock and some transport vessels to cross the river. (In fact, you must first build several Houses to increase your support base before you can build additional Units.)

Once you have crossed the river, take time to reorganize your army before you proceed. Don't allow your weaker Units to take the lead. They may blunder, falling into an ambush and being destroyed before you can come to their aid. You may want to consider building a few Triremes to cover your flanks as you continue down the river. Use the missile attack strength of these boats to destroy the enemy village on the river's north shore.

Unfortunately, the path turns inland at this point, and your ships must be left behind. Hopefully, you still have your Ballistas. They come in handy as you negotiate your way past several fortified positions you now encounter. In the eastern corner of the map, you will discover several Gold Mines. Build a Storage Pit, and have your Villagers mine for gold.

The Artifact you must capture is located inside the walled city, which lies just beyond the Gold Mines near the center of map. Part of the city is elevated on a plateau, which gives the city a plunging fire bonus—namely, a tripling of the normal damage your Units

sustain from missile hits shot from higher elevations than your own. Build a Siege Workshop and begin producing siege weapons with the gold you are mining.

To reach the Artifact, you must first blast your way through the city's wall. Position your siege weapons, so that you receive the plunging fire bonus for shooting at targets at lower elevations than your own. No wall can withstand the force of your siege weaponry for too long. Once you have breached the wall, capture the Artifact. From here, simply build a Dock and a transport, and then move the Artifact to the friendly Government Center at the map's northern corner.

Wonder (331 BCE)

Objective: Destroy all enemies *or* their Wonders.

Scenario Instructions: The return of Xenophon and the 10,000 Greek mercenaries in 400 BCE revealed many weaknesses within the Persian empire, but not until now could anything be done about it. The Greeks have been united under you, Alexander of Macedon. You have marched into Asia Minor and are now surrounded by your enemies. You've got them just where you want them. First, destroy the Great Wonder already built by the Lydians and then the Phoenician Wonder. Beware of Persian interference with your campaign. Wage successful war against Persia and her Allies, and you will be known hereafter as the "the Great."

Resources: Wood—500 RPs, Food—1,000 RPs, Gold—500 RPs, Stone—500 RPs

In this final campaign scenario, even though you may portray Alexander, you have yet to prove that he is—you are—"Great." Your people begin the game precariously sandwiched among three powerful, fortified Iron-Age opponents. Worse, the Alexander Hero Unit is not included among your initial forces.

As the scenario opens, the Lydians (red) are just putting the finishing touches on their Wonder in the map's eastern corner. You have *only* 2,000 years to bring it crashing down. The Lydian Wonder is well-protected by extensive and elevated fortifications. Have your Villagers start work on several Siege Workshops just outside of the range of the Lydian towers. Position your Heavy Cavalry Units nearby to protect your Villagers. When you have built at least a half dozen Ballistas, move them *en masse* towards the Lydian wall. These fast-firing siege weapons will breach the wall in no time.

Once you have breached the wall, your Ballistas should systematically destroy any Lydian towers within range of your troops, as they advance on the Wonder. Smash the Wonder with your Heavy Cavalry before the time limit has elapsed. With the Lydian Wonder gone, you may now turn your attention to the Phoenicians (yellow). They should be finishing their Wonder just about this time.

Once again, concentrate the fire of multiple siege weapons at a single section to breach the walls. If you have some wood to spare, you may want to consider building a Dock on the stretch of water just outside the Phoenician wall. With this Dock in place, begin building warships. Their missile fire, along with the fire from your Ballistas, hastens the destruction of the Phoenician village.

In the map's northern corner, the Persian civilization acts as a spoiler in this scenario, forcing you to defend your village and to fight a two-front war. The biggest threat posed by the Persians comes from their Priests and siege weaponry. It may be worthwhile to stage a preemptive strike. Don't become involved in a protracted fight; keep focused on your victory conditions.

VOICES OF BABYLON

The Babylonian campaign set emphasizes the role of the Temple and the strength of the Priest. These freewheeling games are characterized by numerous religious conversions. Babylonian scenarios

are never boring—they keep everyone guessing until the very last moment as to who's ahead. Sometimes, all it takes is a single Priest with the strength of his convictions to turn certain defeat into sudden victory. These scenarios begin with a scenario reminiscent of Abraham's trek from Ur (set in 1760 BCE) and last until the battle of Nineveh in 612 BCE.

Holy Man (1760 BCE)

Objective: Convert or destroy the Elamites and Akkadians.

Scenario Instructions: The small kingdom of Babylon is growing under the energetic leadership of its new king, Hammurabi. You have been sent down river to bring some enclaves of Elamites and Akkadians into the fold. Use your powers of persuasion where you can, but don't hesitate to resort to war if they prove difficult.

Resources: Wood—200 RPs, Food—0 RPs, Gold—0 RPs, Stone—0 RPs

This is one of the more interesting and challenging scenarios to play. You begin the game with exactly one Unit—a Priest. With this Priest, you must use your powers of forceful persuasion to convince (convert) the heathens to join your cause. You must protect your Priest at all costs throughout this scenario. When the scenario opens, your Priest is located in the southern corner of the map. Slowly move northward along the west river bank until you reach a shallow river crossing. Cross the river and head directly east into the territory controlled by the Akkadians.

The weaker of the two enemy tribes in this scenario is the Akkad (yellow). The Akkadian village is located in the eastern corner of the map. Move your Priest into the village, and begin converting the Villagers. Put these Villagers immediately to work building a Town Center for you. Eventually, you will have converted so many Akkadian Villagers that their tribe will grow weaker while

yours grows ever stronger. Once the necessary infrastructure is in place, use military force to destroy the remnants of the Akkadian civilization.

The Elamites are aggressive people located on the west side of the river. (Their Town Center is located in the western corner of the map.) If you try to take them first, they will kill your Priest— don't even try it. Once you have subjugated the Akkadians, however, you should be able to build an army capable of destroying the Elamites.

Be patient. If you attack the Elamites prematurely, you only trigger an invasion that you may be unable to handle. There is no secret to destroying the Elamites, except to say that they have the characteristics of the Egyptian civilization. You may recall that Egypt *cannot* build several different military Units, but *can* produce a considerable number of Priests. Plan your assault accordingly.

Tigris Valley (1755 BCE)

Objective: Capture two missing Treasures.

Scenario Instructions: The addition of the Elamite and Akkadian towns into the Babylonian Empire pleases Hammurabi greatly. He has a more difficult task for you now. One of your frontier cities was recently sacked, and important treasures were carried off, including a copy of Hammurabi's law code engraved in stone. Push into the area where the treasures were taken, and build up a force to recover them. The prestige of your great king remains tarnished as long as these treasures remain in enemy hands.

Resources: Wood—500 RPs, Food—500 RPs, Gold—500 RPs, Stone—500 RPs

You begin this scenario with a Town Center and three Villagers on an island with abundant resources. Much of the surrounding countryside is dense forest and large deposits of stone to the northwest.

Gold is relatively scarce throughout the map, so plan on seeking Trading partners.

The scenario itself is fairly straightforward. Your objective is to locate two Artifacts and return them to your island. (It is recommended, albeit not necessary, that you bring the Artifacts back and move them adjacent to your Town Center.) At this point, the victory conditions kick in and end the scenario.

As simple as it sounds, this scenario is one of the more difficult ones to win. The Akkadian tribe (yellow) is represented by the Egyptian civilization. (You already know the formidable advantages given to Egyptian tribes.) Your biggest source of trouble, however, is the Elam tribes (red and brown). The red Elam tribe is again represented by the Egyptians, the brown Elam tribe by the Assyrians.

Your initial concern is to fend off coastal raids and amphibious landings. Both the Akkad and Elam are of the mind-set that the best defense is a strong offense. You can expect to see their warships and scout vessels appear with increasing regularity. Some visits simply will be nuisances; others will be outright invasions.

As soon as the scenario unfolds, move your three Villagers to the southwest. Locate the coastline and begin building Docks. You probably only need to build two at first. Luckily, your inventory is well-stocked and can handle this sudden construction frenzy. As soon as the Docks are built, start cranking out Scout Ships—you'll need them.

The first big decision you make is what to do with the food stockpile. You start the game with 500 food RPs, which is enough to get you to the Tool Age. The question is: Do you spend the resources on reaching the Tool Age, or are there more pressing needs for all that food? Judging by the speed at which your enemy comes at you, it is probably better to advance to the Tool Age. You need to begin building Watch Towers and walls fairly quickly. There are no forage sites on your island; therefore, you can build a Granary anywhere you choose.

The red Elam tribe inhabits a small, weakly garrisoned island to the southwest. One of the two Artifacts is held there, as well as a substantial source of gold. Make this your first stop. Invade the island in strength, using your naval vessels for fire support. Take the Artifact and whisk it away.

Use the gold you find to finance the next step in taking on the brown Elam tribe. This tribe lives on another island near the center of the southwest edge of the map. In stark contrast to the previous island, the brown Elam tribe definitely has its act together. You can expect some serious Catapult and Ballista hits before you even get close.

The second Artifact is situated at the island's center. Use your naval vessels to wear down the tower defenses. Expect the Elam to attack you the moment your people set foot on the beach. Have plenty of Priests on hand to convert a few attacking Elamites. Your perseverance eventually pays off. In this battle, reinforce your army, and the enemy will wither with the end of its resources. Concentrate on eliminating Units, not buildings. Capture the Artifact and take it home.

Lost (1595 BCE)

Objective: Destroy the Hittites.

Scenario Instructions: Disaster has struck. A Hittite army has marched down the Euphrates River and sacked Babylon. Although your party is isolated among enemies in a marsh area, it is the *only* hope for extracting revenge. A Hittite force remains in the area and intends to build a new city along the river. Clear your enemies from the marshlands and destroy the Hittite city before it becomes established.

Resources: Wood—500 RPs, Food—500 RPs, Gold—0 RPs, Stone—500 RPs

You begin the game stranded on an island with a band of Archers and a Priest. After a short wait, an enemy Heavy Transport passes

by the northern end of the island. Have your Priest convert the transport—this is your only way off the island. Your objective in this Iron Age scenario is to defeat the Hittites by destroying their village and military Units. Well-guarded by towers and missile Units, the Hittite village is located in the middle of the northeast edge of the map.

Once you have boarded the transport, make your way to the map's eastern corner. You will find a number of Gold and Stone mines. Even though you start with a sizable stockpile of food, stone, and wood, you also must secure a steady supply of gold. Protect your Priest. You need him to begin converting enemy Villagers and enemy buildings once you have disembarked from the transport.

The Hittite village seethes with activity. The large number of Villagers gives your Priest ample opportunities for conversion. The more Villagers you convert to your side, the quicker you will acquire resources, especially gold. You should use these converted Villagers to build the infrastructure you need.

One of the first structures you should build is a Temple. Your Priests, because they have the benefit of Iron-Age technologies, are quite effective in this scenario. They should spearhead your attack on the Hittite village. Priests are vulnerable by themselves; therefore, be sure to provide them with fire support from siege weaponry and Archer Units.

You need not mess with the other tribes in this scenario. You can ignore them altogether and still win. Victory comes when the last Hittite Unit or structure is either converted or killed.

I Shall Return (1125 BCE)

Objective: Destroy the Elamites.

Scenario Instructions: Following the Hittite invasion and retreat, Babylon has been ruled by the Kassites for nearly 500 years. Kassite rule is in danger, however, because of Elamite and

Assyrian intrusions. Another Elamite army is pressing forward at this moment. If the city cannot be held, you are to save what you can and retreat down the river to build a new army. Retake Babylon for the Babylonians and destroy the Elamites.

Resources: Wood—300 RPs, Food—300 RPs, Gold—300 RPs, Stone—300 RPs

This scenario starts out by handing you a serious defeat. You can't save the town, so don't even try. A good general always knows when to retreat. As soon as play begins, gather all your Units and flee for the Light Transport offshore. In a variation of the old adage "women and children first," load your Villagers on your transport first. A Light Transport can only hold five Units. Be sure that you get as many Villagers as possible on the transport. There's much work for them to do.

The scenario map consists of a large island in its center with a smaller island jutting from its southeastern side. (The latter is the site for your Dock at the scenario's beginning.) You may be tempted to hold this tiny island because of its Gold Mines, but don't bother with it. Load your Units on transports to escape across the river.

From the eastern corner of the map, a second land mass extends and offers you refuge—or at least, a temporary reprieve—from the Elamite assault. You must build a new village from scratch on this land mass. With nearby forests, numerous Gold and Stone mines, and ample food—the eastern corner of the map serves as an excellent site for this new village.

Build a Storage Pit first and begin to stockpile resources. Next, build another Town Center and begin expanding your population. (Fortunately, you have some time before the Elamites cross the river to come looking for you. It is better, however, for you to pursue them than to wait for them to come to you.) Concentrate on building up a naval presence. If you can control the waterway, you can prevent the Elamites from transporting troops to your village.

Once you have built up sufficient strength, land your troops on the northern tip of the island and sweep southward. Don't try to retake the island without having at least a half dozen Triremes available for fire support. Luckily, most of the Elamite buildings are within easy range of your missiles. By this time, resources on the island will have been depleted. Hence, the Elamites will be unable to replace their losses, while your army simply becomes stronger.

The Great Hunt (1120 BCE)

Objective: Capture the Artifact.

Scenario Instructions: The glory of Babylon has been restored by the recapture of the city from the Elamites. King Nebuchadnezzar I vows that recapturing the city is not enough, however. The Elamites must feel his wrath in their own homeland. Attack the Elamites in their mountainous strongholds. Find and recapture the statue of the god Marduk that they carted off (represented by an Artifact). Peoples long oppressed by the Elamites will give you aid in your quest . . . if you can find them.

Resources: Wood—0 RPs, Food—0 RPs, Gold—0 RPs, Stone—0 RPs

This scenario is full of surprises and lots of fun to play, but it'll have you pulling your hair out long before you reach the end. You begin with exactly nine Axemen—not a lot of manpower for the job ahead. You must search for, and capture, the statue of the god Marduk (represented by an Artifact). Basically, you must travel a *well-worn path*. (This path will be obvious when you look down at the map.) As your party continues down the path, it must confront wild animals and roaming bands of enemy Units. (Don't dismiss these animals. Watch out for them. Elephants and Lion kings aren't your ordinary, everyday animals.)

Fortunately, you meet and make friends with several mercenary troops along the way. Instead of being weakened by the trek, your

army has the potential to gain strength on its journey. For example, behind the area marked by two blue flags are several friendly Priests. Knock out a section of the wall and send a Unit in to free them. Once free, they join your band.

You can control your troops' actions more easily and efficiently if you separate them into groups based on Unit types. Keep your Archers in one group and your Axemen in another. This way, the two groups won't trip over each other when they move or attack.

Remember that every enemy Unit you destroy is one less Unit you can convert and put to use. This lesson is particularly important with the siege weaponry you will discover on the way. The trick to converting siege weaponry is to move your Priest adjacent to it before he starts his chant. The Priest will be inside the siege weapon's minimum range and, therefore, immune to attack.

Your Priests are so important in this scenario that, should you lose one, start over—or at least start from the point at which you last saved the game. *Save early* and *save often*. No matter how good you are at the game, save this scenario frequently.

The most serious challenge you face during the first part of the journey comes when a double row of (orange) towers blocks your path. Siege weapons come in handy here. Blow a hole through the line of towers. (You don't have to destroy them all.) Attack the middle tower with concentrated fire from your Composite Bowmen and Elephant Archers. (Hopefully, you have been able to convert a few.) Keep a Priest behind the attacking Units to heal them as they shoot.

Once past the towers, you immediately encounter a row of Catapult Units, followed by a row of Ballista Units. Have your Priest convert these Units one right after the other by moving adjacent to them. Repeat this trick as many times as necessary. (Save the game at this point so you don't risk having to start over from scratch.) Use these siege weapons to cut down the Archers and Priests located a little further to the east.

A crucial point in the game. The path to victory lies beyond this row of towers.

Finally, you have reached the sea. Take control of the Light Transport, the first of three Light Transports you eventually uncover. Kill or convert the enemy Units across the shallows before you load your force on the transport. Notice the wooded peninsula to the east of you? Think it might be worth your while to check out the area on the other side? Survey says—yes! You will be pleasantly surprised by this heavenly gift.

Extremely well-protected by Heavy Catapults, Ballista Units, and towers—the Artifact you attempt to recover is located on an island with steep cliffs in the northern corner of the map. To reach this island, you must cross the entire length of the map by sea— but it's not that easy. Along the way, lone siege weapons—positioned in numerous shallow regions between you and the island—will attack you. You can bypass the siege weapons if you choose or try to convert them if you feel daring. But don't risk losing a Priest to gain a Ballista—it's not a good trade.

The only place to gain entrance to the island is a break in the cliff located against the northwestern edge of the map. Disembark your siege weaponry on the shallow area just south of this break. Expect heavy fire from enemy Ballistas and Catapults. You must win this exchange. Use your Elephant Archers against the siege weapons, for these Units can destroy siege weapons faster than they themselves can be eliminated.

Once you have established yourself on land, proceed slowly. Use your Elephant Archers, backed by Priests acting as medics, to take out the towers. Make your way up to the top of the path, capture the Artifact, and win the scenario.

The Caravan (1119 BCE)

Objective: Return the Artifact to the Temple.

Scenario Instructions: The raid into Elam was successful and the statue of Marduk has been recovered, but the statue must be returned to Babylon. There are still bands of Elamites and other enemies loose in the Zagros mountains who wish to prevent the return of the statue (represented by an Artifact). Bring the statue safely to your frontier Temple where it can be guarded before being moved to Babylon.

Resources: Wood—0 RPs, Food—0 RPs, Gold—0 RPs, Stone—0 RPs

You begin this scenario with exactly five Composite Bowmen and the Artifact. You must return the Artifact to the Temple located on the northwest edge of the map. The direct path—the obvious path—is not the way to go. In most cases, you are better off if you take the road less traveled. Proceed slowly and deliberately.

This scenario can be a relatively simple exercise in movement, but don't be lulled into complacency. A quick turn of events can spoil the scenario, forcing you to restart. Begin by moving northward. You will come to a fork where two elephants are grazing. Bear to the right and continue northeast across the plain. Before long,

you will come to a narrow river. Follow the river directly east, and you eventually find a shallow crossing. Avoid the pack of lions near the crossing.

Just over the river is a small village surrounded by steep cliffs. Investigate the village and use the cliffs to gain a plunging fire bonus against the Elam Hoplites to the north of the village.

From the Elamite village (brown), head directly for the Temple. Some Elamite War Elephants (orange) are situated between your men and the Temple. Simply bypass these Elephants. If they try to engage you, ignore them, continuing towards the Temple. Victory is yours the moment the Artifact is returned.

Lord of the Euphrates (648 BCE)

Objective: Destroy the Assyrians and the Chaldeans.

Scenario Instructions: The destruction of the Elamites and the return of the statue of Marduk to Babylon have brought many years of relative peace to the Euphrates valley, but the armies are marching again. The Assyrians are extending their empire and are threatening from the north. The Chaldeans are pushing upriver from the south. You are to revitalize the Babylonian armies and destroy both invaders now encroaching into your territory.

Resources: Wood—200 RPs, Food—200 RPs, Gold—200 RPs, Stone—200 RPs

This scenario is a study in how to fight a two-front war. The Chaldeans are directly to your north, and the Assyrians are to your southwest. You begin the game strong in terms of resources, but quickly build walls and towers. The Chaldeans are particularly aggressive, and they will send raiding parties your way.

A resource-rich piece of land lies to the east. The Chaldeans are aware of its existence and are actively trying to settle in the area. Undoubtedly, this will prove to be an early cause for conflict

between you and the Chaldeans. The numerous Gold Mines in the area are extremely important, as your exploitation of the Gold mines will fund your future war efforts, particularly the construction of Priests and other religious technologies.

Situated in a relatively good location, your village has access to an abundant supply of wildlife, many nearby foraging sites, and stone mines. Your initial goals should be to stockpile food and to expand your work force. Expend a considerable amount of resources on Unit upgrades and on researching technologies.

Consider two technologies, *Metalworking* and *Wheel*, as mandatory expenditures. Of course, to research *Wheel*, you must first build a Market. Build the Market regardless, because it enables you to build Farms. Artisanship (also available as a result of the Market) increases the effectiveness of your missile Units—something that comes in handy when the Chaldeans strike.

The Chaldean village is located directly to your north. Fortunately, a body of water separates you from this village, making an attack by direct route impossible. The Chaldeans (red) are given Greek attributes in this scenario, meaning that they can employ few Archers and Cavalry Units but considerable numbers of heavily armored ground troops and siege weapons. Plan accordingly.

The Assyrians (yellow) are less of a threat at the game's beginning only because they are further away. Again, water—an ocean this time—separates you from the enemy village, located in the far western corner of the map. The Assyrians make their presence known in short order, however. Your introduction comes in the form of naval vessels off your southern coast. For a time, allow the Assyrians to have their fun shooting up buildings that you placed too close to the coast. Concentrate your efforts on defeating the Chaldeans before you turn your attention westward.

Your best weapon against the Chaldeans is conversion. They have no effective response to any form of religious attack, so be sure to have plenty of Priests on hand. Use your siege weapons to smash

their slow-moving foot soldiers, should they appear. Attacking the Chaldean village probably will become quite costly. The numerous towers in the area are sure to take their toll on your men.

Once the Chaldeans have been brought to heel, take on the Assyrians. Your first fight is with the Assyrian navy. Because both the Assyrian and the Babylonian navies are limited in terms of the ships they can build, this battle is settled by numbers alone—whoever has the most ships wins the day.

After the naval battle has been decided in your favor, you may begin to land troops in Assyrian territory. To avoid a fight on your way ashore, make your initial landings to the southeast of the Assyrian village. The Assyrians are known for their fast-firing Archers, but they lack many advantages that you enjoy. Consult Chapter 1, "The Civilizations (The 12 Tribes)" for more information. Once the battle reaches the Assyrian mainland, their lack of resources eventually causes their military to collapse.

Nineveh (612 BCE)

Objective: Destroy Nineveh's Wonder.

Scenario Instructions: The Assyrians have been pushed back from Babylon, and now the tide has turned. The Assyrians have fallen back behind the mighty walls of their capital at Nineveh. Destroy Nineveh's Wonder to break the power of the Assyrians forever. If necessary, destroy any Assyrian Allies that stand in your way.

Resources: Wood—2,500 RPs, Food—2,000 RPs, Gold—2,000 RPs, Stone—400 RPs

The final scenario of the campaign is one of the harder scenarios you will ever face. You begin this Bronze Age scenario with a beautiful city, tremendous resources, and a navy of Scout Ships and Light Transports. The odds are still stacked against you, however. Your objective is to undermine the Assyrian's will to resist by

destroying their Wonder . . . but that's not all! Five other enemy tribes have the potential to interfere with your operations.

Your picturesque city, you may notice, lacks a certain human quality, a certain human activity. That's right—look closely and you can see that there are no Villagers whatsoever. Look even more closely to discover that you have no Town Center either. Basically, you're stymied. The solution lies in having your Priest convert an enemy Villager and having that Villager return to your city. In the city, your newly converted Villager can build a Town Center which, in turn, begins to crank out more Villagers.

Getting Villagers back to your village is only the first step in a very long road to victory. While you are trying to convert a Villager, the Assyrians are hard at work constructing their Wonder. They know that by building a Wonder they are just asking for trouble. You better believe that they are taking the necessary steps to defend it, too.

Your city beams with beauty, but without Villagers, its productivity lies wasted.

Early in the scenario, Assyrian War Galleys and Triremes visit you. Their mission is to damage or to destroy your Docks and naval vessels—the one sure way they have to safeguard their precious Wonder. Fortunately, you begin the game with plenty of wood with which to build numerous warships. Do it! You need to combat Assyrian quality with Babylonian quantity—at least for the short term.

(Let's face it—there's just no easy way to win this scenario. When you sit down to play this one, figure on being here for some time. Have a friend slip food under the door for a couple days.)

Before you attempt to take on the Assyrians, concentrate your efforts on defeating the enemy forces (yellow) to the northwest. You must occupy their village and put their resources to good use.

Beyond eliminating the yellow player, you must advance to the Iron Age before tackling the Assyrians. Unless you are extremely lucky—or the Assyrians get a severe case of the "AI stupids"—you won't win this one if you stay in the Bronze Age. The Iron Age makes a number of new Units available. You need to produce War Elephants and Elephant Archers because of their ability to withstand damage—the kind of damage Assyrian towers and siege weapons will dish out. Your navy will benefit by the addition of two new classes of warship—Catapult Trireme and Juggernaught.

The biggest benefit of reaching the Iron Age, however, is your Priests' newly acquired ability to research *Monotheism*. As you know, *Monotheism* lets you convert enemy Priests and buildings. This technology alone is enough to turn the tide of a battle in your favor.

The Assyrians have fortified almost the entire length of their southern and southwestern shorelines. Their wall extends right to the water's edge, limiting landing sites worth consideration. In fact, the Assyrian coastline nearest to your own is *not* the best place to begin your assault. Although there is ample room to drop off troops, you will find that landing here draws tremendous fire from towers and siege weapons, including two orange-colored Heavy Catapults.

The best place to land your invasion force is further to the east, near the point where the coastline meets the northeast edge of the map. (There's even a little road which runs down to the beach for you.) Four towers bar your way into the city. Use Elephant Archers, Catapults, and Priests to kill or convert them.

The Wonder is just inside the gateway. If you have made it this far, destroying the Wonder will be an easy task, considering how slowly it is being built. Congratulations! Not only have you won the scenario, you have finished the campaign.

YAMATO

Asian civilizations are among the strongest in the game and the most visually appealing. These scenarios give you the opportunity to raise large armies of mounted troops and siege engines. The combination of swift-moving riders and powerful artillery makes the Yamato campaign an interesting tactical study. This campaign begins in 365 AD and concludes in 663 AD.

The Assassins (365 AD)

Objective: Eliminate the Izumo leader.

Scenario Instructions: Yamato spies within the Izumo clan lands report that the Izumo leaders are planning an attack against some of your allied clans. A preemptive attack against the Izumo is not practical at this time, however. It would hurt your relations with other clans with whom you are negotiating. You are to lead a small band of assassins into the Izumo lands, locate their clan leader, and eliminate him. Without their leader, the Izumo cannot attack. This is a dangerous mission, but there are some Yamato friends inside the Izumo lands who can help you.

Resources: Wood—0 RPs, Food—0 RPs, Gold—0 RPs, Stone—0 RPs

This scenario tests your ability to infiltrate enemy territory without detection. Your small force consists of one Yamato Hero (a Composite Bowman), three Broad Swordsmen, and one Yamato Cavalry Unit. That's it—this is all you get to take on this mighty fortress.

If you are to win this scenario, you must do so through guile, not brute force. The Izumo leader lives inside a large fortress, guarded by a contingent of Archers and siege weapons. Clearly, your small force is not strong enough to fight its way through defenses such as these. The best way into the fortress is not the obvious direct route. Enter the fortress through the back door and avoid a large battle.

Your band of assassins begins the scenario next to a river which bisects the map from north to south. Start moving southward along the river bank, but be careful. Numerous Lions lie in your way—enough to put an end to this endeavor before it even starts. Have your Broad Swordsmen lead the advance, and your Hero and Cavalry Units bring up the rear.

Your Broad Swordsmen should gang up and kill any Lion that threatens to injure a member of your party. Be sure to attack these Lions with multiple Units. Never let a Lion take on a solitary Unit. Gang up on them to kill them in a hurry and to minimize their opportunity to inflict damage.

Stay close to the river bank. As you make your way southward, you eventually come to a shallow river crossing. Have your men cross the river individually. An enemy tower is in the vicinity, so be careful not to get hit by its missile fire.

Double back to the north, moving up the river's west bank. Stay as close to the river's edge as possible. Although it looks as though the forest blocks the path, it does not. It may take some effort, but you can squeeze through the trees. Once you have bypassed the enemy tower, you find a friendly Blind Lame Priest. Have him heal all of your injured men before you continue your advance.

Continue north for a short distance, and you come across an Izumo Government Center. At this point, you have made your way into the enemy fortress through the back door. The Izumo leader you must assassinate is a tough, Short Swordsman Hero with an attack strength of 20, an armor rating of three, and a hit-point total of 200. If you start to attack the Government Center, the Izumo leader will try to defend it, giving you an opportunity to kill him as he comes to the rescue.

Island Hopping (375 AD)

Objective: Recover six Stolen Treasures.

Scenario Instructions: The elimination of the Izumo leader brought a temporary peace to that part of your border, but the Izumo are becoming aggressive again. Izumo raiders from islands in the Inland Sea have attacked a number of your coastal villages. They have carried off important treasures from several shrines. You are ordered to attack the Izumo islands and recover the six treasures that they have stolen.

Resources: Wood—0 RPs, Food—0 RPs, Gold—0 RPs, Stone—0 RPs

This scenario tests your ability to conduct simultaneous amphibious operations. Your objective is to capture six Artifacts, each located on a different island. The key to winning this scenario, however, is destroying the Izumo Dock in the center of the southwestern edge of the map.

As the scenario opens, your ground Units and naval vessels are situated on a spit of land in the center of the northeastern edge of the map. Immediately embark your forces on the Heavy Transport and sail towards the center of the map's southwestern edge—almost directly across the entire length of the map. Locate the Izumo Dock. Land your ground forces on the tiny island just to the north of the Dock. As a bonus, you find one of the six treasures on this island.

Use your warships and siege weapons to destroy the Dock, preventing the Izumo from building any new naval vessels. Even after the Dock is destroyed, be prepared to defend your transports at all times. Several Izumo warships have been at sea since the game's beginning.

Another stolen treasure is on a tiny island in the eastern corner of the map. Use your warships to pick off enemy Bowmen on these islands, or land your siege weapons and let them do the work. A third treasure is on the large peninsula which juts from the northwestern edge of the map. A large Izumo force is also stationed on the peninsula. Fortunately, you can usually grab the treasure and jump back on your ships without having to fight them. There's no need to fight them here—so don't.

Always keep in mind that your objective is to recover the stolen treasures. Killing enemy Units is not a victory condition, so avoid contact with the enemy whenever possible. Another area to avoid is the southeastern edge of the map. The islands along this edge are garrisoned and fortified. None of the stolen treasures are located on any of these islands—simply stay away. Priests on these islands have the ability to convert your ships, making you lose the game. Don't tempt fate, especially at the higher difficulty levels.

A fourth treasure is located on an inhabited island in the far north corner of the map. Again, use your warships to eliminate enemy Units, and then move in with ground troops to recover the treasure. The fifth and sixth treasures are located on islands near the center of the map. You should have little difficulty in locating and recovering these last two treasures.

Capture (370 AD)

Objective: Capture the Artifact.

Scenario Instructions: Your successful raid of the Izumo islands has enflamed your enemies, and they have overreacted by shifting too much of their strength out of position. A weakness has been detected on one of their flanks. Penetrate their defenses

where they least expect attack, and carry off an important Artifact that they may not be guarding adequately. If you are successful, this raid can demoralize their people and leave their rulers even more vulnerable.

Resources: Wood—400 RPs, Food—400 RPs, Gold—200 RPs, Stone—400 RPs

This lengthy scenario tests your ability to conduct extended ground operations with minimal supplies. Your objective is to capture an Artifact on an island in the center of the map. The scenario instructions refer to a weakness, but it's unclear exactly what this weakness is—this scenario is just plain tough!

Capturing the Artifact requires you to build a strong navy in order to secure safe passage for yourself. There is a land bridge that links this island to the mainland. The shallow crossing extends from a piece of land centered along the southeastern edge of the map. This crossing is much easier to traverse than to try to land troops via transports. The trick is getting to it.

You can reach the crossing in two ways—(1) the long way, which requires you to move around the outer edge of the map; or (2) the short route, which forces you to fight a pitched battle almost immediately. Should you decide to take the long route, prepare yourself for an extremely long, arduous trek. Along this route, you come in contact with all three enemy tribes (red, yellow, and brown), and you must defeat them before continuing.

If you choose the shorter way—the more direct route—count on a faster-paced game. As your men move to the southeast towards the crossing, you make contact with enemy troops right away. Since you begin the game in the Bronze Age, you can start building high-powered troops right away as well. Priests, as usual, are important for their ability to convert enemy Units.

Siege weapons are required, too. You want to build these missile Units to provide your men with fire support. Enemy towers encircle the island. You must use your siege weapons and warships to

reduce these towers before you attack the island. Tear down the fortress wall that blocks the entrance and then retake the Artifact.

Mountain Temple (376 AD)

Objective: Destroy the Izumo Temple and build a Temple where the Izumo Temple once stood.

Scenario Instructions: The war with the Izumo people is coming to a climax. Your raids and captures have partially demoralized them and weakened their rulers. You are close to crushing their armies and bringing them under Yamato rule. Destroy the Izumo Temple on their sacred mountain and build a Yamato there. There may be Kibi clan forces supporting the Izumo. The Kibi must be pushed out of the way if they interfere with your attack.

Resources: Wood—200 RPs, Food—400 RPs, Gold—200 RPs, Stone—200 RPs

This is one of the more difficult scenarios to play. You won't finish this one in a single sitting. In the northern corner of the map, the Izumo Temple sits atop a mountain, secured by two concentric rings of fortifications and towers. To make matters worse, a large river—in practical terms it's a moat—separates you from this mountain fortress. Take this scenario step by step.

Step one: An island with several Gold Mines is situated to the west of your Town Center. Land on this island as soon as you can to begin mining the gold. Gold is necessary in this scenario because you want to have plenty of siege weaponry later in the game.

Step two: The Kibi tribe (yellow) is a constant nuisance throughout the game if you don't do something about them. Your two towers keep it at bay for some time, but eventually, you have to go after it. At this stage of the game, your priorities are divided. Your land forces should sweep eastward against the Kibi, while you build a sizable fleet of warships and transports back at home.

Step three: You eventually destroy the Kibi, thus removing any overland threat to your village. At that point, concentrate on getting

your army across the river. The cliffs that line the river's northern bank limit the places where you can disembark. Use your warships to destroy any towers that can hit your forces as they cross.

Once you are on the north bank, find the path that leads up the mountain. Unfortunately, you must take this fortress head-on; however, with plenty of siege weapons nearby, you can do it. The Izumo probably will start throwing Priests your way. Watch out. If your siege weapons are converted, this battle is over and you lose. Your Priests should be positioned such that they may reconvert any of your forces that fall prey to enemy Priests.

The Canyon of Death (380 AD)

Objective: Recover the Artifact and carry it to the Controlled Island.

Scenario Instructions: The defeat of the Izumo and Kibi clans has consolidated the southern part of Honshu under Yamato rule. You wish to expand your influence southward now to the island controlled by the Shikoku clan. They showed you great disrespect, however, and have stolen important and valuable items that were being carried by your first emissaries. Rather than attempt an expensive war overseas from a long distance, your small party is to fight through Shikoku territory quickly and recover the items. Carry them to the offshore island that you control. This raid demonstrates the power of the Yamato and the futility of resisting your confederation.

Resources: Wood—0 RPs, Food—0 RPs, Gold—0 RPs, Stone—0 RPs

You begin this well-designed scenario with a mixed force of Cavalry, archers, and swordsmen. This force must make its way through enemy territory to reach an island along the map's southwestern edge. Once there, additional forces you control will enter the game. In order to reach the island, you must move along a treacherous, winding path that stretches the length of the entire map. The

dangers are many, and some of your troops will perish. As long as one Unit reaches the island, however, you have a chance at winning.

Your initial force starts in the eastern corner of the map. You immediately notice the presence of several well-worn paths in your vicinity. Unfortunately, they all lead to trouble. Shikoku towers, Archers, and Catapults block your advance at every turn. Although there are several ways to reach the island, the best and safest way is also the longest.

The first leg of your advance runs along the northeastern edge of the map. Let your missile-equipped troops lead the advance. When you spot enemy Units, concentrate your fire and pick them off one at a time. Quickly bypass any towers along the route—you will sustain unnecessary casualties if you stop to fight with them.

The path leads into the northern corner of the map before it turns south. You will fight several battles and encounter several towers after you make the turn. Scout out the route ahead. You are looking for the coastline. Although the path leads back to the center of the map, stick to the coastline and follow it southward.

Eventually, you come to a fortress wall that blocks your progress. Batter down a section of this wall and keep advancing. Just past the wall are several boats to transport your men to the island. Upon reaching the island, a large force of troops appears. You must use this army to get your Artifact.

The Artifact itself is on another island just to the north. Load your army on the transports and drop them off at the southern tip of the island. Be prepared to fight a considerable enemy force before you reach the Artifact. Once you destroy the enemy force, run in, grab the Artifact, and transport it back to the flagged island to win.

Oppression (385 AD)

Objective: Destroy the Kyushu Government Center.

Scenario Instructions: The success of your raid through

Shikoku lands broke their spirit, and within a few years, they became part of the Yamato confederation. You have turned your gaze further south now to the island of the Kyushu. Your first efforts in Kyushu lands are not going well, however. Your small colony has come under the rule of a powerful Kyushu leader who rules the area nearby. He is now demanding heavy payments to allow you to stay. Due to entanglements to the north on the main island, the Yamato can send you no aid at this time. The Yamato leaders order you to revolt against the Kyushu warlord and gain control of this part of the island. Destroy the Kyushu Government Center.

Resources: Wood—400 RPs, Food—400 RPs, Gold—400 RPs, Stone—400 RPs

This interesting scenario requires tact and patience. You begin the game oppressed by an evil Kyushu overlord. You must continue to pay the extortion money he demands or else. (The "or else," in this case, means that you immediately come under attack by very strong enemy forces.) Count on abandoning your existing buildings at some point. You won't be able to keep up with his demands, and when the enemy attack does come, it will be too overwhelming.

While you are still "friends" with the overlord, explore his city to the south of your Town Center. Send one or two Villagers to have a look around. You must destroy the Government Center inside the city walls to win the scenario.

This scenario is actually very open-ended. Some players feel that their only salvation lies in leaving the Kyushu mainland altogether. If you follow this line of thought, consider settling at the base of the elevated peninsula to the west. This easily defensible site contains several large deposits of stone and ample food. Other players may want to hang on to a piece of the mainland. This course of action is somewhat more difficult.

You only need to destroy the Kyushu leader's Government Center to win the game. There's no need to engage his troops in a pitched

battle. If you took the time to do some reconnaissance, you may have noticed that the outer wall does not extend completely around the town. The town's entire seaward flank lies open and exposed.

Better yet, the Government Center is situated very close to the water's edge. A quick landing in this area will give you a fairly good chance of destroying the building before the enemy can react. It's definitely worth the try.

A Friend in Need (562 AD)

Objective: Protect the Paekche and destroy the Scilla town.

Scenario Instructions: The success of your invasion of Kyushu brought southern Japan under Yamato control. Over the last century that control has spread to the north on the main island and overseas to a colony on the mainland of Korea. There you have become an Ally of the Paekche kingdom but enemies of the Scilla. War has recently broken out between the Paekche and the Scilla. It is in your best interest to aid the Paekche. If they fall, the Yamato colony is sure to follow. Aid your Paekche Allies in any way possible, and destroy the nearby Scilla town to gain control of this borderland.

Resources: Wood—200 RPs, Food—200 RPs, Gold—200 RPs, Stone—200 RPs

Located along the northwestern edge of the map, the Paekche town begins the game under attack from the Scilla. The few Axemen, who resided there at the time of the attack, are quickly wiped out. Don't despair. You have an excellent village of your own in the southern corner of the map with a sizable Villager population and a large standing army.

Your objectives in this scenario are to save your Allies from eventual destruction and then to take the fight to the Scilla. In fact, the best way to approach this scenario is to ignore the Paekche and to concentrate on eliminating the Scilla. Getting rid of the Scilla is the best way to ensure that your Ally survives.

The Scilla town is well-protected by fortifications and towers which runs the length of the northeastern edge of the map. Their large army is primarily comprised of Composite Bowmen and Heavy Cavalry Units. Don't count on them to stay inside the protection of their walls. The Scilla are perfectly content to come after you first and save the Paekche for later.

This fairly easy scenario is a lot of fun to play, and can be won without either side resorting to those pesky Priests. The open terrain is conducive to maneuvering large mounted armies—the kind of army the Yamato is known for building.

Since your objective is to destroy the Scilla town, you need to build several siege weapons. Combine the firepower strength of these Catapults with the volume of fire from approximately a dozen Horse Archers. Systematically take down the towers that surround the town. Should Scilla ground troops sally forth, eliminate them with ranged fire. In fact, you should avoid engaging in close combat as much as possible.

A large deposit of gold and stone and a nearby grove of berry bushes are located to the southeast of the Scilla town. You should take two actions in regard to these resources—keep Scilla Villagers

You must save this Paekche town from destruction by bringing down the Scilla's wrath upon yourself.

away by placing the sites within your missile troops' range, and look for ways to exploit these resources yourself.

Tang Invasion (663 AD)

Objective: Destroy the Tang.

Scenario Instructions: The defeat of the Scilla armies 100 years ago brought peace to the Korean peninsula. The Yamato have been able to benefit from trade in the area, and your influence has expanded. A new threat has appeared, however. Chinese armies of the Tang Dynasty have penetrated the peninsula from the north. One army is marching on your colony, while another deals with your Paekche friends. You must defeat the Tang army or your foothold in Korea is lost. Win the battle to become the greatest Yamato leader and to launch the Yamato as a world power.

Resources: Wood—100 RPs, Food—100 RPs, Gold—0 RPs, Stone—100 RPs

The Tang are invading from the northern corner of the map, driving southward with a large army. Two rivers bisect the map from southwest to northeast. Your only hope is to gain time by defending the shallow river crossings. You start the game with light screening forces already in place. The task at hand is clear—stop the invasion, then destroy the Tang village.

This resource-rich map has a heavily forested wilderness dotted with mesas with steep cliffs. In many cases, the mesas' tops contain valuable gold deposits. The nearest gold deposit is located on a mesa just to the west of your Storage Pit. Since you start the scenario without any gold in your inventory, send some Villagers up to the mesa to begin mining right away.

The trick here is in not locating the resources this time—everywhere you look you'll find some—but holding off the Tang invaders long enough to place the resources into your inventory. Your Town Center should initially produce Villagers as fast as it can. You need

to develop a large workforce before the Tang attack begins in earnest. Definitely research *Wheel*, as this allows your Villagers to move much more quickly about the map.

Your army is divided into three groups, all of which presently screen the shallow crossings of the easternmost river. These groups are not strong enough to hold these positions in the face of a concerted attack. They will provide you with a measure of warning, however, when the Tang invasion force is on the move. These crossings are excellent choke points and should not be abandoned. From a tactical standpoint, you couldn't ask for a better starting point for your own eventual counterattack.

The longer you can hold the Tang back at these crossings, the more time you have to build up a workforce. If time permits, part of this workforce should be sent to fortify these crossings. A few towers in the right locations can inflict serious damage on enemy Units as they attempt to cross the river. If you can, reinforce these positions with fresh troops from your town (as you build them). Send troops to the two northernmost crossings as they are the closest to the Tang village .

In this scenario, the Tang has the cultural attributes of the Shang civilization. Expect to encounter numerous Chariots, Heavy Cavalry, and Heavy Catapult Units. Their attacks usually follow a common form—mounted troops in the lead followed by slow-

A typical river crossing. Choke-points like these force enemy troops to invade at predictable, easily defensible routes.

moving siege weapons. The best time to hit the Tang force, there-fore, is when—due to the Units' different movement speeds—its Cavalry Units have separated from its Catapults.

Terrain favors defense in this scenario. Besides the closed nature of the landscape with its many choke points and obstruc-tions, the mesa formations provide you with many opportunities of inflicting triple damage on advancing troops with the plunging fire bonus. Unfortunately, you will be on the defense only long enough to stop the Tang. To win the game, you must go on the offensive—sooner or later.

MULTIPLAYER SCENARIOS

In addition to the four campaigns, there are a number of specially designed multiplayer scenarios. These scenarios contain symmetri-cal maps with resource sites equally divided among the players. Each scenario can be played with either four players (two teams of two players) or eight players (two teams of four players). The maps are identical.

Because you can tailor these scenarios to suit your personal tastes, they never play the same way twice. It is difficult, therefore, to formulate detailed strategies with any certitude. These games change considerably depending on the skill and demeanor of the other players.

In general, tricks you develop playing Single-Player scenarios have practical applications here. But any game involving human emotions is extremely unpredictable. Accordingly, only universal play hints and tips are offered here.

KNOW YOUR ENEMIES

Pay careful attention to which tribes you are going up against—know their strengths and their weaknesses as outlined in the earlier

chapters of this book. Use this information, so that you don't wind up playing the enemies' game. Make them play yours.

Since you are competing against human players as opposed to computer-generated AI routines, it helps if you know a little about their styles of play. This isn't always possible, especially given the number of new people you may meet online.

If you know, for example, that a certain player has a fascination for building large navies, you can better prepare yourself. (Maybe even get him or her to agree to play on an inland map where there is little water.) Conversely, you would want to convince someone who likes to build Mongol hordes of Horse Archers to try an oceanic adventure.

KNOW THYSELF

Choose a civilization that best embodies your particular style of play. You perform best commanding troops with which you are familiar. Know your own strengths and build on them. Know your weaknesses and look for other players to exploit them.

Personally, I like to build large-walled compounds defended by numerous towers. This kind of infrastructure requires that I mine large quantities of stone very early in the game. Cut me off from my Stone Mines, and I am forced to fall back on alternative strategies that I'm less comfortable with.

KNOW WHAT BUTTONS TO PUSH

We're not talking about the game interface here; we're talking about knowing what motivates the people with whom you are competing. *Age of Empires* gives you the opportunity to act as your civilization's ambassador. The Chat feature allows you to beg, barter, threaten, insult, brag, and even cajole your fellow players. All of this adds a bit of "diplomacy" to the game that the Single-Player

scenarios lack. (Diplomacy is again defined here as the "*art of saying nice doggie while looking for a big rock*.")

Some players can be bought off or bribed for a few gold Resource Points; others can be bluffed into acting favorably towards your civilization. Many times, you can "steal a win" by playing the consummate politician and allying yourself with the winning team. This strategy depends entirely on your skill as a negotiator and on your power of persuasion.

Your reputation goes a long way in multiplayer games as well. People have long memories when it comes to competitive games. If you have developed a reputation as a "straight-shooter," people may be more inclined to deal with you. They will come to your aid more readily because they know you will return the favor when they need help themselves.

On the other hand, if you have a habit of "screwing" your neighbors, you will have a much more difficult time getting others to trust you. As humans, we have a tendency to harbor grudges against those who have wronged us in the past. It will be just your luck to have to deal with an army of Yamato horsemen descending on your town and to find out that a player you "ticked" off in an earlier game is riding his way to your demise.

KNOW THE TERRAIN

Each multiplayer scenario may be studied in intricate detail by using the Edit Scenario feature of the Scenario Builder. There's no excuse for not knowing where everything from a Gazelle to a Gold Mine is located. Since much of this game involves exploring the map, knowing where everything is ahead of time gives you a commanding advantage. While others stumble around in the dark, your people can make beelines for all the best resource sites.

KNOW THE VICTORY CONDITIONS

Each multiplayer scenario has a master theme. They are repeated here verbatim.

Multiplayer Border Patrol

Each Team must move its Artifact through the terrain held by its opponent into the region surrounded by allied player flags.

Multiplayer Come and Get Me

In this resource-rich scenario, each player begins in an easily defended canyon, but must move outside its safety to gain access to more resources.

Multiplayer Crossroads

A balanced affair with plenty of territory and gold to fight over.

Multiplayer Cutthroat

Players start on islands to the east with a small transport and three Villagers. To the west is a giant land mass awaiting colonization.

Multiplayer Gold Rush

This all-land scenario offers plenty of gold for the taking, but the player who can mine out the center has the advantage.

Multiplayer Hill Country

An all-land map divided by a mountain range. Several small passes allow travel between sides.

Multiplayer Hostile Lands

A moderately resource-rich map dominated by a central body of water and numerous rivers. All players begin with diplomatic stances set to Neutral and can readjust as the game progresses.

Multiplayer Intruder

A Post-Iron Age scenario. Player 1 is defensive and begins with four groups of two Villagers spread across the map's largest land mass. Player 2 is the attacker, and begins with a well-established island city. There are several Choke-points on the map that will allow the defender to hold off its attacker for a time.

Multiplayer Marooned

Each team needs to balance production to ensure superiority on land and sea while moving from island to island.

Multiplayer Oasis

Each player must attempt to control the "oasis," a large area in the center surrounded by cliffs and filled with resources.

Multiplayer Passes

Each player begins safely tucked away behind numerous ridges in the center. To gain resources, however, everyone must find a way into this area.

Multiplayer Pathfinder

Each team must leave its island to colonize the continent across the water. A single Ruin exists in the center.

Multiplayer Rising Tide

Each team must work to defeat the other team across a river.